CHARLIE KRAY

DOING
THE
BUSINESS

THE FINAL CONFESSION OF
THE SENIOR KRAY BROTHER

COLIN FRY AND CHARLIE KRAY

JB

JOHN BLAKE

First published in hardback 1993
Paperback published 2000
This edition 2011

ISBN: 978 1 84358 287 8

British Library Cataloguing-in-Publication Data:

A catalogue record for this book is available from the British Library.

Design by www.envydesign.co.uk and BCP

Printed in Great Britain by CPI Bookmarque, Croydon CRO 4TD

1 3 5 7 9 10 8 6 4 2

Papers used by John Blake Publishing are natural, recyclable products made
from wood grown in sustainable forests. The manufacturing processes
conform to the environmental regulations of the country of origin.

CONTENTS

ACKNOWLEDGEMENTS   VII

INTRODUCTION   IX

1 FIGHTING FOR SUCCESS   1

2 PROTECTING THEIR INVESTMENT   19

3 THE WILD WEST IN THE EAST END   41

4 ESCAPE FROM LONG GROVE   57

5 THE GLAMOUR GAME   73

6 HOW TO SUCCEED IN BUSINESS
   WITHOUT REALLY TRYING   91

7 OUT OF AFRICA   105

8 THE KENNEDYS V. THE MOB   127

9 THE CANADIAN CONNECTION   147

10 ONE NIGHT IN PARIS   173

11 HE DID IT HIS WAY   195

12 THE GEORGE RAFT STORY   211

13 NEW YORK, NEW YORK   229

14 NEMESIS   257

    EPILOGUE   269

    POSTSCRIPT   287

To my wife, Eva,
for all her patience and tolerance and to
our children, Alexander and Christian,
for their belief in their father

ACKNOWLEDGEMENTS

I WOULD LIKE FIRST OF ALL to thank my wife, Eva, for listening to me while I have tried to establish the basic idea for this book. I needed someone to bounce my ideas off and Eva, unfortunately for her, was at hand: to discuss, assess and advise on the progression of my thoughts.

Later on I was ably assisted by Robert Smith, my previous publisher, who spent many a day with me finalizing the concept of the book. I will always be thankful for his involvement. This team effort was continued with John Blake at Blake Publishing, who encouraged me to update *Doing the Business*, thus involving previously researched material considered at the time to be too dangerous to include in the original book back in 1993.

A special thank you must go to Richard F. Young of the Hartley Library at Southampton University. Early on in my research, he gave me great assistance and put the university library facilities at my disposal. On a personal note, I would also like to thank Southampton University for my recent BA Hons degree, awarded through King Alfred's, Winchester.

DOING THE BUSINESS

Likewise, I will always be grateful to Charlie Kray (although I could have done without the threats), without whom this book would have been an impossible task. His efforts were relentless and his memory exceptional as he helped me to appreciate the style of business favoured by the twins, Ron and Reg Kray, his brothers.

And last, but not least, I would like to thank my good friend Charles Rosenblatt, without whom this book would never have been attempted. His guidance during the evaluation of my synopsis was invaluable, and I can still remember his opening words: 'Everyone has at least one good book in them.' With 40 years in the motion-picture business, he should know what he is talking about.

INTRODUCTION

CHARLIE KRAY IS DEAD - but he is not forgotten!

On 4 April, just into the start of the new millennium, Charlie Kray succumbed to the effects of a sudden heart-attack and quietly passed away at St Mary's Hospital, only a stone's throw away from Parkhurst Prison on the Isle of Wight. He was, at the time, serving a 12-year sentence for his part in a £39 million cocaine smuggling plot. He died broke, homeless — and alone.

The demise of 'Champagne Charlie' made the front pages — how Charlie would have loved to have seen the obituaries, the media hype, the gossip and the gas. And he would have been thinking all the time of the money he could have been making, selling his story — loads of money, by the bucketful. He would have laughed all the way to the bank!

But the circumstances surrounding his death were all but cheerful, hopeful, colourful — and there was no humour of any kind. The troubles surrounding Charlie

Kray started in 1999 when he suffered his first stroke, causing him to have reduced circulation in his legs and feet. And he never overcame the effects of this, brought on as they undoubtedly were by the trial, the conviction, the appeal process and his imprisonment at Frankland Prison.

To his friends, Charlie had openly admitted his guilt in the cocaine smuggling operation — but he was after the money, and in no way did he intend to go through with the deal. He was put under extreme pressure by the police officers involved to come through with the goods — and being Charlie Kray, he knew exactly where he could lay his hands on £39 million worth of cocaine. That was always the problem — it was his making and it was eventually his downfall. Everyone would confide in Charlie — he knew where the bodies were buried, he knew who was doing what and to whom. He knew but he couldn't tell. That would be breaking his code and Charlie was an old-time criminal — he believed in respect, in tradition, in honesty among thieves.

Certainly, Charlie felt that his current spell behind bars was a gross injustice — it was a sting operation, set up by the 'Met' to catch the last remaining Kray still at large. His feelings of outrage and his unmanageable frustrations were exacerbated by the fact that his first stretch in prison was a horrendous miscarriage of justice — he had served seven years for helping to dispose of the body of Jack 'The Hat' McVitie, when all the time he was safely tucked up in bed, with not a care in the world. He didn't know until the following day any of the events of the preceding evening, when his brother Reg Kray, urged on by twin brother Ron, stabbed McVitie to death. But the police wanted the Krays, all three of them, and there was no hope for Charlie, who was inextricably involved in the Firm's activities. However, it may be well worth noting that Charlie Kray was never on the Board of any of the Kray companies, he was never in charge in any way, shape or form. But Charlie was always there to support the twins, to offer advice — and to make a little something for himself, if he could, in the process.

His first time in prison had not been kind to him — he remembered and remembered, and he regretted and regretted. But it did no good at all. However, he did promise himself that he would never be sent to prison again, never, not for anyone.

One way of trying to come to terms with his life, before and after prison, was to write, and I was privileged to be involved in the writing of this book. All the remembering, all the regretting — it all served a new purpose, a way of redemption and a means of helping him to find his own way in life without the twins — Ron and Reg Kray.

The second time around, first in Frankland and then in Parkhurst, was hard for Charlie Kray. He wasn't a youngster any more — he was 70 years of age and a pensioner. He lost much of his hair after the first stroke and with the blood circulation problems he became a pitiful, frail and ghostly image of his former self. When he started complaining of chest pains, prison authorities at Parkhurst were quick to act — they decided to send him to St Mary's for investigations, medical not criminal. Their suspicions were well founded — Charlie Kray was suffering from a heart-attack.

On the following day, Saturday 18 March, news reached Reg Kray in Wayland Prison, Norfolk. The message said simply, 'Charlie is dying.' He immediately contacted the authorities at the prison and arrangements were hurriedly put together for him to visit Charlie on the Isle of Wight, probably for the last time. Reg hadn't seen Charlie for over five years — not since his twin brother's funeral.

Reg Kray is no stranger to Parkhurst. He served at least 17 years, mainly in isolation, at this establishment — he knows all the rules, all the regulations. He wasn't keen on going back there, and the thought of confronting Charlie, possibly on his death bed, was not what he had wanted.

At around 8.00am on the morning of Sunday, 19 March, Reg Kray, together with three trusted warders, left Wayland Prison in a white van, driving carefully and slowly through the giant main doors of the prison. The van had arrived earlier, at around 6.45am, but it had to be inspected and checked, even by a sniffer dog, before Reg could be safely put inside. They were taking no chances with their prize prisoner.

The van was quickly on to the M11, and then the

M25 around London, to the west. At around 11.00am the warders were hungry so they pulled into Winchester Prison, a scheduled stop for lunch. The meal was the usual thing, something good for the warders, something not so good for the prisoners, but Reg couldn't eat much — he kept on thinking of Charlie. He wanted to get there fast — at any cost.

The white van, complete with its occupants, made the ferry at Porstmouth early in the afternoon and by mid-afternoon they had reached St. Mary's Hospital and the dying Charlie. Reg had endured the entire trip handcuffed to two warders, except for a brief interlude when waiting for the ferry, where he was allowed to smoke a cigarette or two while one wrist was freed. On this first day he was allowed to see Charlie for around 45 minutes, still handcuffed to the two warders, one on each side — plenty of time for a quick chat and a few words of encouragement. Charlie hugged his brother, nothing could dent the Kray spirit, but his legs were already beginning to turn black, and the feeling had gone. Reg was under no illusions — it was all true. At 73 years of age, Charlie hadn't long to live.

The usual words came from trusted hospital sources — Charlie was 'comfortable and cheerful' although he had become 'extremely unwell'. And Parkhurst Prison let it be known that Reg Kray, once gangland crime boss and now a pensioner of some 66 years, was a welcome visitor — he could stay and use Charlie's cell until his brother was well enough to resume his sentence, or until ...

Reg couldn't even manage a smile for the cameras as he left the hospital. He was smart enough though, shirt-sleeved, white casual jacket carefully placed over his arm, not getting in the way of the handcuffs, and the customary blue jeans. Sources at the prison told reporters that the reunion had been emotional — 'Both men are old,' they said, 'and they know they haven't got long left.' Reg settled into Charlie's old cell, and waited. It had been a long day!

The following week passed slowly and painfully, apparently with no end in sight. Charlie was fighting the toughest fight of his life. After all those fights, after surviving all those years, after already witnessing the death of his mother, his father, his brother Ron — was it now to be Charlie's turn? He didn't give up easy — he fought every inch of the way. But there was no quick fix, no easy option, no way out.

The speculation grew as Reg Kray waited for his brother to die. Was he just taking a break from Wayland Prison, spending a few quiet weeks on the Isle of Wight, just for the sheer fun of it? Was he manipulating the situation just to get a few more columns in the press, using brother Ron's favoured media tactic? Well, let me assure everyone — there was no way in hell that Reg Kray wanted to be in Parkhurst, it brought back so many memories, and none of them pleasant. Imagine having to spend all that time — some two weeks in all — in your brother's cell, waiting for him to die. It was one of the worst experiences of his life.

INTRODUCTION

The news was brought to Reg on the evening of 4 April — Charlie had died peacefully in his sleep at around 8.50pm that evening. Reg Kray was alone in his cell, alone in his thoughts — he was the last Kray standing!

He had already made his peace with Charlie earlier in the day, but it was a one-sided conversation — Charlie was so far gone that he couldn't even manage the blink of an eyelid. He told him that they had not always seen eye to eye, that he was dissatisfied with some of the comments that Charlie had made. He told him that he hadn't always been straight with Ron and himself — about the T-shirt deal, where he had kept all the money for himself; about the film deal, in which he accepted the unacceptable and paltry figure of £300,000 since he needed the money urgently to pay off his debts; about the problems it had caused when he was arrested for the cocaine bust, hence spoiling Reggie's own chances of getting out on parole. Reg Kray had much to complain about, but through it all he bore Charlie no malice — they were family and that counted for much; now it could all be forgiven, once and for all time. There was more he would have liked to have said, personal things about the past and the present, but the circumstances weren't right for such a conversation — being constantly handcuffed to two prison warders, always there and always listening, was far from the private, intimate environment necessary for such words.

But Charlie couldn't hear him. He was fading fast and everyone knew it. His legs were now black, his breathing difficult — it was just a matter of time and, after 73 years time, was all Charlie had. The hospital had only recently issued a new statement to the press, saying, 'He has had heart problems and respiratory problems. His condition is giving cause for concern.'

Reg had returned to Charlie's cell, a lonely and embittered man. Soon he would be the last of the Krays — the sole survivor of the gangland wars, the ageing Godfather of UK crime. But, in reality, he was simply a lonely pensioner, waiting for death.

The rush to Charlie's bedside was too late — he'd died. All the good intentions in the world would not bring him back. Reg couldn't help his twin brother Ron, who had died at the hands of his beloved cigarettes, and he couldn't help his older brother Charlie when he really needed help — before the cocaine deal and well before it had all started to go downhill, when Charlie's son Gary died of cancer. This had been the turning point for Charlie — losing Gary was like losing his reason for living. He idolised his son, they were inseparable. But what made matters worse for Charlie was the fact that he couldn't afford to bury him — Charlie Kray was broke, with little chance of employment, with only a few friends around him, with only a fearful dread of what the future held. It was Reg who had stepped in and saved the day, paying for all the funeral arrangements. But it was more than money that Charlie was in need of — he needed a reason to live.

INTRODUCTION

The cocaine deal had been Charlie's last hope, but doing a deal with undercover policemen was not the foundation needed for good things to come and a solid future. Champagne Charlie Kray was just an old time rogue, going nowhere — fast!

Reg wept and wept that first night. There was much to think about — the past, the present, the future. And there were the funeral arrangements to consider. Reg had pulled out all the stops for Ron's funeral, five years earlier — should he do the same for Charlie? Or should he play it low key, and try to placate any inquisitive Home Office officials, keen to keep the last Kray in jail? He was urged by many to play safe — have a quiet ceremony with none of the pomp and circumstance that surrounded the funeral of his twin brother. But Reg Kray is no ordinary Eastender — he had already decided that first night in Charlie's cell. It was to be the real McCoy, something to satisfy the fans, to remind people of the Kray legacy. Charlie Kray would be buried with honours — and everyone would know about it.

Reg couldn't forget these past few weeks with Charlie. 'I visited him twice a day, once in the morning and then a long session in the afternoon,' he told the press, always eager to please. 'He looked terrible,' he told them, 'he was just lying there on his back sucking in air from an oxygen mask. He was breathing really heavily and he was out of it.' Reg paused for a moment. 'It was heartbreaking, his chest was going up and down and he couldn't hear me.'

But the crowds would hear, the East End of London would hear, the entire country would hear — from Reg Kray, as he laid on the accolades and praised his brother. 'I've been through so much and, even though it has been hard coping with the loss, I have remained strong in mind,' he told friends. 'But it has been so sad to lose Charlie — prison was not the place for him, he was too old to endure it.'

The funeral service was held on Wednesday, 19 April, at Bethnal Green's St Matthew's Church. The idea was to bury Charlie, but it soon turned into a tribute to Reg. All the usual suspects were there — Mad Frankie Fraser, Tony Lambrianou, Freddie Foreman, even previous arch rival for the position of criminal boss of London, Charlie Richardson, turned up to pay homage. So too were the police — some 200 or more of them. They lined the route, checking the stretch limousines as they passed by, waiting for a sign of a break by Reg and seeing which villains they could identify among the mourners' *Who's Who?* But I for one definitely think that the two helicopters flying along the route, in the skies above the East End, was a wasteful way of squandering tax-payers' money — and the marksmen, with guns at the ready was a little unnecessary — overkill comes readily to mind. There were more guns around the East End that day than there ever were in the days of the Krays.

The day started at English's Funeral Parlour, where Charlie had been laid out like a king. He had lain in state in an open coffin, well-wishers coming and going, all paying their respects. Some brought wreathes, some best wishes for the afterlife — they paid their tributes to Charlie, one and all, as bodyguards watched over the lifeless body. In fact, there were more flowers in that funeral parlour than Buster Edwards used to have at his stall just outside Waterloo Station.

One wreath was in the shape of a boxing ring — it was fashioned from red roses and white carnations, coming from Reg and his new wife, Roberta. Another said simply 'Grandad' and yet another came from friends on C-Wing at Parkhurst Prison. The lovely lilies came from Barbara Windsor, with whom Charlie had had a fling back in the '60s, and her new husband Scott Mitchell.

By around 11.00am, the villains were getting nervous — the collars were becoming tight. Reg was due any time now and those suits, last worn at Ron's funeral, were beginning to feel the warmth of the day. But Reg arrived on time and everyone could breathe a sigh of relief. It was now Reggie's show, and all the old lags and the new kids on the block could relax and enjoy the spectacle of a true East End send-off.

Wreathes and flowers piled up on the street and on the roofs of the stretch limos, as shadowy figures in shades got ready for the drive to the church. Charlie's coffin was brought out and placed in one of the two hearses, the other was simply there for effect. They were ready for the ride, even the hearse carried wreathes spelling out the word 'Gentleman', and the crowds were lining the streets and hanging out of windows, craning their necks for a glimpse of the ageing gangster. Everyone appeared to have forgotten the fact that Reg Kray was a convicted killer.

The blue Mercedes people carrier, carrying Reg Kray and a woman police officer, handcuffed together, moved slowly down Bethnal Green Road. People cheered and threw flowers as the cortège passed by, stretch limousine after stretch limousine, some 18 in all. At a leisurely walking pace and spear-headed by a white-robed minister and a mourner, dressed entirely in black and complete with top hat, the cortège approached the church. They even managed to pass the top of Valance Road, where the twins had lived with their mother, Violet, and their father, Charlie Kray Senior. Reg caught a quick glimpse of the road, but he wouldn't have recognised it — the houses had been pulled down many years ago and the streets are now clean of crime.

Gradually they neared the church, where enormous crowds had gathered. One by one the vehicles came to a stop, one by one the gangsters got out of their limos, one by one they entered St Matthew's Church. It was all sombre and respectful, well staged and organised. It was just what Reg Kray had wanted — now he had full control of the situation. And he would give the crowd exactly what they wanted and expected.

He waved to the crowds and smiled when he reached

the church even though he was still handcuffed to the policewoman, who towered above him. He looked thin and pale as he straightened himself, brushing down his grey pin-stripe suit and straightening his tie. His hair was almost white and cut short, and he looked frail. In fact, he looked like what he was — an old man.

There was plenty of muscle at the church to keep control of the crowds and there were Hell's Angels present in abundance. As Reg entered the church, he was greeted warmly by the mourners, friends and family — all hugging and kissing in true Mafia fashion like there were no tomorrows. At last he was seated and the show could begin.

The coffin was brought into the church by six pall-bearers to the tune of Celine Dion's 'Up Close and Personal', a favourite of Charlie's. All the gold and the jewellery on display glittered and sparkled as light entered by the main doors, a spotlight on proceedings, that were by now well under way. Even some of Charlie's old showbiz pals were there — Billy Murray, who plays Detective Sergeant Beech in ITV's *The Bill* sat quietly, head down in reflection, and Charlie's old friend and drinking partner, the actor George Sewell, sat patiently and attentively following the course of events as they unravelled. These two were just onlookers this day, extras on the set — the star of this particular performance was Charlie Kray.

The ceremony was conducted with respect and aplomb by father Ken Rimini, who had known Charlie for many years. The songs included 'Morning Has Broken', 'Fight the Good Fight' and 'Abide With Me' — and there were enough heavies around to see that everyone sang, but everyone! The tears flowed and everyone stared at Reg, as father Ken spoke of Charlie.

'Many things have been said about Charlie,' he told the mourners, 'some true and some very untrue and hurtful. I can't judge him. He now stands before a greater authority than this life.'

As he continued, he told of the last time that he had seen Charlie Kray — at Charlie's son Gary's funeral, some four years earlier. Gary, a young man who would do no one any harm and a most cheerful character, just like his dad, had died suddenly of cancer at the age of 44. 'It broke his heart,' he told everyone.

Reg couldn't hold back the tears as the good father spoke of his older brother, now deceased. He laid his head on the young shoulders of his wife Roberta as he tried to take it all in — the hurt, the frustration, the pride.

Tributes were read out loud from friends and family alike. Jamie Foreman, son of Kray cohort Freddie Foreman, told of how 'Charlie's smile will be engrained on my heart' and others read poems in tribute. But the finale was a recording by Reg of a poem he had written for Charlie — it rang out on the speakers in the church, filling the air with nostalgia. His voice was weak, his tone sympathetic as he spoke the words.

'I am not there, I did not die. I am a thousand winds that blow. I am diamond glints on snow.'

INTRODUCTION

A true tribute from someone who many would call a diamond geezer, freed for the day from his prison home, to pay his last respects to his older brother — a man who had died without a penny to his name, a man who had made a pitiful living on the name of Kray, a fake and a fraud and a relic of bygone days. But Charlie Kray was nothing like his brothers — he was a crook, yes; he was a criminal, yes; he was a man who would do almost anything to make a dishonest living — but Charlie Kray was a loveable rogue, a charming womaniser, a cheerful and light-hearted soul who was always welcome company in any company. And I for one will miss him.

The oak coffin was led from the church to the sounds of one of Charlie's favourite singers and old-time pal, Shirley Bassey. The sounds rang loud and true from the speakers, 'As Long As He Needs Me', as Reg leaned forward and kissed the coffin. The service was over — now to meet the crowds.

As he emerged from the church, Mad Frankie Fraser yelled out three cheers for Reg Kray. Naturally enough, the crowds were eager to comply and Reg had his tribute well rehearsed and planned — well worth the 50-minute wait. A few bear hugs later and he was once again back in the Mercedes and on his way to Chingford Mount Cemetery.

The four-mile trip was a formality. The crowds lined the streets, as they had done five years earlier. The procession of cars kept in line, orderly and calm — just like a military campaign. Once inside the cemetery, more heavies were there to protect Reg from the crowds as he wandered among the graves. A glance around the family plot lead him to the grave of Frances, his first wife, who had committed suicide at the age of 23. He stopped and stroked the headstone, waiting for the photographers to catch up with him. The policewoman, still handcuffed to Reg, took it all in her stride — she did her profession proud as she showed the kind of respect and consideration that many other officers would have found difficult to handle.

Flanked by the policewoman on one side and his present wife, Roberta, on the other, Reg Kray waited for the coffin to be lowered. As Charlie was laid to rest, Reg threw a red rose on to the coffin — a last, lonely tribute. Many hugs and kisses later, Reg Kray was ready for the journey back to Wayland Prison, Norfolk.

Diane Buffini, Charlie's common-law wife, was one of the last to leave. 'Charlie would have loved the sunshine,' she told reporters, as once again the shouts rang out — 'Free Reg Kray,' and 'Take the handcuffs off.'

Big Paul, the heavy in charge of the bodyguards, thanked the crowd for coming to support Reg Kray.

'Reg wants me to thank you all for coming' he told them. 'He wishes you all well and he hopes to be among you soon!'

More cheers followed as Reg was led away to the blue Mercedes — it had been a long day, but the gangster, once the head of one of the most powerful criminal organisations in the country, had taken it all and more, and he was still fighting.

This fighting game is in the blood, as it was for all three Kray brothers. And with some 32 years behind him in jail and no date fixed as yet for his release, Reg Kray needed all the strength he could muster. Ron lost his fight back in 1995, Charlie had only recently lost his — so was Reg now to succeed where his brothers had failed? Could Reg survive to be set free, to stroll the streets of London once again — to be a celebrity, to be a man of stature, a man to be reckoned with within the society he scorned? Maybe that was the true meaning of 'Fight the Good Fight'.

Colin Fry
May, 2000

1

FIGHTING FOR SUCCESS

RON KRAY HAD BEEN HIT time and time again and his face was showing the signs of the night's work. His cheeks were bruised and grazed and his left eye was completely closed, but he had finally beaten his man to the floor in a sudden flurry of pure aggression; winning was the name of the game for Ron and he didn't care how he did it. His brothers hadn't fared much better, but it was without doubt Charlie who had come off worst of all. He was in complete agony, doubled up in pain from the severe beating he had taken. It wasn't a good night for the Krays and it marked a fatal turning point in all their careers.

They vigorously washed the blood from their aching

1

hands as they vowed never to be beaten like that again. Ron and Reg talked about the future and how they would get even; Charlie could only talk of getting out — he had had enough! The purple blur of half-shut eyes, the mangled hands and the bloodied features would soon be a thing of the past for all three Kray brothers. Never would they let this happen again, never would they allow themselves to fight on someone else's terms.

The day was the 11th December 1951 and the brothers had all been fighting on the same bill at The Royal Albert Hall, the only time this feat has ever been achieved. The boxing days were over for the Krays. Next time they would fight by their own rules — street rules.

Charlie had been a fighter most of his life, both in the ring and on the street. In London's East End in the 1950s, fighting was a way of life — and death. It was about survival of the fittest. Street gangs and street people all settled their scores in the same way: with their fists. Fight first, ask questions afterwards. Careless talk cost lives.

The Kray boys had pedigree. Cannonball Lee was a champion bare-knuckle fighter. He was also their grandfather, Jimmy Lee. Lee had fought in the days when boxing didn't have many rules. Just the street. It was every man for himself. He'd entertained the boys for years with tales of prize fights and fighters; the same stories over and over again. They never tired of them. Fighting was in their blood.

When Charlie decided to pick up the gloves, he met with strong resistance from his mother Violet. As Cannonball's daughter, she had lived through years of watching her father come home hurt after bouts of fighting. She had spent her childhood helping her mother to pick up the pieces of him, only to wait for him to dust himself down and start all over again. but she didn't want to watch her own boys do that.

Their father, though, took a different point of view. If they wanted to fight, then that was OK with him. After all, he couldn't do much about it, even if he'd wanted to. But he knew of the advantages that boxing had brought. He had fought as a youngster and was pleased to see his boys carry on the tradition, to keep the punch in the family name. He would help them all he could, if he could. He had his position in the East End to think about. At home, however, it was his wife Violet who ruled the roost; but even she could not persuade her boys away from the boxing ring.

In the East End of London, the name of Kray had become well known in boxing circles. And old man Charlie commanded a lot of respect through the reputation of his three boxing sons. He liked the reflected fame and glory. Life had been tough early on. During the Second World War, Violet had taken Charlie and the twins Ron and Reg to Suffolk, where they could live safely away from the German bombings of London. Although he had visited them every weekend and supported them through it, it hadn't been easy.

Old man Charlie felt that he hadn't always been a good father to his sons. Not that he had mistreated them. Not in any way. On the contrary, he'd always tried his best with his family. Even when he had been on the run as a deserter during the Second World War, he had made every effort to go home as much as he could. But he had been absent so much during the War. He had missed much of their growing up then. He could remember when the twins were young, though, how they would always side with their mother Violet in any argument. And how he could never win.

Although old man Charlie may have been the breadwinner in the family, it was Violet who always took care of her boys: their school days, their ill days, their happy days. Violet was always there for them. Old man Charlie went away again, later on, after the War, taking care of business. He travelled extensively throughout England, the south in particular, buying and selling whatever he could. Sometimes gold. He made a good living, enough for Violet and the boys — and just enough for regular nights out with his pals. The drinking and the fighting were both an important part of life in the East End.

Nothing could make up for the fact that old man Charlie hadn't been part of the family much — not enough for his liking, anyway — in the early years. So, it had become his job to prepare his sons boxing kit. It was his contribution to the smooth-running of the pre-match organization — and his way of showing that he, too, wanted to help out and join in with family life. The three sets of kit were laid out in neat piles in the front room: the black, highly polished boots; white socks; blue satin dressing-gowns; an array of towels and protective cups; and the shorts, black and white for the twins, and light blue silk with a yellow leg stripe for Charlie — a present from the twins. They were Charlie's first pair of silk shorts, a special memento for what Charlie wanted to be his last fight.

Henry Berry had trained all three boys. He had started with young Charlie, whose boxing career had begun at senior school — and he'd been training ever since. But Charlie hadn't trained for the Albert Hall. He'd been asked to compete rather late in the day and had decided that although he'd give it a go, this would be his last professional fight. He was only doing it for the money this time. The £25 purse was too tempting to resist. His chances he realized were not good. Lazar came from a great boxing family and was a well-fancied contender. But Charlie had decided to accept the challenge. He didn't have anything to lose, except his pride. And the money was guaranteed.

Charlie had been in training three nights a week since he was fifteen. He went to a local club and continued when he got home too. Cannonball Lee had rigged up a gym with a canvas kitbag as punchbag in an upstairs bedroom. Once he'd left school he worked during the day as a messenger for Lloyd's insurance brokers in the City, but at night he would train relentlessly. With a heap of training, no smoking or drinking, he became a good clean boxer.

A few weeks off with rheumatic fever weren't enough to stop him. He fought to recover quickly and went back regularly to a boxing club in Hoxton. Everything was going well, and once he'd joined the naval cadets at Hackney Wick, he didn't look back.

With the help of good training facilities and an iron will to succeed, Charlie became increasingly serious about boxing. As a decent welterweight with a string of successful amateur tournaments behind him, he decided to turn professional. It was just post-war and there was good money to be made –often as much as £10 — for just a night's work. Good money in those days. The coins thrown on stage by fans at the end of a match would have been a bonus, but most of this went to the helpers.

As Charlie once said, 'Have you ever tried picking up coins with boxing gloves on?'

What young Charlie did collect, though, was a row of trophies, a flash of silverware that had pride of place on the mantelpiece at home in Vallance Road. His success and enthusiasm were enjoyed and envied in equal turn by his younger brothers. They wanted to join in; they wanted to fight their way to the top too. Ever mindful of his by now high standing in the East End community, old man Charlie was eager to help any way he could. The gymnasium upstairs was improved, and the boys trained day and night.

Charlie had been encouraging his kid brothers to spar with him from when they were so small that they had to stand on a chair to reach the punch bag. Six years younger than Charlie, they made up for in enthusiasm what they lacked in experience, and with regular work-outs in the homemade gym they became fighting fit. With its speedball, punchbag, weights and skipping ropes, it was the place to be. There was a steady stream of aspiring young fighters going in and out of Vallance Road all the time. Young Charlie would organize competitions for the youngsters, and the twins had already decided to form their own boxing club, operational from the back upstairs bedroom.

In spite of her fears for the well-being of her boys, Violet Kray found herself enjoying these training sessions. She was pleased to have young men around who were appreciative of how she kept things in order and looked after their kit. She liked the involvement and attention.

When after a year of training like this, they moved on to the Robert Browning Institute in Walworth, South London, Violet was sorry to see them go, but they knew they could rely on her support. The twins had been agitating to join a real club, and once there they didn't have to work too hard at catching the eye of the trainers who were to be their key to stardom.

'How old are they?' asked one trainer. He was hanging out at the Institute, surveying potential talent.

'Ten,' replied Charlie. 'And they have never boxed.'

The trainer's jaw dropped. 'They are amazing,' he said. 'We'll sign them up.'

Around this time, the Kray twins, aged ten, boxed their first public match together in East London — at a funfair boxing booth in Victoria Park. This later became a rare occurrence, and, once they reached their twenties and operated in business together, the twins never, ever fought. Like most brothers, they argued a lot, but nothing would happen. Although the atmosphere would get so thick and heated sometimes you felt sure there'd be all hell let loose.

The boxing booth that day took all comers, and when nobody proved willing to spar with a particularly beefy fighter, Ron Kray chanced his arm. He was quite keen to earn the prize money, but it was his notorious bravado that took the upper hand.

'I'll take him on,' he shouted.

Taking one look at the size of him, the manager of the booth just laughed. He thought it was a good joke, as did the gathering crowd, who hooted and catcalled. It wasn't possible for Ron to fight the big man. No, it wasn't on. There was no one small enough for him to fight with.

The anti-climax became too much for Reg Kray. Without a second thought, pointing at Ron, he yelled above the roar of the crowd: 'I'll fight him.'

There was silence for a moment. It was obvious that the boys were brothers and evenly matched. If they were both willing, then why should anyone want to stop them? The twins climbed into the ring and prepared themselves for the fight. Although they had sparred together many times before, this time it was the real thing.

They proved to be great entertainment for the crowd, both determined to win and hitting each other furiously. Finally the booth manager called it off. The match, he decreed, had ended in a draw, and he paid the boys a few shillings for their efforts.

But, for Ron and Reg it had more significance. They had enjoyed themselves, the boxing, for sure, but more so being the centre of attention. The applause was more than gratifying, it was the way forward. Through boxing, they could get what they wanted. The roar of approval from the crowd was for them; they were in charge, calling the shots.

In time, Reg became a good boxer, quietly confident. Nothing ever seemed to shake him, and he had a confidence in himself that was strong. He could be relaxed and easy going and he never appeared to get tense or edgy before a big fight. He'd shadow box with himself as he jogged up and down the street or on the spot. He'd train hard. He didn't like losing, and he was sure that he wouldn't.

Ron also boxed well and was as fearless in the ring as he was proving to be outside it. His nerves always showed, though, as the match drew near. He tried to take everything in his stride and accept his life without argument, but it wasn't that simple. The prospect of losing face — anywhere, anyhow — spurred him on to success. And there was the family name to consider. He had to win. But the fear of failure never left him.

The Krays were driven to the Albert Hall on the night of 11 December 1951 in Jack Jordan's Riley. Jack had been their manager for years. He'd got the Kray party good seats at the Albert Hall, all the family and friends who wouldn't want to miss the fights. All that is except Violet; she was staying in that evening. The sight of someone hitting one of her boys was just too much for her.

The car pulled up at a side entrance in Exhibition Road, South Kensington. They all piled out, rushing off in different directions — old man Charlie to find his seat, and Ron, Reg and Charlie to the changing rooms.

Ron was on first. Followed by Reg and then Charlie. No sooner were his hands bandaged than the whip knocked on the door: 'Ron Kray, you're on.'

Ron left the dressing room with Jack Jordan; Reg and Charlie were close behind. The roar of the crowd was deafening as Ron walked out into the spotlight, along the red carpet to the ring. The atmosphere was electric. As Reg and Charlie watched backstage, they were aware of Ron's apparent indifference to his opponent, Bill Sliney. He, Ron, was giving all his attention to Henry Berry who was drilling him one last time.

It was roasting hot in the Albert Hall, and the buzz from the crowd was deafening. It was getting smoky, as though a fine mist were falling in the hall. In the arena, Ron was beginning to sweat; it was running steadily down the sides of his face.

'And, now,' the master of ceremonies bellowed over the speaker system, 'on my right, Bill Sliney from King's Cross and on my left, Ron Kray from Bethnal

Green.' The referee called the two men into the centre of the ring.

He briefed them, 'We want a nice, clean fight. No butting or holding and no punching low. Go to it. Have a good fight.' Back in their opposite corners, the boxers waited. They were alone in the boxing ring. Some say it's the loneliest place in the world.

'Seconds out,' the time keeper shouted.

Now it was all down to Ron. The fight started well, and Ron soon had Bill Sliney down for a count of eight. It looked as if it was going to go Ron's way, he was really on top. Although Bill Sliney was putting up a courageous defence, Ron was definitely ahead. Don't count your chickens though! Always keep in mind that the fight's not over until you've won — or lost.

It was a nasty blow to Ron's eye from an accidental clash of heads that turned the fight round in Bill Sliney's favour. When it happened, the crowd went quiet. No one stirred in the Albert Hall. The referee inspected the damage, and even as he did so Ron's left eye was closing fast — but not enough to call off the match. Ron was forced to fight on with the use of only one eye.

In the second round, Sliney used Ron's injury to his advantage, circling Ron anti-clockwise, making sure to keep to his blind side and at arm's length.

'Jab, jab, jab,' came the cries from Sliney's corner.

Ron Kray only knew one way to fight and that was to go forward, keep going, with aggression. His pride and courage would not let him give up — even though half the time he couldn't even see his opponent.

He had fought hard fights in the past, such as one time at Lime Grove Baths in West London, when he had been caught by a right hand and took a count of eight.

Everyone saw it, except Ron. He came round just in time to see the match through to a win in three rounds. It was sheer guts and will power that carried him.

The same thing had happened at the Sporting Club in the West End. Felled early in the contest, he had regained his strength sufficiently to knock out his opponent in three rounds. But, this time it was turning out differently. Maybe he was just a slow starter, but on this occasion he couldn't catch Sliney. He tried relentlessly, but he couldn't land a good, clean punch. After six gruelling rounds the referee announced Bill Sliney's victory.

The decision against Ron was a slim one, made on points. It had been close, but Sliney had got the verdict. Disappointed but gracious in defeat, Ron slipped through the ropes and strode back along the red carpet, through the applause to the dressing room. He'd been unlucky this time.

Reg was on next against Bob Manito, a South Londoner from Clapham. Reg had psyched himself up; he was feeling confident. He remembered the time he had fought Ron in the finals of the London Schools' competition. Then he had had to face Ron over three consecutive years. The first two years he had lost, but on the third occasion he had made up his mind not to lose. He had given himself a good talking-to. Nothing was going to stop him.

It worked — he won on a unanimous points decision. But there was hell to pay at home. Violet made them promise that they would never fight each other again. She'd been disappointed in them. The family must stay together, stand by each other, play together and stay together. No in-fighting. It was something that was bred into the roots of their lives and stayed with them for ever.

That night at the Albert Hall he was sure his mother would soon be more than proud of him. He'd see to that. And sure enough it worked like a dream. He beat Manito in each of the six rounds. He had won. Strength and will power, combined with careful attention to his trainer's advice, had proved a heady and triumphant brew. It was strong stuff: the stuff that dreams are made of.

In the ring now, Charlie was not in good shape. He knew that if he were knocked down in the course of the fight, he should stay down. Lew Lazar was going to come up with a hard fight. Harder than his boxing bouts in the Royal Navy, harder than the knock-out tournaments when he would fight three times a night. There was nowhere tougher for him to be than in that arena at the Royal Albert Hall. It was now time for Charlie to face himself and what he wanted; there is no place to hide in a boxing ring.

It was as early as the second round that Charlie started to slide, to lose his grip on the match. He didn't see a left hook to his stomach and promptly went down on his knees. The referee started counting as Charlie tried to get his breath back. It wasn't easy. He looked across at his trainer who was motioning him to stay down for the count of ten. Charlie couldn't do it. His pride made him get to his feet as the referee reached the count of eight.

'Box on,' came the command from the referee, and both boxers resumed their fight.

It was getting harder for Charlie Kray, but he had to go on. The end of the round was near, and he relaxed for a brief moment, just to regain a little composure.

This proved a mistake. Charlie's guard had dropped, and Lew Lazar caught him again with another vicious left hook to the stomach, and the result was the same as before. Charlie sank to his knees, hardly able to breathe. He was gasping for air as the referee counted, 'One, two, three ...'

A quick look over to Berry, who was frantically signalling for him to stay down, was all he could manage as he fought within himself to regain the strength that had gone completely from his legs.

'Four, five, six ...,' continued the referee, as he stared into Charlie's eyes, looking for signs of recovery.

Charlie's mind raced. Was this really the end of a good boxing career? Should he continue, or should he follow the instruction of his trainer? Questions, questions, questions filled his head. There were always questions to be answered.

'Seven, eight ...,' said the referee.

The pain wasn't so acute now, after a short rest. Maybe he could continue. His pride made him get up at the count of eight. But Charlie Kray was lucky. As he rose to his feet, the bell was sounded for the end of round two, and, even then, he only just managed to hobble back to his corner.

'That's enough, Charlie. You've done enough' were the words that greeted him from his corner. 'Don't go on.' Henry Berry was emphatic in his advice to his boxer. But Charlie chose to ignore him this time.

Could he make it? Could he survive? Could he win? There wasn't time for Charlie to think. He was down on his knees again in the third round, and there were still three more rounds to go. Lazar had landed him yet another left hook to the body, and the referee was counting again: 'One, two, three ...'.

Getting up at the count of eight was becoming a habit, and Charlie dragged himself up by clutching at the ropes. The referee checked him over for a few moments, just to make sure that he was in a fit state to continue, and then he let the fight resume once again. Surely it couldn't last much longer.

It was only halfway through the third round, and things weren't looking at all good. All those fights over so many years had given Charlie the will power to continue, but by now even he knew the end was near. It was almost inevitable.

It was another left hook to the stomach that finally did the trick for Lew Lazar. He had made every punch count, and his left hooks to the body were executed with exact precision. Lazar's timing was superb that evening. He really was a good boxer.

Charlie Kray collapsed to the floor as the crowd rose to their feet. Everyone was cheering; they had done so throughout the fight. They weren't cheering for anyone in particular, as they appreciated the effort put in by both boxers.

'One, two, three .. .,' counted the referee, as Charlie looked across at Henry Berry.

The signals back were the same as before, and Charlie could almost hear his trainer's words: 'Don't be a hero, Charlie.'

'Four, five, six ...,' said the referee, peering into Charlie's eyes.

It was time for Charlie to summon all his strength. He reached out for the ropes and grabbed at them. This time he was successful, but it just wasn't enough.

'Seven, eight, nine .. .,' continued the referee, who realized that the inevitable was about to happen.

Charlie just couldn't do it — he couldn't stand up. His pride couldn't help him. The bell couldn't help him. No one could help him in this loneliest of places.

'Ten and out,' said the referee at long last. It was all over.

The crowd was applauding both fighters as the referee counted Charlie Kray out. Charlie just stayed on his knees for a while, looking fixedly at the floor of the boxing ring. This was it. His final fight, and he had lost. But, he had done so to a good fighter and a possible champion, and there was no disgrace in being beaten by a better man.

Back in his corner, Charlie felt better. Henry Berry consoled his boxer, confirming that he had expected him to lose, given his lack of fitness. It had been a fair fight. And now it was over. Lew Lazar had deserved to win.

Charlie walked back along the red carpet to deafening applause from the crowd, who always gave a good loser a warm send-off. He thought to himself how thankful he was to have been the last of the brothers to box that night — so neither Ron nor Reg had seen him beaten.

Charlie entered the dressing room with Henry Berry and sat down immediately to have his gloves removed. He still had his blue satin dressing gown around his shoulders. He was feeling much better as the twins came over to offer him their condolences. Ron said not to worry; it was only a fight. Reg told him that he had done his best, though he really should have trained more.

Slowly Charlie regained his composure, something he had sought to do that night in the ring. By the time Jack Jordan came into the dressing room to hand the men their pay for the evening's entertainment, all three brothers were laughing and joking among themselves.

DOING THE BUSINESS

For Charlie, Jack Jordan had made an alteration to the normal rules of professional boxing. He didn't take his percentage from Charlie's pay packet that evening, since he knew it was Charlie's last fight. This was a big gesture from Jordan, who remained a life-long friend of the Krays. Henry Berry, too, had been with the Krays right from the start of their boxing careers, and he would continue in boxing for many years to come. The Krays would always be grateful to these two men's dedication to their fighting success.

Old man Charlie travelled back to Vallance Road in Jack Jordan's Riley with his three sons and their trainer. The atmosphere in the car was light-hearted and fun. Everyone was in a good mood. Jordan and Berry were busy lining up Ron and Reg with more fights. Both men were confident that the twins could become really good boxers; Reg, in particular, could possibly become a champion. He was certainly skilful enough.

Violet received the men at the front door, inspecting each of her boys as they entered the house. She wasn't bothered about the results. All she was concerned about was her sons' well-being.

'What have you done to your eye, Ronnie?' she said as she greeted Ron.

'It's all right, mum. It don't hurt,' replied Ron as he reached out for a cup of tea.

Jack Jordan and Henry Berry came into the house for a few minutes to say hello to Violet, but before long it was just the Kray family alone at home, drinking tea and eating sandwiches. All they thought and talked about was their fights that night. Old man Charlie had enjoyed himself immensely, as he always did on such evenings. Violet was just happy that it was all over.

But for Charlie, Ron and Reg it really was all over. The three Kray brothers had made their first and final appearance at the Royal Albert Hall, and they would never, ever, fight professionally again. They had other things to do.

Charlie simply wanted out, knew he had to move on. The twins had no choice: they had just been conscripted into the Army. But they had all left while the going was still good, and, although their days of sparring in the ring were over, they were just about to begin their fight for success in another arena: the streets and clubs, casinos and pubs of London's East End. If the three Kray brothers had made their mark on British boxing, they were about to impress themselves indelibly on the world in other ways.

2

PROTECTING THEIR
INVESTEMENT

THE REGAL WAS IN ERIC STREET, just off the Mile End
Road in the heart of the East End. Before the War, it had
been a cinema, but by the early 1950s it had become a
derelict and rundown, fourteen-table billiard hall. In
April 1954 the Kray twins had hoped for better days, too.
Just demobbed from the army, they had served nine-
month sentences at Shepton Mallet jail for desertion. But
they were young enough and ballsy enough to feel
resilient, and brash enough to ask for help — especially
from the family.

They were a staunch family, the Krays, and would

always help each other out of trouble. This time it was Charlie's turn to fork out.

He was not known as being very generous when it came to lending money — he was more the borrowing type himself. But his brothers were different, so uncharacteristically he dipped his hand deep in his pocket to get them started in one business deal or another. It was probably this supportive gesture by Charlie that led the twins to involve him later on when they began to dominate the gangland East End.

But the twins didn't have much success — not, that is, when it came to regular up front dealing. Their intention was to achieve, but without any definite goal in mind they drifted aimlessly from one deal to another. So with plenty of time to kill and little money in hand, they turned to petty thieving — and even did a little fire-bombing or two for the local heavy mob who were trying their hand at protection and extortion. One day they would steal a truck load of goods, the next it would be dealing in stolen documents. Sometimes they would cheat the local bookmaker. It was a case of anything goes for Ron and Reg Kray — and they loved it!

Hanging around, at loose ends, they heard about the Regal. A few visits there confirmed to them that it might be possible to turn the place around, to improve its fortunes. Apart from its derelict air and no-hoper clientele, they knew for sure that it had possibilities.

Their takeover bid was slow but unstoppable, an echo of how they would come to operate in the East End throughout the fifties and sixties. Reg would play billiards in the hall with his pals, while Ron held court for his friends and acquaintances. He was a charmer, Ron, flamboyant and witty, quite eccentric. The violence at the Regal, which had always been there, escalated during the first few months of their attendance. As they became regulars, so did the brawling — and damage to the billiard hall.

The aggression around the place got so bad that the manager bought an Alsatian dog to help protect his property — and himself. It didn't help; the animal had fireworks thrown at it, and the dog soon went mad. By the summer of 1954, the manager had had enough too. He was ready to quit.

Ron and Reg made the owners an offer; one they couldn't refuse. For £5.00 a week, they would take over running the hall, confident that they could do it smoothly. No one would mess with them, they'd make sure of that. They'd keep the money from the tables, and the takings from the refreshment bar would be split between the owner and the twins. It was all cut and dry, no angles, no messing. And it was to become their first really successful business operation — and legitimate at that — run entirely by them, their way.

In 1954, aged twenty-one, Ron and Reg were just getting to establish a name for themselves in London's East End. The Regal was the start of it all. They were at the beginning of what became a run. And it was only natural that other young men would want to flex their muscles, to test them out. To find out how tough they really were. The violent eruptions that had increased with their presence were an attempt to suss them out.

If the three years in the army had done just one thing for the Kray twins, it was to have made them fitter and tougher than ever. Their reputation as hard men spread like wildfire in their patch around the Mile End Road.

The twins were not to be provoked. No one willingly messed with them. You don't fight them, they fight you.

When the Regal was refurbished and reopened by the Krays, it became an overnight success. Packed to the roof with their mates, old and new, and their mates' mates, it was the happening place in the East End. No one wanted to miss a night there. With the place so full of so many friends and relations every night, there was no room for strangers. Other gangs stayed away. Sensibly. And violence and aggression was becoming rare.

What finished the violence at the Regal once and for all was what happened to a Maltese gang, also from the East End. They made a big mistake one night when they decided to call by for their protection money. It was just after the billiard hall had reopened. Now it's a joke to think of anyone mad enough to try to extort money from Ron and Reg, but their reputation at that stage was slight.

A number of Maltese gangs operated in the Mile End Road area in the 1950s. They were well established and confident. Confident enough to call on Ron and Reg at the end of a long hard night.

Alone in the Regal, the twins were stacking chairs. Immediately they sensed trouble. The Maltese strolled casually around the hall, striking the smooth green baize of the new tables and examining the cues in a detached but menacing way. Eventually, the gang leader approached the twins. Before the word protection was fully out of his mouth, he was out of the door with his mates, flattened.

'Protection from what?', Ron had replied as he lashed out at them with a cutlass.

Seconds later, Reg drew out a knife, and the battle

that followed would have been bloody and fatal if the Maltese gang had not fled in terror.

Cool as ever, Reg Kray was heard to comment, 'They've not got a lot of bottle, these continentals, especially when the knives come out.'

Other incidents followed, but nothing major ever happened again there. An occasional fight that flared and died down as abruptly as it had started. The East End was a tinder box, but Ron and Reg kept a firm grip on the sparks that might set it alight. The word was out. The Regal was a peaceful club where you could enjoy a bevvy with your mates; it wasn't a place to start trouble. In a different way, though, it did just that.

The twins got the lease on the Regal renewed for three years. They now had a base from which to operate and somewhere they could meet their old friends and contacts. Charlie Kray watched it all happening. How the billiard hall became a meeting-place for young tearaways and villains, even old friends from the glasshouse in Shepton Mallet. They all somehow found their way to Eric Street.

Charlie didn't like it, but he simply had to put up with it. The Regal soon became one of the places in the East End to discuss and plan such business activities as robbery and burglary — quite openly. It was just the beginning: the Kray twins were starting to discover that crime can pay.

Reg Kray handled all business arrangements at the Regal. Where he could he kept it in the family — his uncle Billy served behind the bar. Reg took the Regal and its spin-offs very seriously. If someone wanted to dispose of stolen goods, then Reg would deal with it. He'd find a contact, someone to negotiate a sale. He'd even arrange storage of the merchandise at the Regal until a buyer could be found.

But it wasn't just the goods Reg dealt with; he'd arrange to look after specialist tools and equipment, used on jobs by local villains. He'd hide them away, sometimes under the benches at the Regal, but always at a price.

The scale of the villainy escalated; soon they were hiding guns. And Ron, it was known, had an arsenal of fire-arms. It had started with knives. He was fascinated by them and had also begun to collect cutlasses, of which he had a huge collection, including swords, sabres and bayonets. Anything with a blade. He would sharpen them from time to time in the back yard at Vallance Road. He would spend hours happily honing them on an enormous grindstone.

His gun collection was also vast, most of which was hidden under the floorboards, upstairs at Vallance Road. He didn't consider why he collected them or what he wanted them for. What was obvious was that it had become an obsession.

What was also becoming an obsession was the need to stay in control, to keep the Regal running their way. According to their rules. Sometimes this backfired.

As the months passed, business at the Regal flourished. Takings at the tables and the bar peaked, and the crowds kept on coming. While Reg was in charge of business, Ron had set himself up as entertainments manager. It was an informal arrangement, but it included the role of bouncer. One evening when Ron was holding court as usual from his chair, a gang of young men came. They were just another East End gang looking for trouble. And it was Ron's job to deal with it.

Ron was always fearless. His instant reactions always operated from this blind aggression. Fiercely he picked out one of the youths, and dragged him off to one side to frisk him roughly.

As he searched, he brushed down the boy's legs and yelled out, 'You should have known better than to come in here with weapons.' He looked furious and triumphant.

It went very quiet in the hall. The silence in the eye of the hurricane. The thunderous rage to come was palpable. Everyone held their breath for what felt like a long time, knowing that something had to give. And give it did. One of the youths asked cautiously if he could have a quiet word with Ron.

They went off behind the bar and in an audible whisper the youth said, 'He's wearing leg-irons — he's partly crippled. It isn't a sword.'

The timebomb had been defused, and Ron, this time, was able to laugh it off.

But looking after business meant taking care of real bother, and Reg was equally at home with this. He would deal with disorder directly, famous for his trick cigarette punch. He practised it for hours on a punchbag, determined to perfect his technique. It worked. He would offer a cigarette with his right hand and then hit out at the other man's jaw with his left. He broke a lot of jaws in his time, including that of a local trouble-maker by the name of Tony Schnyder.

Schnyder was always hanging around the Regal, often up and down the nearby New Road area of the East End, where the rag trade was centred. His trouble was negotiable but complicated by the fact that he carried a gun. He took great pleasure in showing it off to all and sundry; it was a big part of his image. He liked to create the right impression: I'm tough, so don't mess with me. And part of this involved bad mouthing the Krays.

'Is that Tony Schnyder, the big tough guy?'

The buzz went round the Regal. Schnyder had just been felled by a swift right hand, which had cracked his jaw. The injured man collapsed on to the floor in agony, blood pouring from his mouth. Reg Kray had just had enough of his brash talk. In the bar, Schnyder had made one too many remarks within hearing distance of Charlie and Reg and now he had had to answer for his big mouth.

'He doesn't look very tough to me,' someone sneered. 'He walks through the door, and he's carted out feet first.'

A ripple of disdainful laughter and chat washed around the room. Schnyder did not find the incident at all amusing. As he scraped himself off the floor and crawled out into the street, he had revenge fixed in his head. Staggering down the street, he drew no comments. This was a common sight all around the East End. What was not common was Schnyder's next course of action: he had decided to report the incident to the police.

Involving the law was to break an unwritten East End code: Thou shalt not talk to the police. If you brought in the law, you lost your reputation and credibility. The Krays didn't slag off the police, but they didn't talk to them much either -unless they had to, in which case they were pointedly polite. But to go to them for help with East End business — never. There's loyalty, always, to your own kind. Schnyder knew this, but he was angry and humiliated enough to break it.

As he neared the police station, he was lucky that he met Georgie Woods, a man with a web of connections in the East End, a man whose word counted. Woods cautioned him about taking his grievance with the Krays to the law.

'That would be stupid,' he said. 'Forget it. Straighten it out some other way. Involve the law and you'll lose your reputation.'

Schnyder knew he was right. That night there would be no trouble with the law at the Regal. That would come later. For now the policy was to keep one step ahead and out of trouble.

The Regal had become the centre of attention, a hangout and the focus for a gang of youngsters who were regulars. This was the start of the firm, the inner circle of young men about the East End, up to tricks. There was always some excitement there. When there wasn't, then Ron would organize a trip outside the manor to make some. It was good to be on the firm, you could do what you liked if you stuck together. You tried not to fall foul of the law, but you fought for your patch. Any way you could — clean or dirty. You were ready for anything or anybody.

Ron had read everything there was to read about Al Capone and the Chicago gangsters. Capone became a real hero to him. Ron even began to copy his style of dress and tried to organize the firm along military lines, as Capone had done. He became known as the Colonel. Always immaculately dressed, he would sit in his favourite seat in the smoke-filled billiard hall where he was in his element. To make the atmosphere even more thick, Ron liked the crowd to smoke as much as possible — sometimes even asking them to smoke more if he thought there wasn't enough of a fug.

Ron would often surround himself with young men at the Regal, just as much as he would attract women when he was out and about. A lot of people, men and women, found Ron attractive. He was a flamboyant person, gregarious and generous with those in his circle.

He'd told his brother Charlie that he liked men and women equally; his preference was bisexuality. Charlie found this hard to swallow. How could someone as manly as his kid brother -a man's man even — a hard nut, macho and unbeatable, want to have sex with another man? To fight with them, yes, to spar with backchat and jokes, to hang out and play pool, but not sex.

Charlie could never get his head round this. It was a gulf that was unbridgeable and came to represent something that stood between them that would never mend. Although family ties kept them together, Charlie would never feel really close to Ron and was never able to reach the intimacy of affections that existed between the twins. He remained and was often treated as an outsider, and this spilled over into their business deals. Charlie often went it alone.

In the summer of 1954, Charlie Kray was involved in his own business. He had set up a travel company that specialized in all-in holidays to the south of France. With two good friends, Stan Davies and Lenny Bearfield, he'd tour-drive a minibus to the Villa Roches Roses in St Raphael.

In the villa, which he'd leased for the summer, he put up his guests. The villa had been occupied by troops during the Second World War, first by the German occupying forces and then by the Allies. It was now a solid source of income for its owners, with whom Charlie became friends, as he did with many of his clients. One of whom he never forgot.

Vic Streeter was a big man, six foot three in his bare feet, with a face threaded with scars and a prominent broken nose. He'd obviously seen tough times, but he was a real gentleman — and, as it turned out, a policeman. Vic was a talented rugby player, a skill that was put to the test against the French Navy who were billeted nearby, looking for a one-off friendly. Charlie was enlisted into Vic's team along with Stan and Lennie, and they beat the French at a game one Saturday afternoon in the main football stadium in St Raphael.

Years later Charlie and Vic were to meet in very different circumstances, at the West End Central Police Station. It was 1968, the year when the three Kray brothers were arrested by Detective Chief Inspector Leonard 'Nipper' Read, who'd been leading an inquiry into their activities for some time. The officer in charge at the station that day was none other than Vic Streeter. He booked them without saying a word to Charlie.

Once locked up, Vic Streeter came down to the cells to talk to Charlie. He hadn't wanted to speak upstairs, it wasn't appropriate and might have proved embarrassing for any of them. But he'd never hidden his friendship with Charlie from his fellow officers. It was common knowledge that he and Charlie knew each other, and it was an acquaintance that did neither of the men any disfavour. Vic was an honest policeman and a good man, and his association with Charlie reflected well on him.

Honesty and goodness were qualities that Charlie understood, but with which he hadn't had much truck by the late sixties, embroiled as he was with the increasing corruption of the firm. The ties of East End family were binding, they were strong and unbreakable. At that point, they had broken Charlie.

Business at the Regal was profitable, and, apart from a little assistance given to the local criminal fraternity, it was on the level. It had to change.

By the end of 1954, the Kray twins had built up a considerable reputation around the Regal in Eric Street, which had spread to include Mile End. In particular, this had got up the noses of three local dockworkers who unofficially ruled Poplar and the Mile End Road. But dockers had an unbeaten reputation for toughness themselves. To be a docker you were at the top of the heap. A real man's man, a tough-gut who took no shit from anyone. The time had come for a showdown.

The challenge to the Krays came in the form of an invitation to join the dockers for a drink at one of their locals, a pub in the Mile End Road. This was language that the Kray twins understood. They often invited men for a drink, only to beat the living daylights out of them when they turned up. Fight dirty, fight tough, keep on top. Don't let the bastards grind you down. The buzz was that the dockers wanted protection money from the twins; they could have done worse than to have heard the story of the Maltese efforts in that direction.

Ron and Reg were both extremely strong. Their early boxing training and their tough military service had seen to that. Although neither man was what you'd call big — Ron stood five feet ten and weighed in at twelve stone, Reg was slightly smaller at just over five feet nine and eleven stone -they made up for in grit and iron determination what they may have lacked in size. They never, ever held back in a fight and always gave it their best, 100 per cent. They had rules of their own and had never been defeated in any conflict.

Even though most of their adversaries were often much heftier than them, they had never lost a battle. Well, they were looking forward to winning the war in Poplar, anticipating it with a grim pleasure and unshakable confidence. Much like their first bout in the ring at the funfair, all those years earlier. Only this time it was really for real.

The meet was to take place early on a Sunday morning. On the evening before, they went out on the town with some of the firm. The others were anxious for them. They were about to take on three ex-heavyweight boxers with reputations to match. The twins didn't seem that bothered, anyone would think it was just another night out, getting ratted and laid, followed by a regular Sunday down the Regal.

Sunday did find the twins at the Regal, clearing away glasses and empty bottles, brushing down the green baize of the billiard tables — everything as normal. They were early risers anyway. Work done, the place was filling fast. Though crowded, it was unnaturally quiet with anticipation. But the twins behaved no differently from any other Sunday morning. As the appointed time approached, they calmly put on their jackets and walked slowly but resolutely along to the Mile End Road.

The three dockers were drinking light ale in the private bar of the pub, and apart from them the place was empty. Only a barman to take their order. As their drinks stood on the counter, one of the dockers reached over to pass them along the counter to Ronnie.

'Here you are, sonny. You're just about old enough for a shandy,' he said.

This was provocation enough. All hell broke loose. The barman retreated to the safety of the public bar. He heard the fight rage for a matter of minutes. When everything had gone quiet, he walked back into the private bar. So confident was he that the dockers would win outright, he uncapped three bottles of light ale and carried them through on a tray.

The scene that faced him is now legendary. Two of the dockers were sprawled unconscious on the floor, and the third man was just about conscious but obviously in a terrible state. There was blood and glass everywhere. He watched as Reg had to drag his brother off the third docker.

Ron never knew when to stop and without Reg's intervention would almost certainly have killed the man. They pushed by the barman, frozen in shock and fear for himself, brushed down their suits, straightened their ties and walked casually out of the pub as if they'd just been in for a swift half.

The story soon became a part of gangland folklore in the East End. Don't mess with the Krays was the message. They're different. They had reached a turning-point in their status in the east London fraternity — there was never to be any going back.

If what the dockers offered were protection, you could keep it. Ron and Reg knew the time had come for them to move in, to exploit the situation. The brawl with the dockers was the second time they had been asked to pay protection money, and it was the second time they had come out on top. Enough was enough. It was glaringly obvious that they should come up with their own plans to muscle their way into the lucrative protection rackets. They were rife in the East End, and Mile End and Poplar were theirs for the taking. They'd fought for them and won.

From now on the Regal would no longer function simply as a legitimate business venture. It would be the operational base for Ron and Reg and other members of the firm. From there they would arrange the collection of their pension, as they called the protection money. From there they would, as Reg says to this day, supply a real and necessary service to their customers.

Reg believed that the firm should protect their clients from rival gangs, who didn't operate in such a fair-minded way as they did. They would be peacekeepers — at a price — and customers had to pay that price, regardless. It was a good investment.

Protection was rife in the 1950s and still remains big business in any major city. The idea is simple enough: an organized gang or firm offers to protect businesses such as clubs, pubs, restaurants and amusement arcades for a fee. Some of these premises attract violence, especially at the weekends, when people would go out and get blitzed on booze or drugs and want to rampage through the place, tearing it apart. Heavies were needed to stop this happening. Other places were threatened by rival gangs, whose unwanted attentions would need frightening off. These businesses were pawns in the gangs' games, but still in need of protection.

Whatever the situation, if any business approached by the firm refused to pay up, then they would soon find that their place of business would be burgled, torched, or just busted up. Business proprietors were over a barrel, between the devil and the deep blue sea. They paid up.

Whether ethical or not, the Krays prided themselves on providing a form of order in the East End. And they felt they were scrupulous and fair. Businesses were guaranteed safety and they generally had to pay protection money once, and not in various amounts to any number of rival gangs, each operating the same scheme. In that sense they were the best. Although they played on people's fears, they were fearless themselves and unbeatable.

They provided a service that was unrivalled. Trouble was dealt with quickly and quietly by the twins, or by members of the firm acting on orders from them. They were always adamant that violence was to be used only as a tactical weapon, and in particular only against rival gangs and troublemakers. Nevertheless the threat of violence was the hub of the protection business. It never went away.

Reg Kray believed that the protection rackets, as they existed in the East End of London in the 1950s, were an ugly form of business. When the twins devised their own system, they wanted to give it a form of dignity and went out of their way to stress its advantages to their customers. They likened their system of operations to that of an insurance company. To them the protection racket was a business with something to offer, not something for nothing or extortion. They were quite prepared to supply a service and called it doing the business, which they did very diplomatically. Rarely did they demand money directly or violently.

The firm offered two forms of protection: nipping and pension. If you were on the nipping list, the Krays or one of the firm, would nip into a shop or pub and nip out again with a token, consumable payment, such as a crate of gin or cartons of cigarettes. Anything that they might use then and there, themselves or to hand out to their family and friends. Generosity opens doors and stores up favours.

Or they might spend an evening in a pub or club, standing drinks for everyone and anyone. At the end of the evening, with a word from the firm, the bill for the night out would be torn up and the evening's entertainment paid for courtesy of the house. Sometimes a gold watch or pair of gold cufflinks engraved with RK would be left as security for a loan to the firm. A week or so later someone from the firm would call; Reg or Ron needed his cufflinks for a special outing. The question of the loan was never raised again.

The twins particularly liked this form of payment. It was the way friends operate, saying, 'Forget it, this one's on me,' or 'Your money isn't any good here.' To Ron and Reg, it made the scheme more acceptable and dignified. Always say please and thank you, even when you're thieving it. With no money changing hands, no one got their hands dirty. In return, the twins emphasized that they were always on call to help. Just give us a call. Mates doing each other a good turn.

The pension list was altogether more businesslike. The arrangement would be worked out in advance by Reg. He based it on turnover. It was a percentage of the weekly takings and always strictly cash. Collection would be made on the dot, at a fixed date and time. The pension was where the real money was made, especially with those businesses that operated illegally, such as unlicensed gambling houses, clubs or bookies. No one could ever complain to the law. It was a watertight earner, though sometimes not just in cash terms. Occasionally, the twins liked to gamble and took a share in the business itself, instead of a cash payment. By the mid-sixties they'd expanded to about thirty share interests. It was boomtime.

The twins' nose for business was unbeatable, but once or twice someone would slip through their net. One such was Peter Cook, entertainer and club owner. He was approached by Ron and Reg at the opening of his London club. Never ones to miss a commercial opportunity, as the Krays mingled and downed a few glasses of champagne, they approached Peter Cook with an offer he couldn't refuse. Or so they thought.

The conversation began with the infamous opening gambit, 'Don't you think you need . . .'?

Cook's reply was direct — and probably simplified by the fact that, at that time, he'd never heard of the Krays. He told them straight — he wasn't in need of any protection. If any trouble cropped up, one of London's largest and busiest police stations was right next door. Without losing face, the twins left as soon as they could. It was not a story ever to remind them of.

Failures were not that common in the firm, but as with every other business venture, they happened. Like any insurance company, the Krays were asked to cough up from time to time.

This happened with a car dealership, in the early days of their protection, towards the end of 1955. The twins had more car dealers on their books than they'd had hot dinners. They knew exactly the strings to pull to get you a motor. It was all legal and above board, except that you didn't keep up your payments. You could bank on keeping it for a couple of years, the repossession from the finance company took that long at least.

On some occasions you didn't need a deposit, but what had gone wrong this particular time was that a used car had been sold to a customer — and it had broken down the next day.

The man wanted his money back. Full stop. No excuses. When the dealer refused, the customer said he'd be back the following day — with some friends from south of the river. They were going to rough up the dealer and try to get the money back. As the dealer had been paying protection money to the twins, he called them up at the Regal and explained the situation.

Ron got really excited. At last a chance for some real action with a south of the river gang. He sent along a minder to babysit the dealership premises, who was to phone him at the billiard hall as soon as the gang turned up. But he was to be disappointed. The client showed on his own, full of apologies for how he'd behaved the previous day. With this climbdown from the customer, the dealer relaxed, and the two men started to sort it out in a friendly way.

Making friends was not on Ron's mind when he stormed in ten minutes later, not aware of the new found common ground. Following the principle of shoot first and ask questions later, he emptied his gun, a Luger automatic, into the astonished customer.

Dressed in a Capone-style overcoat, he looked every inch a gangster. Fortunately, Ron was always a terrible shot, and the first bullet missed from point-blank range. Nevertheless one bullet lodged itself in the customer's leg, and he writhed on the floor of the office in considerable pain.

Once he'd cooled down, Ron took stock of the situation and realized he had no enemies there. But possibly to hide his embarrassment or perhaps just in a blind fury that there was no opportunity of a shoot-out in the Wild West of the East End, he stormed off much as he'd arrived — unannounced and unexplained. Mopping up was left to Reg, as it often was. He made sure that the wounded man didn't talk. He visited him in hospital and had a friendly chat. Reg could be very persuasive.

The twins were nearing their twenty-second birthday, with the firm a successful and thriving outfit. The Regal had proved an excellent base from which to develop their business activities, and the twins took advantage of any good idea or crooked scheme for making easy money. Even this early on it was clear that neither Ron nor Reg believed it possible to make a substantial living out of a legitimate business operation although they had turned the Regal round into profit, legally. Both twins felt sure that there was much more to be made from illegal or criminal activities.

One of the drawbacks of a life of crime came, however, when Ron was eventually arrested for grievous bodily harm and sentenced to three years' imprisonment on 5 November 1956. He wouldn't be back at the Regal till the spring of 1959. Reg had been able to smooth things out for him in the past, but this time he couldn't help his brother.

The tables were turned in 1960, when Reg landed an eighteen-month sentence in Wandsworth Prison for his apparent involvement in a shady protection deal. Reg had accompanied a man called Shay on a visit to a shop in the Finchley Road, north London. Shay had been paying

Ron Kray for the use of his name in some business deals. Reg was there to help Shay, but Shay had not filled him in on all the facts. At the shop, Shay asked the owner for £100 and said that if he didn't pay up, he'd be cut to pieces. At this critical moment, the police appeared from the back of the premises, arresting and handcuffing both men on the spot. Ron, himself out of prison now, was powerless to help get Reg off his conviction.

Through his friends and acquaintances at the Regal, Ron had established a network of his spies all over the Bethnal Green and Mile End areas of East London. The system worked well, and nothing escaped the attention of the Krays. Ron lived up to his name of the Colonel and ran the firm in a very strict fashion. Those who did well were rewarded; those who didn't were dealt with most severely.

The information gathered by Ron's spy network helped to form the basis of rackets that ran and ran — for the next fourteen years, until the twins' arrest and imprisonment on 9 May 1968 — and were only slightly interrupted by their spells in prison. Most of these schemes still operate somewhere in Britain, only the names of the protectors have changed. The game goes on and probably will for decades to come. Some things just can't change.

3

THE WILD WEST IN
THE EAST END

Bow Road was deserted on a miserable winter's night. Bone cold with a drizzle that fell like a fine mist, cutting visibility by half. It was impossible to see across the road, the houses on either side were quite invisible to each other. On a street corner, two men had been hanging about for a while, only the occasional flare from their lighted cigarettes breaking the gloom from time to time. In that part of town, at that time of night, under those conditions, you jump to conclusions. Filthy weather for dirty business.

The truth couldn't have been more different. That piss awful night, when only fools and villains might be out, Charlie and Reg were on a mission, but with no trouble in mind. The Kray empire was expanding. They wanted more outlets. A suitable building to house their new club. This is what had brought them out on a night that would have been better spent shooting pool and chewing the fat. A few drinks and jokes with the lads.

It was a huge and impressive-looking building with a large, adjacent car park. Ideal for a club, somewhere the punters could drive to in their cars. No problems with on-street parking. The house stood several stories high, and although in need of considerable refurbishment, it seemed pretty much right. Charlie and Reg mentally mapped out how it would be as they reccied in the dark, flashlights picking out the best and the worst bits. The only snag, as Reg saw it, was the large building on the opposite side of the car park that faced directly on to the main road: Bow Street Police Station.

Clubs opened and closed regularly in the West End. But a club on Bow Road, in the heart of the East End, would it really take off? Is this what people, staunch East End family people, wanted? Charlie and Reg had discussed it on and on. In the end it had come down to Charlie's faith in Reg's business sense.

Charlie had been chuffed when Reg asked him to join him in his latest business venture. Of course, with Ron banged up in prison for three years, it was only natural that he'd keep things in the family and ask his big brother. But Charlie was still encouraged. Blood was thicker than water, but so much of it had been spilt one way or another that you could never be sure.

Charlie only got involved in the business end of things. He liked to enjoy himself and keep a low profile. This was the way he did things. Ron's enforced absence meant that Reg was more accessible to him. Separate from his twin, Charlie knew he had a million times better chance of getting on with Reg. Running the club would be much easier with just the two of them; threesomes could be difficult, especially as the twins made such a dauntless pair. Stuck like glue and more than the sum of their parts.

Charlie was on to a good thing, and he knew it. Ron's being away for the next two years would give him and Reg a good crack at getting the club off the ground. Not necessarily megabucks, but good clean money, maybe with a bit of an edge on the side. A touch of the criminal fraternity but mostly straight up.

Spring 1957 saw the opening of the new club. Reg was still in his early twenties, but he found himself at the hub of the thriving Kray empire. And alone, with Ron inside. Charlie would help him. Of course he would. Plans had to be made quickly to secure the lease of the building, and Reg set the ball rolling in the only way he knew how — with raw, determined energy. There was never any time to waste for Reg. He was always well fuelled and became, with a good sense of direction, unstoppable.

Reg had got money to fund the new club from various sources. He'd done his sums carefully. With the money in hand, Charlie didn't want to know where it'd come from. He just wanted to get in gear and get going, get the show on the road.

He had been back to the house with Reg to inspect it by daylight. Yes, Reg had done his homework and come up with a good investment opportunity. Why should Charlie worry? There was even a bonus. They had taken on the lease with sitting tenants in the upper storey.

'I thought they could act as caretakers,' Reg said. 'It's

good to have people living in,' he continued, and added without a hint of irony, 'There's a lot of thieves around.'

Neither of them was interested in the day-to-day details of the refurbishment, but one thing that grabbed Reg's instant attention was any fine tuning on the fitting out of the gymnasium he'd insisted on installing. They had ordered a punchbag, a maizeball, weights and assorted weightbuilding apparatus, a sweatbox and a speed ball. Complete with a full size boxing ring, it would be a knockout in every way. All that was left to do was to decide what to call it.

The solution was simple. It was Charlie's idea. Everyone around town called this area of London the Wild West. The East End was a lawless land, just like the early days of the Wild West in America. Yet it had its own laws and code of ethics. They were rigid and inviolable. Don't shit on your own doorstep came high on the list. Never steal off your own, be it cars, cash or wives. Don't accept the lawless — the craziness of drug dealers and ponces.

Inspired by all of this, Charlie came up with the name: the Double R Club. A cowboy, lone plains' drifter tribute that was equally applicable to his brothers: Reg and Ron.

On a Wednesday evening in 1957, the Double R opened its doors for the first time. It proved an overnight success. Big Pat Connolly and Tommy the Bear Brown were taken on as doormen.

Hiring them all fitted in with how the Krays operated, playing largely on fear. Tommy the Bear was a pussy cat in a bear suit, a huge, gentle giant, whose bark was worse than his bite. In fact Tommy rarely, if ever, even spat or snarled. He didn't have to. He was a scarecrow frightener, part of the Kray twins' furniture. But if he didn't work, then Charlie and Reg knew how to look after themselves. They were always there to defend themselves when push came to shove.

Connolly and Brown were on the front line. And they looked the part. Both big and ex-boxers, no one got past the door without their approval. Those who were allowed in were warned not to cause trouble. It was a house rule: no trouble. If there were any disputes, they would be settled well away from the Double R.

Punters tended at least to follow the letter of the law. After all, the Krays were supplying a service, a nice place where a bloke could take his wife or girlfriend for a good night out without the risk of fights or shootings or bother of any other kind. In-house entertainment was good, too, with Fred Merry, a famous fifties pianist. He and his drummer played every night of the week. The audience were encouraged to participate. On stage there was a full-height microphone for anyone who cared to sing, though, later, Queenie Watts was taken on as the house voice.

Reg knew all the tricks in the book when it came to giving people a good time. He was always open to anything that would make the club more professional and up to date -and capitalize in every way. He wanted to attract people in, give them a good time and show the West End establishments a thing or two. There are some things money can't buy. Personal credibility thrived in the East End, even though the West End could boast flash cash flows.

The arrival of the jukebox at the Double R was all part of this. It kept the place humming. Customers played it during breaks in the live music and danced to the latest sounds. There was even room to jive, twist, rock and roll, or just plain old-fashioned cheek to cheek.

Club hours were from three in the afternoon to eleven at night sharp. This was the same every day of the week. After-hours drinking was discouraged, except behind closed doors for family and close friends. Weekends were always busy, and it soon started to attract so-called respectable customers from the West End. Local villains mixed with celebrities. Everyone loved it. Sybil Burton, Barbara Windsor, Jackie Collins would all drop by to enjoy an evening out and take time to chat with Reg or Charlie. Men with money started to show, looking for excitement. Reg was only too happy to oblige.

Life was good. Reg and Charlie had made a success of their business venture together.

But it wasn't all plain sailing. Trouble, when it started, normally broke out during the day, especially the afternoons.

This was when most of the new customers came by. It was just such an afternoon, when Charlie was serving behind the bar, that three brothers walked in. They'd enrolled and hence been vetted in the usual way, so they got past Big Pat Connolly, no trouble.

Reg was standing at the bar with a gin and tonic in his hand, chatting. It was quiet, even slow, mid-afternoon. One of the three men invited Reg to have a drink with them. Reg refused. The man ignored him and said he'd buy him one anyway.

'You're having a drink,' the man ordered. It was a stupid remark. 'I'll get you one, and you will drink it.'

He didn't let up. The intruder ordered a gin and tonic for Reg, which Charlie prepared and put on the bar counter with his hand held out for the money. Calmly Charlie put the note in the till, rang up the cash register to give the man his change. The man held out the gin and tonic for Reg.

Without a word and as the sound of the cash-register bell died, Reg hit the man hard on the jaw with a vicious left hook. It laid him out flat.

It was then that Charlie joined in, to assist his brother, and before they knew what had hit them, the three brothers were bundled up and thrown out bodily into the street.

The regulars just carried on as normal. Most of them hadn't even moved from their seats and were sitting drinking and chatting as if nothing had happened. All of a sudden, with the men now well out of earshot, Reg turned on Charlie.

'What do you think you are doing?' he yelled.

'What d'you mean?' Charlie replied. He was surprised by Reg's reaction. 'I came to help you, of course,' he continued.

'No, you don't,' Reg screamed. He pointed wildly. 'You stay there — behind the bar. I'm quite capable of taking care of myself and those three fellas.'

Reg had been insulted by Charlie's chipping in like that, as if he, Reg, couldn't handle things himself. He had his reputation to protect. Charlie should have known that.

It went all quiet for a moment in the bar, until someone started to laugh. When Reg realized he'd made his point and reasserted his dominance, he managed a laugh too. The situation was defused. For the time being. But it was always a delicate balance with the Kray twins' sensibilities.

Reg's fierce and fearless attitude to danger, physical and emotional, was something that the regulars at the Double R talked about for years to come. His reputation as a tough guy was well earned. He didn't suffer anyone gladly, although you'd often never know it until you got hit. But, he didn't always use his fists to make his point. With more minor upsets during the evening he would sort them out quickly, negotiating. He was very good at that, Reg.

There was one particular incident that happened when Violet and old man Charlie were round the club. Queenie Watts had just started singing there, and they'd heard a lot about her, how good she was and so on. They would have come by anyway, so proud were they of their sons' achievements there, but she was the specific draw that evening.

Violet was sitting in her favourite chair by the bar with old man Charlie, enjoying Queenie's performance, when a big man, well over 6 foot, got up on stage and grabbed the microphone. He started singing rude songs but was soon shouted off by the other customers: 'We want Queenie. Get off. We want Queenie.'

Reg spoke one word, quietly, in Charlie's ear: 'Trouble.'

It wasn't until the man, obviously the worse for drink, walked up to Violet and tried to get her to dance with him that Reg made his move. As the drunk grabbed his mother, the entire club went quiet, and all eyes were fixed on Reg.

Without a change of expression, Reg walked straight over to the man and knocked him to the floor with his favoured left hook. Charlie then took over and dragged him out of the club, past the front desk and outside into

Bow Road, where he dumped him unceremoniously in the street.

'Don't come back,' he warned. 'Just keep away, if you know what's good for you.'

Outside on the pavement, the man had begun to come to. He was confused. What had happened? He couldn't remember. Charlie hung about for a bit and told him. The man was genuinely apologetic — and embarrassed — he didn't know what had come over him. It must have been the drink talking.

Eventually the two men shook hands, and in the months to come the drunken stranger became a club regular. But he took care to behave himself.

It was incidents like these that reinforced the idea of the club as neutral territory. As long as you did things the Kray way, you could come along, but you had to toe the line when on club premises. The Double R became a place where members of different gangs could meet without fear of trouble, and this earned it the nickname, Switzerland — neutral territory. The Krays had started to provide a service for all comers but always on their terms. They ruled OK or all out.

Reg had started to become a bit of a playboy, spending his time up West with young ladies. This was something new for him. When Ron was around, they didn't make much time for women. Or rather, as an apparent womanizer, Ron didn't actually take much interest in women.

Reg, on his own, operated differently. Charlie let him get on with it. He was married. Other women weren't on the agenda. Live and let live. Reg's behaviour wasn't his business. But ironically, with the two brothers getting on so well, the only area of disagreement between them was to become Charlie's wife Dolly.

Charlie had been married for years and had two children. He, Dolly and the kids lived in Stepney. Charlie made great efforts to keep out of trouble. Anything criminal and he was out of the way. It was going on all around him, but he wasn't interested. But, it wasn't this that got up Reg's nose, it was Dolly.

Reg just didn't like the way that Dolly would act. With the Double R, you'd think she owned it, the way she went on. It caused a lot of animosity. To top it all, Reg got the idea that Dolly was carrying on behind Charlie's back, having an affair with one of the regulars at the Double R. Years later, when Charlie was in prison, the affair did come out, it was public knowledge. And no surprise to Reg, who'd suspected it all along. Reg really disliked Dolly.

The Dolly problem did interfere in Charlie's relationship with Reg, but on the whole they got along fine, particularly because both agreed not to let Dolly interfere with their business arrangements. Charlie was as shrewd as Reg when it came to business. He urged to Reg to expand, to invest in more clubs, including gambling halls, and car dealerships. The adjacent car park often served as a showroom for the car dealing.

Reg acquired the Wellington Way Club in spring 1957. Here members could play blackjack, rummy and faro. Reg even started illegal bookmaking in a back room at the club. They made good money. And it was all in and around the same part of the East End. Their budding empire was easy to get to and to run, by keeping it so much together. It looked like nothing could stop them. Everything Charlie and Reg started turned to gold. With strict rules of conduct for the clubs and for themselves, they got on well with everyone, even old enemies.

Billy Hill, in the 1950s one of the old bosses of the London underworld, of the West End in particular, had begun to give Reg and Charlie a few good ideas, tipping them off with inventive investment opportunities. Billy Hill and Jack 'Spot' Comer were self-styled kings of London's underworld from the forties, but by the time Hill started handing out advice to the Krays he had taken himself into retirement.

Charlie and Reg appreciated Hill's help. Hill, in turn, needed his protégés, heirs to his business. He also wanted someone he could trust to keep an eye on the remaining business interests he still had in London. Through him the Krays became involved in all kinds of business, though their preference was certainly for the legitimate or at least semi-legitimate deal. Billy Hill was a shrewd operator, who had been successfully running protection for more than a decade.

Hill introduced Reg and Charlie to the West End of London, particularly to the gambling clubs. He had been a man of influence there and was still not without his contacts. The Krays' visits to Soho with Billy Hill were a real eye-opener as to where the real money could be found and made. With changes in the gaming rules about to be instituted, Charlie and Reg knew it was an ideal time to get involved. And the ideal place would be the Double R. Prosperity, fame and a life of ease, without crime or at least almost so, seemed within reach. Charlie and Reg were on their way. There was, however, one major obstacle: Ron.

Ron had been inside for two years, and Reg and Charlie had made the most of this time. They'd had a good two years. But, it couldn't last for ever and Ron would be out soon. He had made a fleeting visit to the Double R during his escape from Long Grove Hospital, where he'd been sent during his prison sentence. It was a plan that had been engineered by his family and friends. That visit had been brief and unremarkable in terms of running things. Once Ron came out for good, though, in 1959, and joined them at the club, everything changed for the worse.

Ron started to take over. He would invite his friends to the club, and he was uninhibited about spending the 'house' money. He enjoyed the club, and he behaved as he always had. He would run up a bill and have it wiped clean at the end of the evening, just like one of his protection deals. But this was his home patch, not some protected public house or drinking club.

Ron's behaviour became a real problem. He was out of prison and a bit out of his head. Not at all well. He was very moody, up and down. No one could handle him. His paranoia was knife-edge and high, and one of his beefs was the way he thought Charlie had taken his place with Reg. Although Reg had tried to explain to Ron the practicality of his and Charlie's business arrangement, Ron was not prepared to understand or even to listen. He thought both Reg and Charlie had been disloyal to him. For a while he wouldn't have much to do with either his twin or Charlie, spending much of his time away in the country, in Jersey or just out.

Reg and Charlie wanted to get on with their lives. To make more of what they'd started with the Double R and their new business deals. The living was good. It was legal, or near enough, and they had no problems with the law. They didn't want trouble, full stop. They had made a truce with all the other gangs to try to secure peace. But Ron soon changed all this.

Ron caused major fall-outs with other gangs, and he began to rule the roost again, in much the same way as he had done before his sentence. He stirred everyone up. He wanted fame, and he wanted to fight for power. That was Ron's way. Reg and Charlie could only sit back and watch everything they built up together dissolve right in front of their eyes.

If you can't beat 'em, then join 'em. Reg felt this way. Ron's influence was too strong for him to resist, and before long he was following his twin's example. Reg began to take less and less part in the running of the Double R along the lines he and Charlie had established. It was the beginning of the end. No one could control Ron, and eventually he won. Violence, which had been a rare occurrence at the club, became a regular, nightly event. It got even worse when one night someone tried to shoot Reg as he was shutting up for the night. And then the police took to raiding the Double R all the time.

One such raid occurred early on a midweek evening. The police poured into the club on the pretext of checking the customers' membership. When Ron saw the police enter the club, he rushed up on stage and stopped the music. Fred Merry had been entertaining a few early evening customers with some old favourites.

Ron snatched the microphone from Fred and announced, 'I'm sorry about this. It's a police raid.'

He paused for a moment, before adding, 'Since none of these gentlemen is a member, they will be leaving very soon. We are not allowed to serve non-members here!'

Ron just had to have his little joke, at any expense.

The police were there to search the place. They didn't know what they were looking for — they were just looking. Reg really got mad when some of the police raced up the stairs to the gymnasium. It was in use by regular punters, just men training who didn't have any edge to them other than boxing. It was a popular training establishment for many champions and boxers alike, men such as Barney Bill, Ken Johnstone, Tommy McGovern, Terry Allen and from time to time even Henry Cooper. They didn't like interruptions at the best of times.

Reg got so furious as he watched the gym, his pride and joy, overrun by the law. He took off his jacket and sprang into the boxing ring, yelling, 'Come on, then. If this is what you really want. If any of you young officers want any trouble, then just come here. Then it'll be all legal.'

It was clear that Reg wasn't just mouthing off. He meant every word. No one took his challenge and, ignoring him, the police left the club as abruptly as they'd arrived.

For that evening at least, there were no more uninvited guests at the club. But things could really only get worse. And they did. After three years in operation, they were refused a spirits licence and had to close down.

Over the preceding year, the police had shown increasing interest in the club, and it had been under police surveillance for some time — from the time when Ron had first been on the run from Long Grove Hospital. With Ron around full time, relations with the law had gone from bad to worse. But the final nail in the Double R's coffin had come when Reg had refused to help the police to find Ronnie Marwood.

Marwood had killed a policeman, and it was common knowledge in the East End that Reg Kray knew where he was hiding. Reg blankly refused to help with their enquiries, not because he was a good friend of Marwood but because he could not bring himself to inform to the police. No grassing was an important part of his code of ethics. He wouldn't budge. It would have been unthinkable.

Reg's silence annoyed the police, but they couldn't break it. What they could do was to return the disfavour.

When the Double R's licence came up for renewal, they refused it. There was a distinct difference in attitude between the law that ran the East and West Ends of London. In the West End, money talked, bribery worked, and problems were ironed out with hard cash. In the East End, however, any slight disagreement was dealt with quickly and harshly by the police. One of their favourite secret weapons was to withdraw or refuse a spirits licence. It was highly effective.

Maybe it had something to do with respect or regard for people of influence. Maybe it was the lure of a large wad of notes in their hands. Maybe it was a more fluid society with greater social mobility than the East End. Whatever the reason, a lot more police bribery and corruption occurs in the West End.

The Double R was forced to shut its doors. It was a sad occasion, especially for Reg. The club had been his baby, his idea in the first place. He had put a huge amount of effort and energy into it and had made it very successful. The gymnasium had been a major part of it. Reg was immensely proud of his achievement, but it all had to go. Ron Kray, the Colonel, had woven his spell and made sure of that.

There was one loose end that remained to be tied. Down in the club cellars there was enough booze to open an off-licence. But that wouldn't be the Krays' style, to do something so obvious — or so legitimate. Instead, they boarded up the windows of the Double R and held a huge party for all their family and friends. They drank and partied for days until all the spirits, wine and beer had gone, every last drop. They'd been stopped for the time being but had fun ending it. They'd be back in business before too long. That much was certain.

With the closure of the Double R there was no longer any neutral territory in the East End, where rival gangs could try to settle their scores without resorting to violence. There was no longer any club where a man could take his wife without fear of fighting or drunkenness interfering with their night out. There was no longer a hope for Reg and Charlie Kray to run a purely legitimate business. They had shown themselves capable, but Ron hadn't allowed this to develop.

Charlie and Reg had been driven back underground. If the Double R had carried on, then maybe they would have found some way of integrating Ron — of controlling his unfocused energy. Of bringing him out of himself — and in with them — above ground and within the law.

Ron hadn't wanted that. He wouldn't try for the straight and narrow. He remained complicated, difficult and wanted to operate only on his terms. From here on it became the laws of the Wild West that reigned supreme in the ever expanding frontiers of the East End underworld.

4

ESCAPE FROM
LONG GROVE

WHAT HAPPENED EARLIER IN JUNE 1958 and led up to the closure of the Double R made it obvious that the Krays would go to any lengths for each other — the ties that bound the brothers, especially the twins, were unbreakable silken nooses. What wouldn't they do for family, for each other, for brotherly love — and ultimately destruction? For the moment they survived on loyalty and fear. Blood brothers.

Four o'clock in the morning was a good time to think. Reg and Charlie had been endlessly going over the same ground for weeks. They both had the same thing on their mind: how to get Ron out of Long Grove Hospital.

In the summer of 1958 there were over 1000 patients at Long Grove. Of these only a handful had come from prisons or other state institutions. Ron and the other prisoners were treated exactly the same way as was any patient there in need of treatment. The doctors who treated Ron were only given limited information about him and had no idea of his background and criminal record.

Long Grove was an institution for the criminally insane, and Ron had been there for the past four months, on a transfer from HMP Wandsworth. Although his condition had now improved due to medication, his request for a transfer back to the prison had been refused. All Ron Kray could think about was his close friend Frank Mitchell: he was detained in Dartmoor during Her Majesty's pleasure, indefinitely. Ron feared the same fate.

On each visit Ron told Reg about the goings-on at the asylum. One time, he said, when he was sitting quietly, minding his own business, a fellow patient had come up to him and slapped him in the face. For no reason at all. A nutter, Ron called him. Ron had retaliated and had had to be calmed down by the strong male nurses.

Another time Reg and Johnny Hutton, an old family friend, were on a visit, and one of the patients just walked over to them and, without saying a word, spat in their faces.

Outraged, Ron had turned slowly to his brother and said, 'I've had just about enough of this place.'

They were right to be worried about Ron. Long Grove wasn't the place for him, not now that he was looking and feeling so much better. They wanted him out.

The number of visits Ron could receive in Long Grove were stepped up. Old man Charlie and Violet would visit twice a week; young Charlie would go with Reg whenever they could. Friends and family all turned up to help Ron out, to keep him afloat, his spirits up. But on each successive visit some new ghoulish fact would come to light about the place, even more reason for Ron to be moved on.

It all seemed hopeless till, on one of these visits, Reg got wind of the six-week rule. If anyone serving a prison sentence spent time away from Long Grove for a period of six weeks or more and did not cause any trouble or commit any crimes during that time, then on their return they were required to be transferred back to prison, their certification of insanity nullified. How Ron would spend time away from Long Grove if he were not back in Wandsworth was another matter. They'd just have to work on that one.

The important thing now was for Ron's certificate of insanity to lapse, by making sure he got out of Long Grove for six weeks — and stayed clean. Of course, then he'd have to go back to Wandsworth to serve out what remained of his sentence: maybe another twelve months at Her Majesty's pleasure.

It was a tall order: to get Ron away from Long Grove and keep him hidden for six weeks, at least.

There were so many locked doors and attendant restrictions at the hospital that stood between Ron and his freedom. They couldn't afford to fight their way out, as this might affect Ron's chances when he surrendered himself six weeks later. If anyone got hurt or the place turned over, there'd be a price to pay. And Ron would be on the front line for that. Guns were definitely out, as were knives and other instruments of violence. For once it was vital that they were subtle.

Reg and Charlie sat together in the Double R, despondent and without a clue about what they could do to help Ron. Get him out of Long Grove at least. But how? They'd considered every option. Or so they thought.

The last customer had gone, but the air in the saloon was still dense with tobacco smoke and the stench of liquor. Charlie got off his stool and went behind the bar to pour them both a drink: a gin and tonic for Reg and a whisky for himself. It was Reg who broke the silence. He smiled triumphantly, as if he'd cracked it, seen a way out. Literally.

'We'll swop places. I'll be Ron and he'll be me,' he said.

Charlie wasn't sure. Trading places. It all seemed too simple. Sometimes, though, what was simple was right. Straightforward and on the nose. The obvious wasn't always obvious to everyone. What did they have to lose? Why not give it a try?

The organization around Ron's escape was planned in minute and elaborate detail. During visits Ron was informed of developments. Accommodation was arranged for him, once he got out. Cars and all the firm were on stand-by. It was all carefully random, with no discernible pattern of movement. They would play it by ear and keep their options open, see how the escape went. As a failsafe, Reg had located a caravan in the woods, deep in the Suffolk countryside, near a friend's farm. Ron would be well supported by friends and never left alone.

The drive to Long Grove Hospital in Epsom,

Surrey, took just over an hour from the East End. It was a Sunday morning, and Reg and a chosen few travelled down there in a convoy of two sleek American cars. One was a black Ford, packed with three of Ron's old pals, Billy Nash, Bernie King and a man by name of Mick the Hammer, the other a blue Lincoln with Georgie Osborne, an old friend of the family, and Reg, driving. A third car was hidden on route, just in case a quick change became necessary on the return trip.

They aimed to reach the hospital just before three o'clock in the afternoon, official visiting time. It was the busiest day of the week, a Sunday, when a lot of people were free to visit. Only two people could see Ron at once, so the idea was that Reg and Georgie Osborne should go in. The others would wait outside the gates in the car, beside the high wall that surrounded Long Grove and just out of view of the gate keeper's cottage.

At five to three the two cars pulled up outside the hospital. Reg parked the Lincoln in full view of anyone in or around the cottage. The black Ford slipped out of sight. If anyone approached, the three men inside had been briefed: they were waiting for family to come back from visiting a friend in Long Grove, a story that was not a lie but simply economical with the truth. As it turned out, they didn't have to account for themselves at all.

Billy Nash, Bernie King and Mick the Hammer sat patiently in the Ford, chainsmoking from a huge supply of Ron's favourite Players that they had brought along for him. They were men who were not unaccustomed to dealing with the law, having between them a variety of skills.

As the men waited in the car, Reg and Georgie

Osborne set off up the gravel drive of the hospital. The gardens there were beautiful, full of flowers in bloom and the twittering of birds. But they were not there to enjoy nature and the countryside in summer.

The walk seemed endless. Reg thought about Ron. If all went well, he, Ron, would soon be retracing Reg's footsteps, back up this drive. This would be his route to freedom.

Back at the Double R, this was hardly Charlie's mood. He was glued to the phone until he received a message from Reg. He kept his fingers crossed. He sipped a stiff whisky as he served customers. If you'd known him well enough, though, it would have been obvious that he wasn't as cheerful as usual. A bit preoccupied and downcast. No one else in the bar knew what was about to happen. Charlie looked at his watch. It was ten past three. He knew exactly where Reg and Georgie Osborne would be at this moment.

It had turned out a pleasant summer day in the East End, although the forecast promised rain later that evening. The weather was much the same in Epsom, so it wasn't so peculiar that Reg was sporting a light raincoat over his dark suit. Apart from the weather prospects, Reg had good reason to wear the coat. It was all part of the escape plan.

Reg and Georgie walked briskly into the hospital through a maze of corridors, past the canteen and finally into the closed section of the building, where Ron was housed. They didn't talk much as they entered the waiting room. Reg approached the man at the desk and told him that they had come to see Ron Kray.

The attendant strolled over to the double glass doors that lead into the locked area of Long Grove. He unlocked first one door and then knocked on a second. Then they were led through by a second guard. The place was secure all right. Other than being invited in, there was no way of entering — or exiting for that matter — except with the aid of dynamite.

In a large room, full of tables and chairs, Reg and Georgie chose a table near the corridor, closest to the double doors that served as both entrance and exit to the closed area of the hospital. It was light in there, with tall windows all the way round and a pleasant view out on to the gardens. The room started to fill with people.

Reg had brought along a photograph album, which he leafed through as they waited for Ron. He sat slumped in his chair, still wearing his overcoat. When the room was almost full, Ron appeared, delighted to see Reg and his old pal Georgie. Reg took off his coat. Without it, he and Ron were dressed identically in dark suits. Behind them, the guard watched as they settled down for the visit.

The first thing the men did was to look at the photos, which reduced them to fits of helpless laughter. The guard looked amused, too, as he walked away from them to pace up and down one side of the room. He noticed everything — and nothing.

By 3.30 p.m. it was teatime. The noise level in the room had reached a high pitch, with everyone talking at once, and there was a lot of toing and froing. It was Reg's job to go and fetch the tea from the canteen, back through the locked double doors in the main section of the building. As the guard passed their table, Reg, Ron and Georgie were still weak with laughter.

A moment or two later, Ron stood up and put on Reg's overcoat, taking a pair of spectacles from the pocket, identical to those that Reg was wearing. Reg slipped off his own glasses and stuffed them into his trouser pocket.

No one remarked as Ron asked Reg cheerfully, 'Would you like a cup of tea, Ron?' and walked nonchalantly towards the double locked doors.

'Just getting the tea,' he explained lightly to the guard on the door.

As he was ushered through, unchallenged, he smiled in brief acknowledgement at the man behind the desk in the waiting room. They'd seen each other before on visits, after all.

Ron continued walking, without a change of pace towards the canteen — and right past it, following the signs for Way Out. Outside in the grounds, he still wasn't free. He still had the endlessly long walk along the broad gravel drive to the main gates to accomplish.

Ron didn't notice the birdsong or the flowers; he was aware only of his own heavy breathing and echoing footsteps, a loud crunch on the gravelstones. Was he walking too fast, or maybe not fast enough? Maybe Reg had been discovered back in the visiting room, revealed to be not Ron, but his twin. Then they'd be after him. With great restraint, he quickened his pace only slightly.

It took an eternity to reach the big iron gates that spelled freedom. But once past the gate keeper's cottage and through them he was away and into the waiting Ford. No one said much; Billy just offered Ron a Players, before they drove off in a relaxed and unhurried way. No engine revving or squeal of tyres that might attract attention. No one said anything much at all until they were miles away from Long Grove. Then it was time for a good belly laugh. They'd pulled it off.

Reg was laughing too, but it was more of a snigger by

now. After twenty minutes or so, the guard began to suspect something was wrong. Where was Ron's brother with the tea? What was taking him so long?

The guard moved closer to the two men, bowed over the album in stitches. As he did so, he took a good look at Reg.

'You've pulled a flanker,' he announced.

'How d'you mean?' Reg asked, as if he didn't quite understand.

'You shouldn't have let him go to get the tea. You should have got it,' the guard said, now angry and less confused.

'Well,' said a relaxed Reg, 'it's your job to look after him, not mine.'

The sound of the alarm was deafening, and it scared the wits out of patients and visitors alike. Men in white coats came running from every direction. Suddenly there were more guards, nurses and attendants in the visiting room than there were patients. The room was cleared, except for Reg and Georgie Osborne.

Everyone was still confused. The guard who had raised the alarm kept looking at Reg. Eventually he had the sense to ask him if he could prove who he was. Ron not Reg? Reg not Ron? From his jacket pocket, Reg produced his driving licence.

'Here,' he said, 'check that if you like.'

When the police arrived, they questioned Reg and Georgie Osborne for over an hour. The two men stuck to their story: they hadn't done anything except to wait for a cup of tea that had never arrived. It was the guards and attendants who had unlocked the doors to allow Ron through.

The police still had to make absolutely sure that it was Ron who had got out and not Reg. The twins were very alike. In the end Reg's identity was confirmed by a police check of their records. Both Ron and Reg had numerous scars, but it was the scars on Reg's hands that showed him to be who he claimed he was: Reg not Ron Kray.

The shit should have really hit the fan there and then, but the police could do nothing — except go out and hunt for Ron. They couldn't detain Reg and Georgie Osborne a moment longer. There was no legal reason to do so.

One hour after the alarm bells had rung in the hospital, Reg and Georgie Osborne made their way out of Long Grove, just as Ron had done some time before.

Reg made a brief phone call to Charlie on their way back to Bow Road. 'It's OK,' he said and hung up.

Now Charlie knew that Ron had been smuggled away to a safe house in Walthamstow. They'd just have to wait for the heat to die down.

Monday, the next day, was very quiet at the Double R. Reg opened up as usual, and Charlie joined him there around lunchtime. Though they couldn't swear to it, they were both sure that the club was under surveillance. But it just turned into a watching and waiting game. Nothing happened.

The following day, a Tuesday, Reg and Charlie were in the club. Charlie was helping to restock the bar, and Reg was organizing everything and nothing, productive and busy as ever. Even though the Double R was owned jointly by the two brothers, Reg felt the club to be his own. It was his patch; Charlie had rights there, but they were limited. Reg made sure of that by being knowing about everything that went on. He didn't miss a thing, or let anything go.

It was Charlie who answered the phone when it rang early in the afternoon. They'd been anticipating a call from the police. After all, they were hunting for someone widely described in the press as a violent criminal.

What the brothers were not expecting was a call from the superintendent at Long Grove. He wanted to see them both as soon as possible. He felt that the brothers should be made fully aware of the situation — as he saw it. An anxiety in the man's voice made Charlie realize this was a serious request, not some attempt to bamboozle him and Reg into taking a false position.

On the drive to Epsom, Reg and Charlie orchestrated their story. They hadn't done anything; it had been Ron's idea, something he'd suggested on the spur of the moment. They'd gone along with it, but only by not stopping him. They'd just waited for a cup of tea that had never arrived.

At Long Grove, the superintendent was polite — but to the point.

'I must congratulate you,' he said. 'That was cleverly done, and no one was hurt. No violence at all. Well done.'

Reg and Charlie were taken aback by this approach. They'd expected all manner of things but not to be congratulated on Ron's departure. On the surface, they were unfazed and kept to their story. They had no knowledge of how Ron had escaped.

The superintendent was not put off by their admirable show of innocence.

'I realize that you were both behind the escape, but I do not expect you to admit it,' he said.

He went on to tell them in no uncertain terms that

he thought they had made a mistake. Ron was not well, still mentally ill. He could very easily have a relapse without proper medication and adequate care. His remarks, he assured them, were all based on informed medical fact and not personal opinion and prejudice. He was prepared to be proved wrong, but he did not feel it would be sensible to test it out.

'Thanks for coming to see me at such short notice. If you need to reach me, you have my telephone number. Please feel free to call at any time.'

On the drive back to London, Reg and Charlie did not totally ignore what the superintendent had said. It wasn't all water off a duck's back. They realized there was some truth in it. After all, they knew Ron well — his mood swings, irrationality, charm, persuasiveness and anger. For six weeks, though, their hands were tied. It was a sobering moment, especially as the brothers had planned everything down to the smallest detail. But they hadn't allowed for this.

When they saw Ron later that day, they were relieved to find him in good spirits. It was vital to keep him company, which is what he had staying with friends in Walthamstow, to keep him cheerful. But equally it was important to keep him on the move and out of the way, preferably in the caravan hideaway in Suffolk. It was not far from where the boys had been evacuated with Violet during the War. Ron might feel at home and relaxed there, it might do him good.

An old friend accompanied Ron to Suffolk, where they lived in as much luxury and ease as a caravan provides when you're on the run from the law. Ron and his minder walked, talked, exercised to keep fit and even spent the odd night at the local cinema. But Ron was easily bored. And it was hard for him to be discreet. Not only him, but the friends who visited on weekends. When everyone left on a Sunday night, Ron's mood would slip from a euphoric haze on to black ice.

Reg thought increasingly about what the superintendent at the hospital had said about his twin. He decided that Ron might well benefit from medication, and he took some pills down to him at the caravan. They helped a bit, but Ron was still not right.

Ron became more and more difficult. He wore down Reg to the point at which he agreed that Ron could come up to London. For a night out in the East End. It was against Reg's better judgement, but at least a trip to town might shut him up for a bit and make him easier to handle in other ways.

In the early hours of the morning, Ron did the first of a run of reappearing acts. They became famous in underworld mythology. With all the customers gone, save a few friends and members of the firm, he showed up at the Double R.

He gave quite a performance. First of all, they'd had a dummy run outside the club, using a decoy car, and someone who looked like Ron. When the police didn't turn up, they waited a bit longer. Then Ron came in for real, making quite an entrance, one that captured the imagination of the criminal fraternity. The Krays were the talk of the East End. The very front and balls of the guys.

The star turn in Ron's new repertoire was his appearance at a pub, often frequented by Reg. The locals thought he was Reg, and they joshed with him as he ordered drinks and sat around in a suit just like one Reg wore. They even asked him how Ron was doing.

'Very well,' Ron replied, unfazed.

It may have been fun and games for Ron, but it was very much business as usual for Reg. In Charlie's eyes all was not looking good — trouble was brewing.

Charlie didn't want all the notoriety, especially with the police right next door. They were constantly on the look-out for Ron. Charlie could also see that Ron, with his charismatic, manic personality, was beginning to take over completely at the Double R. It wasn't what Charlie wanted, and he didn't like it.

Unstoppable as ever, Ron continued to do the rounds of the East End over the next few weeks. He was continually moved from one safe house to another and seemed to be taking life on the run very much in his stride. There were signs, though, of a deterioration in Ron's personality, which Reg would get wind of from time to time. Someone or other would tip him off about something weird that Ron had done somewhere. Ron was really not in good mental shape.

Everyone began to second guess Ron, trying to keep him sweet. It became intolerable. Ron still had to be kept hidden away. There couldn't be any possibility of bad behaviour. That might attract the wrong kind of attention.

In the end, the strain got too much for Charlie. He persuaded Reg to take Ron to see a psychiatrist, who prepared a report on Ron.

The psychiatrist's assessment, when it arrived, proved a tremendous shock for the whole family. It stated quite clearly that Ron was both schizophrenic and paranoid, a danger to both himself and others. That was it. Now they knew something had to give. They'd have to act —

Above: Ron, right, and Reg left, in Tangiers with mentor Billy Hill, lying low after Ron killed George Cornell in the Blind Beggar.

Left: A thoughtful Charlie Kray. The twins' elder by six years, he worked closely with them – although he often found Reg easier to deal with.

Above: In the company of the twins. Sonny Liston, centre right, and Terry Spinks, centre left.

Left: Meet and greet… Joe Louis with Ron.

Right: Henry Cooper was a friend too, to be seen from time to time at the Double R Club's gym.

Above: Ron bought the racehorse Solway Cross for his mother. It cost him 2000 guineas.

Right: Charlie Kray once said to an antagonist: 'My mother is an Eastender from a poor background, but you aren't fit to lick her feet.' On her lap is a cuddly toy, made for her by Ron in prison.

Diana Dors was a good friend of the family, seen here with the Krays mother, Violet, and Charlie. In 1981 she visited Ron in Broadmoor with Alan Lake, her husband, and young Charlie.

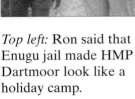

Top left: Ron said that Enugu jail made HMP Dartmoor look like a holiday camp.

Top right: Africa treated the Krays well – at first.

Above: Reg befriends a young Nigerian. He needed all the friends he could get when his Great African Safari company proved as volatile as its abbreviation, GAS.

Right: Ron wonders what to do with his Nigerian souvenir. He might have used it to cool down later, when the heat was on.

Top: George Raft, second left, the boxer turned actor, at his Colony Club in London's Berkeley Square with companions who include Charlie and Violet Kray, right. The Krays never did understand his shabby treatment by the Home Office.

Bottom: Ron with top club man Paul Raymond and Lita Rosa.

Above: In the movie *The Krays*, Reg Kray, played by Martin Kemp, shows one of the ways in which the Krays could do the business.

(RANK FILM DISTRIBUTORS)

Right: But, there were others… Ron, left, and Reg, right, with boxing impresario, Barney Ross.

and quickly — before Ron exploded and caused God knows what kind of a stink.

The Kray family got together one evening at Vallance Road and had a long talk. Ron's mental health was deteriorating visibly by now. They decided to send him back to the hospital -a terribly hard decision for them. Throughout his breakdown, they had stuck together. Blood was thicker than water. Blood brothers.

Enough was enough, though. Ron was too ill not to be in hospital. Even if it went against everything the Krays as a family believed in, they had no choice. That is if they were to have anything left in which to believe. Ron was becoming totally out of control, and no one knew what he might do — either to himself or someone else.

Reg made all the arrangements, and Ron was readmitted to Long Grove. When he later recovered from his breakdown, life at Vallance Road and the Double R was never quite the same.

At Long Grove, Ron's certificate of insanity had lapsed, and he was soon declared sane and well enough to return to HMP Wandsworth to complete his prison sentence. Ultimately the plan to spring Ron from the hospital had worked. As usual, the Krays had got what they were after.

But the escape had been successful in another way, too, that the Kray brothers had not anticipated. It had brought the Kray name into the forefront of the criminal underworld.

5

THE GLAMOUR GAME

'IS THAT YOU, CHARLIE? It's Barbara.' The bubbly blonde wasn't at all her normal effervescent self — in fact she was deadly serious. 'We've got a problem. Can you help?'

Charlie Kray had known Barbara Windsor for years. They had dated regularly at one time, but Charlie had refused to divorce his wife, Dolly, and Barbara wanted marriage, nothing else would be tolerated. They had enjoyed an intimate relationship even after Barbara had become an East End success story, a sexy blonde bombshell of stage and screen. But Barbara couldn't accept their lifestyle, where every passionate evening would end with Charlie crawling back home to his wife. She wanted a home — and a man of her own.

Since those days things had gone from bad to worse for Charlie Kray and his off/on marriage floundered on the rocks when Dolly's affair with small-time crook George Ince became public knowledge and Charlie's position untenable. He was, after all, the brother of Ron and Reg Kray, the two most powerful underworld figures that London had ever seen, and he couldn't allow himself to be the laughing stock of Bethnal Green.

All that, though, was now firmly in the past, but through it all Barbara and Charlie had remained good friends. She was, at this time, only recently married to one of Charlie's old pals from The Regal days, a man by the name of Ronnie Knight who would later on, in 1983, become famous in his own right as Britain's 'Most Wanted Man' for his part in the £6 million Securities Express Robbery in Central London. The twins had also known her for some time as she had been a regular back in the days of The Double R club and naturally enough they knew her husband very well indeed; Ronnie Knight had grown up with the Krays and had always been a loyal friend.

But now, Barbara had a problem. 'There's some dockers who are trying to stop us filming.' Could Charlie help out?

'Don't worry, love,' Charlie reassured her. 'Tell me all about it, and I'll take care of it for you.'

This was bread and butter for the Krays, like a good work-out. A couple of phone calls from Charlie ironed everything out. It was a favour to his old friend, but it wasn't difficult for him. The name Kray sent a tremor down any telephone line these days.

The Kray empire may have suffered a hiccup with the closure of the Double R, but it had not been life threatening: the Double R is dead, long live the Kentucky Club. For once the twins had listened to Charlie's advice: You have to speculate to accumulate. Well, that's just what they'd done. The Kentucky Club was just off the Mile End Road in the East End, and it was their new investment. Something concrete for the money they'd made from protection rackets, long firms and gambling clubs.

The Kentucky was a swankier version of the Double R, and with it the Krays hoped to attract a more up-market clientele, people on the make in the East and West Ends. This time Ron and Reg had really pushed the boat out — their interest in the club wasn't just a shareholding. They'd had too many partnership deals made in exchange for protection. This time they wanted all or nothing, and that was what they were going to make of the Kentucky. They had their rising status in the community to consider.

The essence of the Kentucky was pure sixties and swinging. They were going up, and that meant up West. Plush, brash and gaudy: a statement of intent. To establish Mayfair in Poplar. Only the class was missing, but they were out to attract that too.

The club looked stunning: a black leather and glass bar, trompe l'oeil windows complete with curtains and window boxes in bloom, exotic red walls and the piece de resistance of the four-foot high stage, fully lit and wired for sound. It could take a five-piece band plus singer, no problem. Just in front of the stage was an intimate dance floor, backed by discreet clusters of tables each lit with the moody opalescence of a small lamp. It was flash, and the Krays had made it that way. This was what they wanted now.

A taxi pulled up outside the entrance to the club. In the early evening light the neon sign KENTUCKY CLUB made a welcome splash of colour in the otherwise nondescript drag of the Mile End Road.

'Mind the steps, love,' Barbara Windsor's chirpy voice rang out along the empty street, as she entered the Kentucky with a woman, slightly older than her, well-dressed, stylish, in tow.

'Are you sure this is right?' the woman asked.

The place didn't look that prepossessing from the outside. Barbara took her friend's hand and dragged her in with her. They came face to face with Big Pat Connolly, then employed by the Krays as a minder at the club. He looked offputting, but that was the intention. The warmth of her welcome disarmed him, which wasn't hard to do with Pat Connolly. His face creased into the folds of a huge grin as he ushered her in.

'Go right through,' he said. 'I think you're both expected.'

Charlie was sitting on his own at a table in the corner when the two women walked in.

'Charlie Kray, meet Joan Littlewood.'

Barbara introduced them. Charlie and Joan Littlewood shook hands. Hers was a firm handshake. She was a strong and determined woman, well-known in the East End as a popular show-business figure with her own theatre company and a string of theatrical achievements.

'Good to meet you, Charlie,' Joan said. 'And thank you for the other day — I didn't know what to do. I couldn't think of anyone to help.'

She was directing a new film in which Barbara was one of the stars, and it was she who'd had the problem with the dockers.

Reg and Ron were sitting at the bar. Charlie took the women over and introduced them. They were made to feel welcome, in an amusing, lighthearted way. As the drinks flowed, the Krays silently congratulated themselves on their show-business success — they were really beginning to rub shoulders with the stars. The twins in particular were keen on the glamour of showbiz names to enhance their own increasingly celebrity status. They were good club owners, knew how to make a go of it, enjoyed playing the glamour game.

Joan Littlewood enjoyed her evening at the Kentucky so much that she wanted to use the club as a location in her new film. There was a night-club scene that would go well there.

A movie starring Barbara Windsor and James Booth was high-profile stuff. Classy. The Krays were more than pleased. The film shoot and its later release would enhance their reputation no end. It was a great idea.

'Funny,' said Ron, whose wit at times could dry up a monsoon river bed, 'we don't normally allow shooting in here.'

His humour hid his delight. He was all for it, even to the extent of suggesting that some of the firm might join the film crew on location — just in case of any future trouble on set.

Joan Littlewood accepted Ron's offer gracefully, and they celebrated with more drinks. The twins introduced her to all the staff, particularly to Eddie Woods and John Davis, who served behind the bar. They'd have a chance to get to know one another during the shoot. The club manager, a big man by name of Staff, was dragged out of his office to meet Joan and celebrate the good news. The film's première was planned at the Empire Cinema, just across the road from the club.

'We'll hold a party here afterwards,' Reg suggested.

He was too shrewd a businessman to pass up that good an opportunity. It turned out that there might even be a royal presence. Lord Snowdon and Princess Margaret had been invited. You couldn't get much classier than that. It would be a shot in the arm for the cockney sparrows.

When the première of *Sparrows Can't Sing* — a cockney comedy tale about a merchant seaman, played by James Booth, who returns to his native Stepney to find his wife, Barbara Windsor, living with another man — came around in March 1963, Lord Snowdon and Princess Margaret came to the screening at the Empire. It was an appropriate place for the film to be shown for the first time, as it had been filmed almost entirely on location in the area, with the added bonus that Barbara Windsor was a local girl made good.

Unfortunately for the twins, due to a prior engagement, the royal presence was absent at the party held over the road at the Kentucky Club. Ron, Reg and Charlie were there, though, holding court in their own inimitable way. They greeted their guests with great style, fully aware of the publicity mileage the event carried with it.

A glittering array of the rich and famous turned up.

Barbara Windsor and her new husband Ronnie Knight, co-star James Booth, Roy Kinnear, Avis Bunnage, Barbara Ferris and Joan Littlewood herself, who'd also invited along actor Roger Moore, at that time known as the star of *The Saint* on TV. Bond was still to come. Queenie Watts was booked to sing her sentimental cockney songs.

The Krays had a guestlist of their own. It included one of Charlie Kray's favourite drinking pals, George Sewell, Lord Effingham, who had taken time off from his duties at the gambling club, Esmeralda's Barn, and an old friend of the Krays, Freddie Foreman, the South London gang leader, who was later acquitted, along with Reg and Ron, of a murder charge against their old pal, Frank Mitchell. Freddie Foreman later went on record, however, to confirm that he was indeed the man who fired the fatal shots into the heart of the 'Mad Axeman', as Mitchell was known. The orders did come from the twins, who also supplied the guns. The law, unfortunately, were never to get their men since none of them could be tried again for the Mitchell murder, once acquitted at the Old Bailey. But that was still to come and far from the minds of the future conspirators.

It was a fabulous evening, when the East End put on its best face and showed the West End how to have fun. The mix of East End villains and famous, sixties show-business personalities made a prestigious cocktail for the Krays.

The Kentucky Club had become like a second home for Ron, who had always enjoyed his star role as court entertainer. It was Ron who found the special guests who put in appearances from time to time at the club, entertaining the club regulars. They'd range from the frankly weird, such as a dwarf who would sit on a donkey and play the banjo, to the celebrated, such as Eddie Calvert, the trumpeter, who performed there one unforgettable evening.

On another equally memorable occasion Billy Daniels also showed up, after his performance at the London Palladium. He put on a show for nothing —

because he wanted to. The charisma of the Krays could be magnetic.

During one of their regular Monday morning business meetings at the Kentucky, the Krays were talking debt with Staff, their manager at the Kentucky, and Laurie O'Leary, the manager of the night-club turned casino, Esmeralda's Barn. The amount of money lost through bad debts was escalating. It was becoming more than just a headache, collecting, juggling and writing off money owed by some of the wealthy clientele of Esmeralda's Barn.

Uncle Alf was their main debt collector. He was completely straight, a reasonable man — and absolutely not right for chasing money from the posh nobs of London's West End. Alf was continually harrassed on the job, once even threatened with imprisonment — by a policeman. Extracting money from the wealthy could be like getting blood from a stone.

Something had to change — and fast. By the summer of 1963, the level of debt had risen to over £20,000 — from Esmeralda's Barn alone. It was ironic this, because Esmeralda's was the most valuable piece of property ever owned by the Krays, one which had come into their possession during the early sixties.

It had all begun back in the late autumn of 1960, the start of the swinging sixties in London. Esmeralda's Barn was in Wilton Place, Knightsbridge, one of the most prestigious and expensive addresses in town; it was a three-tiered barn of gold, a licence to print money.

In fact it was a pub and a night-club, a discotheque, one of the first and best in London, and a casino, where the wealthy and aspiring were to be seen gambling into the early hours of the morning. For the Krays to get a foothold here would be to strike gold.

Some time during that late autumn, Charlie had received a telephone call from one Commander Diamond.

'Why don't you hold the meeting at my place?' he invited.

There was a pause at the other end of the line while Charlie flicked through the pages of his heavily booked diary and decided when he could make time to meet the Commander. He, Charlie, was busy these days.

'That's OK with me, Commander,' he said. 'I'll look forward to seeing you again.'

The Commander chuckled knowingly.

'And I'm looking forward to the meeting too, Charlie.' He added, 'I just can't wait to see their faces.'

Commander Diamond was an elderly gentleman of means.

He lived at a smart address above the Scotch House in Knightsbrdge, a stone's throw from Harrods and Hyde Park.

He owned a Rolls-Royce, which he always drove in the company of his dog, which sat in the passenger seat.

The Commander was a well-known and greatly respected character in and around London's West End. Not much escaped his eagle eye. He was a great source of news, often even before it became gossip worthy. He knew everyone and everything there was to know about the West End social scene — its glitz as well as its dirty washing.

He had heard about the club in Wilton Place just recently, on the grapevine. It was in trouble. The owners — there were two main shareholders, Stefan de Faye and a Mr Burns — couldn't agree on a strategy for the business, and it was heading rapidly downhill. Commander Diamond realized that a takeover of Esmeralda's Barn, at least new management, would be a golden opportunity for somebody. He also knew that his friend Charlie Kray was looking for a foothold in the West End, for himself and his brothers, Ron and Reg, that is. He decided to give Charlie a call.

In fact the Commander's main reason for phoning Charlie was not so altruistic. His strong dislike for the two owners, combined with the knowledge that he couldn't trust them further than he could throw them, spurred him into tipping Charlie off. As he knew a lot about de Faye and Burns, he thought it might be advisable for him to be in on a meeting, at least to begin with. Anyway, he wanted his fun.

It was all set up. De Faye and Burns would meet with the Commander to discuss investment opportunities or possibly a complete takeover bid for Esmeralda's Barn. It would take place in the Commander's Knightsbridge flat. Charlie Kray would be invited too, but at this point neither de Faye nor Burns knew his name, although if they had perhaps they would have come better armed.

Charlie was well prepared. He arrived at the Commander's apartment early, accompanied by Ron's business manager, Leslie Payne, and Freddie Gore, their accountant. De Faye and Burns showed up on time and were quite nonplussed by the mention of the Kray name during the Commander's introductions. Negotiating with any Kray was a strenuous task, and they weren't really up to it at that moment. Neither were they prepared for Charlie's forthright challenge.

'Let me first of all say how pleased we are that you could meet us here today,' Charlie started politely.

De Faye and Burns glanced at each other, nonplussed. What is going on here? they must have wondered.

'Now we know you're in trouble — and if we wanted to, we could just take over the place,' Charlie continued.

De Faye didn't respond. He just waited to see how close to his chest Charlie was going to play his cards. Burns, though, couldn't contain his anger. It got right up his public-school nose that he was about to be put down by an East End barrowboy. 'Do you East Enders really think you can come over to the West End and tell us what to do?' he ranted.

He was furious, but not so blazing angry as Charlie.

'I told you that we could, if we wanted to, just go in and take it all over — perfectly legally,' Charlie replied with quiet rage.

Finding it impossibly hard to disguise his fury, he conceded, 'But we are perfectly willing to make you a fair offer for Esmeralda's Barn.'

Burns still wasn't having any of it. He persisted in insulting Charlie.

'You,' he said, in a derogatory tone, 'can't run a business in the West End of London.'

The room just went quiet. Charlie felt no need to defend himself against such a pathetic allegation. He took a few deep breaths to calm himself and spoke again.

'I don't like your attitude,' said Charlie.

He didn't want one second more of Burns' lip.

'Just because I come from the East End of London,' he continued, 'doesn't mean that I can't do the business.'

Commander Diamond nodded his head in furious agreement at this.

'Let me tell you something, Mr Burns,' Charlie went on, this time walking across the room towards him.

For some moments he stood inches away from Burns. Any closer and they would have been dancing together. But it wasn't dancing that Charlie wanted to do. He felt like tearing the man apart. Instead, he just stood quietly and stared unflinchingly at Burns.

'My mother is an Eastender from a poor background, but you aren't fit enough to lick my mother's feet.'

He said this slowly, in a calm, contained voice, enunciating every syllable perfectly. At that moment, Burns must have felt himself to be very alone in that room. He must have wondered, could he really behave like that to a Kray and get away with it? He was soon to find out.

'To be truthful,' Charlie said in a voice no louder than a whisper, but with more impact because of it, 'to be truthful, I feel like knocking you both up in the air. But I'll do it your way.'

With the effort of tremendous restraint, Charlie turned away from him to face Leslie Payne and Freddie Gore.

'My friends here can explain the details, but we're willing to give you £2000 in cash tomorrow for the Barn.'

De Faye and Burns were too bewildered to say anything remotely sensible. In any case, without waiting for either de Faye or Burns to react, Charlie continued.

'If you say yes, then that's fine, and you'll always be welcome at the Barn,' he said.

There was a heavy silence as they waited for the inevitable but.

'If not,' he added, his voice registering a degree of menace, 'then we'll just take it over — all perfectly legal — and you'll get absolutely nothing.'

The following day, a delivery of £2000 in cash to Stefan de Faye completed the transaction, and that evening the three brothers walked in and took possession of the club.

Ownership of Esmeralda's Barn was a fresh start for the Krays; with it they began to play their biggest part in the glamour game. Best of all, it had given them their slot up West. And the kudos of mixing and meeting with prominent people and celebrities on their own turf. The Krays had just found a new credibility other than the street.

They soon learned to appreciate the differences between the East and West Ends of London. West End was a completely new scene. But the Krays were nothing if not adaptable, and it wasn't exactly hard for them to learn how to enjoy their new access to wealth.

There were certain disadvantages in debt collection in the West End, with the police often involved in helping out the debtors. Indeed, the police seemed to take the whole Barn deal very seriously, personally even — they went out of their way to hinder the Krays whenever they could.

Life was good, or so the Krays felt. And nobody and nothing was going to take that away from them. They would use the glamorous style of the casino and discotheque to their very great advantage. If you want to be big, think and do big -and go for it.

With this in mind, they invited Eric Clapton to play at the Barn, and the talented Walker Brothers, whose song 'The Sun Ain't Gonna Shine Anymore' had just topped the record charts. Topping was the right word here, for it was this chart hit that played on the jukebox when Ron Kray shot and killed George Cornell at the Blind Beggar in Whitechapel.

Friends, old and new, visited Esmeralda's Barn to wish the Krays welcome. For a while the club became the brightest star in the London club firmament. Actress Honor Blackman, of Avengers fame, and Maurice Kaufman would drop by from time to time, as did David Burglas, the magician, and Pauline Wallace.

One evening Laurie O'Leary came looking for Charlie, who was having a quiet drink with Lord Effingham.

'There's a fella downstairs asking to see you,' he said.

'Can't you deal with it?' Charlie replied, sipping his drink.

'He says he wants to come up and play in the casino, but he's not a member,' O'Leary continued. 'He's American.'

Charlie didn't know many Americans in those days, so he was intrigued enough to go downstairs and find out who was there. The young man hanging around in the reception area looked familiar, but Charlie couldn't quite put a name to him. He didn't need to. The man introduced himself.

'Hello,' he said. 'Remember me? I'm Phil Everly.'

At that time, the early sixties, the Everly Brothers were world-famous rock stars, ranking ten on a star scale of one to ten. Fame opens every door, and Phil Everly was made immediately welcome.

Some well-known faces, unfortunately, also became well-known debtors. Lucian Freud, the painter brother of Clement Freud, one-time politician and television personality, ran up a debt of £1400, big money in those days. He was not able to pay it back. Instead he offered Ron a painting.

Ron refused — and told Freud that he should consider the debt cancelled. Because Ron liked him, simple as that. Ron told Freud he could come to the club and play in the casino whenever he liked. He just liked to watch Freud enjoy himself, he explained. You really never knew which way Ron would turn. You just never really knew Ron.

Ron lost the Barn a huge amount of money like that. Other times he would be very persistent with debtors. When he asked for a debt to be paid, then it was normally settled on the spot, preferably in cash.

Ron felt that he had a reputation to live up to and, if threatened, he could react with enormous physical strength — sometimes with horrendous consequences. One time he threw one of the croupiers down the stairs. Just like that, almost out of the blue, after he'd suspected him all evening of working with an accomplice at one of the chemmy tables.

'We don't like cheats here,' said Ron, holding the man firmly by the lapels of his jacket. 'I think you'd better leave,' he said, helping him on his way by tossing him downstairs.

Seconds later Ron behaved as if nothing had happened. He could be very unpredictable. But this was a rare incidence of violence. Fighting wasn't common at the Barn. It would have given a bad impression of the place, and good impressions were what the Krays were after in their new-found land of money and privilege.

Their reputation was growing daily in this glamour game. The more they mixed with the rich and famous, the better they felt about themselves. Being celebrities, the Krays were discovering, was one way of cutting through the class structure that entangles Britain. Their high profile was even immortalized by David Bailey when he took a set of photographs during the sixties, and it was the same fashionable photographer that recorded Reg's marriage to Frances Shea.

Fame allows most barriers to be crossed. You can move rapidly into life in the fast lane, and there you make connections. Sometimes they send you into a spin, and you lose control, at best facing back from where you've come. Other times into more connections, which is what business is mostly about: knowing the right people, being in the right place at the right time, being seen charitably to recycle your excess profits. This is how you play the glamour game.

To take part fully, you had to get involved in charity work and the Krays were first-class players. Not simply for the publicity fringe benefits but also because they were genuinely interested in helping people.

Folk, as they saw it, less fortunate than themselves and especially disadvantaged children.

Never deprived in their own East End childhoods, they nevertheless knew what it was like to be East End poor — and that there was much worse than that. They always felt that the public relations side of their charity operations was a welcome bonus, but not the main reason for their generosity. They genuinely enjoyed helping people. They even felt that way about their protection business.

Perhaps the most spectacular charity event staged by the Krays was the raffle of the racehorse, Solway Cross, at the Cambridge Rooms, a club the Krays owned near Kingston, Surrey. Ron had originally bought the animal for 1000 guineas as a present for his mother Violet. A kind gesture, but the horse proved inadequate on the racetrack, and Ron decided he would offer it as the first prize in a grand raffle for charity.

The Peter Pan Society of Brighton was chosen as the beneficiary of the raffle and invited along to handle the money collected. The Krays themselves would not do this, just in case something went wrong and they were accused of stealing charitable funds. Ever cautious in business — of whatever kind.

On the day, in that summer of 1963, Ron put the horse on show in a marquee, specially erected for the event, the floor even covered with imitation turf. No expense was spared. A buffet, plenty to drink, celebrity guests such as bubbly Barbara Windsor and the actor Ronald Fraser.

The turnout of support was good, but no one really wanted the horse. In the end it was won by a publican friend of Charlie, who immediately put it up for raffle again as he couldn't possibly keep a horse in his public house. The drinking and bidding then continued all night, but it wasn't until the morning that Charlie's good friend Ronald Fraser awoke to discover he'd acquired a racehorse along with his hangover.

Rubbing shoulders with celebrities at charity events wasn't the whole story by any means. Some of the celebrities the Krays met became good friends — and much of their charity work was done in the proper spirit of generosity, with no angles, no edge. New friends and acquaintances included a variety of people, such as Freddie Mills, the boxer, and a string of American actors and singers, Judy Garland, George Raft, Billy Daniels, Barbra Streisand, Richard Jaekel and Robert Ryan.

Late in 1981 the actress Diana Dors and her husband Alan Lake, who was to take his own life shortly after his wife's untimely death, went to see Ron in Broadmoor, the maximum-security psychiatric hospital to which Ron was eventually admitted. Charlie Kray arranged the visit and accompanied his friends on their trip there.

The outing was a success, Ron his best charismatic, charming self. As they left the visiting room, Ron turned to give all his visitors a regal wave of farewell. Diana Dors was amused by this.

'I don't know what it is, but your Ron's got it,' she laughed. 'If I could only bottle it, then I would make a fortune.'

'And, then,' replied Charlie, 'maybe by this time next year we'd all be millionaires.'

But doing the business by playing the glamour game hadn't got them that far, yet.

6

HOW TO SUCCEED IN BUSINESS WITHOUT REALLY TRYING

YOU GOT THE STYLE, I got the looks, let's make lots of money. It was Leslie Payne who had explained it all. He often did all the talking. A big man with a strong upper-class accent, always smartly attired, he'd been a member of the firm since 1960 — as Ron's business consultant and financial adviser.

Payne and Ron had met through some low-key motor deals. They'd worked together a bit, but after Payne had so successfully masterminded the smooth takeover of Esmeralda's Barn in autumn 1960, their relationship moved into a different gear. Payne knew business; he could make the Krays wealthy — make them millionaires — and do it with the power and status that the brothers were so in thrall to.

Until Payne had joined forces with Ron, he'd been involved primarily with a small-time operation of his own, which was almost entirely concerned with car sales and finance. In 1960 he was a very minor player in a major league — but he had a sharp intellect and an acute sense for business.

Payne the brain, as the twins came to call him, had impressed Ron and Reg Kray with his well-spoken, educated manner, his clean-cut appearance and his ability to discuss business in a way that others, including the twins, could understand and appreciate. Payne's roots were right side of the tracks. He made a good foil to Reg and Ron, and they were learning about status by association. Payne's spin-off in the partnership was the Krays' wealth — he could take a short cut to success through them and make himself, and them, a lot of money.

What was also good about Leslie Payne from the Krays' point of view was that he was a man of ideas and not ideals. He knew where he wanted to go — and the end always justified the means for him. In this way he thought like the twins. Principles are for rich people.

Well, the Krays may have been getting richer by the hour, but they could remember only too well from where they'd come. And they didn't want to go back there. Leslie Payne was their ticket out, executive class, Concorde style.

The Krays had the three things that Payne most wanted: money, money and more money. Payne had the outward appearance of respectability, but he had a criminal mind. It was the perfect relationship — they had a lot to offer each other, an ideal match between the aspiring underworld and a restless and frustrated member of the middle class.

Payne's way was canny. Apart from Esmeralda's Barn, he'd come out of the shit smelling of roses, time and time again. As co-director of Esmeralda's Barn, he'd earned more than his crust, much more, and he had proved his potential. The next step had to have been the Kentucky Club, early in 1962. This, too, was an overnight success. Everything considered, the twins were eager to listen to Payne. When he spelled out his plan for how to succeed in business without really trying, he had their undivided attention.

Starting and running a business is always risky. The likelihood of a new company becoming highly successful and profitable in the short term is not high. Similarly the chance of a new company surviving at all, long term, is nowhere near guaranteed. The logical solution, Payne reasoned, was to set up a business with the certain knowledge of and commitment to its failure, to plan to go broke and thereby maximize your profits.

In spite of his acute commercial sense, or maybe because of it, Payne would never agree to draw up a business strategy along normal lines. This, for the Krays, was his great strength. With unsuccessful business ventures as their goal, the Krays and Payne made a formidably successful team with their astonishingly simple version of long-firm fraud. A short-term way to make a huge profit by defrauding suppliers, involving the establishment, operation and deliberate collapse of a company. The Krays liked the idea, after all it had the added frisson of being illegal. Payne described it to the twins, step by step: nine steps to heaven — or hell.

STEP ONE Find a suitable front man. This was vital. The person selected would be the face of the whole operation. They would provide a front door of honesty, charm and charisma, behind whose credibility threshold the scheme would either win or lose. The front man would also have to be someone whom the twins could trust implicitly, whom they could control. The front man was top man. He could also become the underdog if he failed to toe the line.

The scam began well in advance of setting up the company. First, the front man would have to tie up any professional interests of his own, since once the new company was underway he could not afford to have any possible ghosts in the closet. His slate had to be squeaky clean. Second, the man would initiate his own personal banking facilities, which would involve opening foreign bank accounts, ready for his share of the long-firm collapse profits. Being a front man was not without its risks, but they were calculatedly good, especially in the early 1960s, when the chance of getting caught was virtually zero. For some men it was a way of life; they made a lot of money, saw the world and never faced prosecution. Simple as that. Not quite.

STEP TWO Set up the business. This would be done by the front man himself. The Krays would not get involved in this phase of the scam at all. The front man would have had his briefing from them, so no further contact between them was necessary at this stage. He would also have received a small cash float, enough to start things up. There was an understanding that proper funds would be in place when banking arrangements were sought. With cash in hand, he would go about his business.

Under a suitable name, the venture would be registered as a new limited company. This took a matter of days and was an inexpensive process. Then office and warehouse space had to be found, and a company identity established with the business stationery and logo. All administration forms and publicity material would be printed up with the company logo. Both these stages were preceded by the obvious need to find a good trading product. These ranged from electrical goods, such as televisions, hi-fi equipment, radios, refrigerators and washing machines, to basic consumer products, such as furniture, clothing, toys, bicycles, cars, suitcases or even crates of wine.

Once a product or range had been determined, Ron and Reg did move in. They would supply the rest of the staff: the floor manager, warehouse personnel and secretarial and administrative staff, all hand picked by them for their loyalty. They would earn good money for a while, no questions asked. And they would do whatever was asked of them.

STEP THREE Set up a business bank account. Tricky things to establish, Leslie Payne had come up with a foolproof way of doing so — by starting several companies at once. Maybe five or six at the same time. This way the companies could supply references for each other. Without this, the trade references were a real headache for the long firm. And, without them, there was no bank account. Without a bank account, the company could not trade. Without trading, the company could not arrange for the purchase of goods on credit terms. Without goods, there would be no profitable sell-off when the time came to close the company. It was a chain of deception that relied on every link.

The front man would arrange this. He would look around for a suitable bank, not too close to the business premises from where he intended to run his long firm. The rule of thumb was the more gullible the bank manager the better. You learned to spot them, the easy targets. Then a large sum of money would be deposited into the new account as start capital.

Over the following weeks, various amounts would be withdrawn from the account and redeposited, just enough to show the bank manager that the company was trading, that he had a thriving business on his books. And, of course, to build up confidence, which is what a long-firm fraud was: a confidence trick. With the bank fully behind them, the company could set up credit accounts with all their suppliers. This was imperative.

STEP FOUR Start trading. The company would buy in goods and sell them on as quickly as possible at a discount. Speed of turnover was essential. To facilitate this, the company would take out adverts in the local newspapers, to enhance the image of it being a bona fide operation. It was looking good — even close up.

The Krays would also make sure that all bills and invoices were paid in full and on time. The company would have all the trappings of a securely based, profitable business venture.

STEP FIVE Set up accounts with all suppliers. Suppliers would by now have been lulled into a false sense of security. Goods had been supplied, and invoices paid in full. All proper and above board. Even the bank manager could confirm that the company appeared sound, a solid investment, which would help the company get its credit accounts. Everything was set for the next and vital stage of the long-firm operation.

STEP SIX Buy, buy, buy. When everyone has grown used to having the company around and in good shape, trading normally, orders would be placed by the front man or warehouse manager — for anything and everything they could get their hands on, on credit. They would try to fill the warehouse as fast as possible. They would order and order, until goods piled skylight high in the warehouse.

This step was triggered by Ron and Reg, with Leslie Payne the brains behind it, keeping a watchful eye on things. They watched the operation at every step of the way. It wouldn't have done for the front man to have got any bright ideas of fixing his own business deals.

If there were any trouble from the front man, then one of the twins would go and have a word. That was all it took to reach what they called a compromise. The front man would then do whatever was asked of him by the twins. He knew quite clearly what non-compliance involved.

STEP SEVEN Sell, sell, sell. The timing of this express sale would be organized by Ron and Reg, masterminded by Leslie Payne. The idea was to sell off the entire product or range as quickly as possible. A huge clearance sale with everything going for cash, at whatever prices they could get on the spot.

The order for this, when it came through, would just be, 'Hit the floor.'

This was the signal. Normally it took only 24 hours to clear all warehouse stock. They would have sold the warehouse too, if they thought they might get away with it. Some people other than the Krays themselves got lucky at this stage. If the goods didn't shift fast enough, Ron and Reg would donate them as gifts to charity, thereby improving their respect and standing in the community.

After the cut-price sale, the front man would hoard the cash, including all the money from the bank account, for a few days. With the knowledge and consent of the Krays. Then, when it was safe, Ron and Reg would move in and relieve him of it.

STEP EIGHT The disappearing act. Everyone would vanish: the front man and staff. Everything would dematerialize: the money, the company paperwork, the filing cabinets, desks, typewriters, even the waste-paper baskets. There would no longer be any goods, employees or company; the offices would suddenly empty. After a few days, the only reminder that the company had existed at all and was not a figment of a fertile imagination would be the pile of unopened letters and invoices on the floor of reception. By the time the suppliers realized what had happened, the goods, money, manager, company would all have evaporated into thin air.

STEP NINE Enter the law. Better late than never? Not in this case. Eventually, often months later, the police would appear on the scene and start to look for the front man, who by this time would be sunning himself on a beach in Rio, or some exotic point south. If and when the law did catch up with him, he knew better than to admit to anything. If he were booked and arrested and went down for a term of imprisonment, then this was the price he sometimes paid. But no ratting on the twins. That would be betrayal. And the price for that was too high even to consider.

Laurel and Hardy, that was how the twins referred to Leslie Payne and his sidekick, the accountant Freddie Gore, who had originally kept the books at Esmeralda's Barn. The Krays made the bulk of the profits from the long-firm fraud — and had nothing to connect them to the company. The perfect crime. But it was Leslie Payne with his able associate Gore, who was the brain behind the scam.

The long-firm frauds were highly successful operations, netting well over £100,000 in 1962 alone. A reasonable profit from a single long firm could be as high as £20,000. Long-firm business fraud became a way of life in the East End after this. All the gangs started to operate them, the Richardsons as well as countless others. They had discovered one of the simplest and most dishonest ways ever devised for making money. But what could the law do about it? The answer was very little.

Police procedure went in three initial phases. First, the company had to go bust before they could become involved. This took time, enough to allow the front man and everyone else involved in the company to escape. Second, complaints had to be received by the police from creditors before there was any reason to act. Again, time was against the police. No evidence, no crime. Until much later.

The procedure moved into its third phase when the police referred the case for fraud-squad investigation. This was a slow process, too, which could easily take another year. By now all witnesses would have gone. The front man would be languishing abroad, waiting for the heat to cool down. It was this intractable factor of time that made catching the perpetrators of long-firm frauds so immensely difficult. The fraudsters, too, knew that the chances of their being caught were minimal and so the scams continued. It was a vicious circle.

To begin with the police would try to find any employees of the erstwhile company. Since most of these people were only employed on a temporary basis, often just for a week or two at a time, and were carefully selected beforehand for their tact and discretion, this was a trail that quickly died out.

The rapid and discreet staff turnover made it almost impossible for the police to gather evidence. Even the orders with the suppliers had been placed over the phone, so no one could physically identify the person who had actually ordered the goods. Warehouse managers could not be prosecuted, since they were only obeying orders and carrying out their duties. The front man was the only person who could help the police with their inquiries — and he had vanished. No evidence, no crime.

The police were quite aware of what was happening right under their noses. They were fixed on the Krays' case and this included Leslie Payne and Freddie Gore. Sometimes they would trail the Krays, hoping accidentally to uncover one or other of their myriad schemes. But they never succeeded.

Detective Inspector Leonard 'Nipper' Read, the detective in charge of investigating the Krays, interviewed endless people about them during the sixties. No one would ever open up, and the Krays themselves always had a failsafe in any scam, which kept them at least one step ahead of the law. Using the great wall of silence that surrounded them, the Krays conducted their activities with uncanny invulnerability — and great caution and cunning.

As no one would ever admit to any involvement with the Krays, the police were frustrated in their efforts to try to link long firms with them. Indeed the Krays were never prosecuted by the police for running long firms, although they successfully operated several between 1962 and 1968, when they were eventually arrested and imprisoned — but they were never prosecuted by the police for long-firm fraud. The Kray empire collapsed in the late sixties for altogether different reasons.

On the Krays' arrest in May 1968, Leslie Payne and Freddie Gore tried to distance themselves from any involvement with the long firms and other dubious operations. Ultimately, though, both men went down too. The Carston Group of Companies had been an impressive West End front behind which they operated from Great Portland Street. With its investigation and collapse, the rats sank with the ship. Payne and Gore both received prison sentences, although they were given their freedom after the trial. But the police never forget their names and never forgave what they had done. It was freedom at a price.

Along with the ups and downs of the rip-offs connected to long-firm fraud, and the wheeling and dealing that accompanied it, there were often hilarious side-effects. On one occasion in the mid-sixties, a business acquaintance of Charlie Kray went for a drink in his local, a pub in the Mile End Road.

As he stood quietly sipping his drink in a corner of the saloon, he gazed idly round the room. With the comfort of a pint of John Bull bitter in one hand, and no one in particular to talk to, he did a quick double-take as he took in the bar full of men. Several of them were smartly dressed in identical brown check suits. He found this odd and highly amusing.

He turned to share the joke with the bloke sitting next to him, but his neighbour was able to offer him a simple explanation. Some rolls of imitation Burberry cloth had been left over from a long-firm fraud. The prices hadn't got rock bottom enough to shift the cloth — or demand had just run out — so another way of getting rid of the rolls of suiting had to be devised. Why not turn their overstock into gold? The cloth was made up into suits.

One of the lads in the pub had then treated himself to a made-to-measure suit and become the envy of his pals. All the young dudes would look cool in brown tweed. Within a week everyone thereabouts was sporting snazzy, brown check suits — all with identical and matching shoes, which had been part of the same scam. The saloon bar looked like a film set for Elvis Presley's backing group, the Jordanaires.

Getting rid of company stock was almost as vital as destroying the company paperwork. And sometimes this called for measures that were not so much hilarious as desperate. In Shoreditch, East London, in the mid-1960s one George Cornell — posthumously infamous when he later fell foul of Ron Kray, who shot him dead in the Blind Beggar pub — was assigned by Kray rivals, the Richardsons, to dispose of any incriminating evidence that had accumulated in a warehouse from one of their long-firm frauds. He had to ensure that all accounts and other paperwork were completely destroyed.

Cornell took his job seriously. He burned all invoices, sales ledgers and suchlike in a metal waste bin, having doused them in petrol before setting light to them. His paranoia was not satisfied with this, though. He returned some hours later with a bundle of dynamite and blew the entire building sky high.

It was a tactic that was as heavy handed as the Kray empire was proving it could be in the East End. For the twins, the sky was not the limit. Their horizons appeared limitless. Soon their careers in crime would go further, still further than even they had imagined. All the way to Africa, in fact.

7

OUT OF AFRICA

WHEN LESLIE PAYNE FIRST MENTIONED a business project in Africa, to the twins, they thought it was a good joke. In fact they enjoyed it so much that they asked him to tell them another one. It was this curious sense of humour that led them to darkest Africa, where they found themselves in deep trouble.

Leslie Payne and Ron Kray shared one important characteristic: they both lusted after fame and fortune, although in different measure. The twins entrusted Payne with their money and he used it, together with their reputation, to cut corners and change the rules of business. Why should he operate like a regular guy, when he could move ahead much faster, riding bareback on the Kray name?

Early in 1964 Leslie Payne paid his first visit to Africa. It was to be the first of many. He flew on a BOAC flight to Nigeria with a colleague whose construction project in Africa was the business focus of the trip. He had been trying for some time to interest investors in his far-fetched idea to build a new township near Enugu, Nigeria, but despite meetings with financiers, politicians, architects and engineers, he had failed. He had their support, but he just could not raise the necessary capital. It seemed that he had used up his lifetime's quota of goodwill. Until, that is, he bumped into Leslie Payne — and the Krays.

This might be our break into the real, international big time, they thought. As white benefactors of their disadvantaged black brothers, they felt the promise of status beyond their wildest hopes. The fact that the Richardsons, a rival South London gang, and their main contenders for the title of 'Gang of the Month', owned a goldmine in South Africa was no mean spur to the Krays' ambitions. It was well-known throughout gangland that Charlie Richardson had invested heavily in the mining business and he had already had one of his so-called allies killed, because he didn't pay. And Charlie Richardson didn't appreciate people who didn't pay their debts. This showed ambition and determination in the eyes of Ron and Reg Kray and they couldn't let the Richardsons top them at anything; it would upset the status quo within the gangs. So they wanted to show two fingers to Charlie and Eddie Richardson. Anything you can do, we can do better.

The Nigerian's scheme for dreamers also had a singular advantage: it was legal. That is apart from all the backhanders that they could collect from builders, electricians, architects, in fact everyone and anyone. The project had the twin essentials: a heart of gold and a seam of black duplicity.

Spring in Lagos was always warm and humid. Payne and his colleague were to stay overnight at the airport hotel, before taking a connecting flight to Enugu. What was to meet them was a shock of jungle, in the middle of nowhere and exceedingly hot. The only luxury that Enugu had to offer was the President Hotel, into which they checked for a couple of days. They were there in the heart of the bush to discuss the construction of 3000 houses and a shopping precinct. Improbable but true.

Payne's main preoccupation at this stage was to ensure that whatever he was asked to do by the Nigerians would be repaid in hard cash. He was reassured to discover that money talks and is understood, no matter what the language. When he returned to London, he reported confidently to the Kray executive committee of Charlie, Ron and Reg Kray and Freddie Gore that they could hope to make a profit of £120,000 from the deal.

With this in mind, a company called Great African Safari was set up under the umbrella of the Carston Group of Companies, which had by that time become the Krays' trading front, based in London's Mayfair. The name's abbreviation spelled GAS. It was a word that was to prove singularly appropriate for the hot air of future events.

It was now time for the Krays to follow in Leslie Payne's footsteps and visit Enugu. In fact they visited the isolated site more than once, only the first time they went together. Thereafter someone had to stay home and keep an eye on business on the home front. Never forget basics, even when you're flying high. Keep those home fires burning. Most often the twins stayed minding their patch, and it was frequently Charlie Kray who would accompany Leslie Payne.

Ron and Reg were very pleased with what they found on their initial trip to Enugu. A finding that was not unconnected to their star reception there. Treated like top government officials and taken from the airport in a cavalcade of cars and motorcycles, they had met local businessmen and representatives of the Nigerian government, including a number of ministers. Dr Okpara, the regional prime minister, showed the twins great respect that extended to him loaning them his Rolls-Royce for the duration of their stay. They visited the jungle and cruised around town in it, where they were wined and dined and generally treated like kings.

Ron's behaviour was much as it was at home. He was undaunted by Africa and its foreign ways. On his second trip to Enugu he asked Dr Okpara for a guided tour of the local jail, explaining that he was interested in sociology. Tough as he was, Ron was shocked by what he saw. Enugu jail made HMP Dartmoor look like a holiday camp. And he didn't like what he heard either. Not a day passed in Enugu without a murder being committed, sometimes within prison walls. Ron felt it would be wise to stay out of trouble in Enugu.

But other kinds of danger he was not afraid of lurked deep in the jungle. He wanted to visit there, despite the frequent reports of gang warfare, of attacks on innocent locals, which involved robbing them of all their possessions and leaving them for dead. Just outside of Enugu, it was the law of the jungle. Gangs of men would terrorize the community with the threat of a machete, used to cut off a man's head as easily as a coconut. And the leopard men were infamous. They would attack villagers using a glove-like device with claws like a leopard's.

In the jungle, life, it was clear to Ron, was very cheap. But he didn't see any home truths in this. He was equally clear that the law of the jungle was not that of the East End. There Ron saw himself as Robin Hood: robbing from the rich and giving to the poor — after you've taken your own fair share, of course.

Ron spent a lot of time on trips along jungle paths in Dr Okpara's Rolls-Royce. He watched tribal dancing, he ate monkey meat, he drank palm wine. He even made friends with the son of a tribal chief and taught him a boxing trick or two. Ron treated his friends and acquaintances there in much the same way as he did those back in London. What Ron wanted, Ron got. There was never any question of it being otherwise. Ron was afraid of no one.

Charlie Kray accompanied Leslie Payne on a trip to Enugu shortly after Ron Kray's celebrity tour. The two men left Heathrow around lunchtime on a VC-10 bound for Kano in northern Nigeria. Charlie always enjoyed a drink or two on the way out: a glass of champagne or a couple of whiskies.

Kano Airport was located a long way out of town, and it looked and felt like landing in the middle of the Sahara Desert. The extra hour to Lagos could have transported them into a world of the extreme heat and humidity of the monsoon season. This time, though, they were lucky. The monsoon was just over, and they could breathe and move freely.

In Lagos they relaxed for a while, talking intermittently about business. Their main topic of conversation was the first expected pay-off from the Enugu township project. A payment of £5000 was due from one of the contractors, to be the first of many.

The flight to Enugu was uneventful, except for the flying skills of the Sikh pilot who flew the small aircraft as if it were a car on a rollercoaster. Feeling jaded after their journey, Payne and Charlie checked into the Enugu President Hotel for two days, and soon got down to business. Jet lag and flying tricks didn't stop them from taking their first payment that evening. They accepted a brown paper envelope from a young Nigerian building contractor, who spoke excellent English. In it was £5000, the Kray's first return on their £25,000 initial investment.

Things were looking good. The pay-off had gone like clockwork, and a celebration was in order. During the evening, in between drinks, Charlie helped out a young member of the hotel staff called Jai whose monthly pay packet of £3.50 had been snatched by one of the machete gangs. Charlie took pity on the lad and slipped him a compensatory fiver. It was later to prove one of the best fivers that Charlie had ever spent.

On his return to London, the twins congratulated Charlie on the successful outcome of his trip. They were keen to get him to return at once to pick up some more hard cash payments, but Charlie knew that the next trip would have to wait — until new investors could be found. He had heard that Hew McCowan, the son of a wealthy Scottish landowner, might be interested. And someone whom the Krays had been told about — Lord Boothby.

It had all started innocently enough. The Krays, through a close friend by name of Leslie Holt, had a direct contact to Boothby. They asked Holt to set up a meeting. Leslie Holt was the perfect choice since he had been having secret homosexual relations with the Lord of the realm for some time and Boothby could not deny him anything.

It was May 1964. Ron Kray, Leslie Holt and another friend, 'Mad' Teddy Smith, a gangster and writer, who had had some success with placing one of his plays — on robbery — with the BBC, went to meet Lord Boothby in his home in Belgravia's Eaton Square, London. It was on the surface of it an unlikely encounter — with an equally bizarre outcome.

That day the meeting went well. The Enugu project was discussed, and the construction plans provided by Turif International examined in some detail. A week later Lord Boothby had a second meeting, this time with Ron and Leslie Payne.

Unbeknownst to Ron, someone else was also keeping an appointment in the vicinity. In fact across the road, on the pavement opposite Lord Boothby's home. It was Nipper Read of Scotland Yard, who was continuing his investigation into the Krays' activities. This had grown to include possible homosexual links between Ron Kray and prominent members of London society — such as Lord Boothby.

So delighted was Ron to be rubbing shoulders with society's upper crust, that he had taken along his own photographer, Bernard Black, to record the occasion. With Boothby's permission, Black took some twenty photographs. But the meeting did not end a total success. Lord Boothby had decided against investing in the Enugu project.

Watching the peer's palatial apartment out in the square, Nipper Read was not aware of these developments — or indeed of any of what he might have considered the fine tuning. He cared not. He was content with the fact that he had hit upon a possible link between Ron Kray and Lord Boothby. He knew he had much to report to his boss, Detective Chief Superintendent Frederick Garrard and, in turn, to his boss, the Metropolitan Chief Commissioner, Sir Joseph Simpson.

He might have paid more attention, though, if he'd realized how someone was about to steal his thunder.

PEER AND A GANGSTER — YARD INQUIRY was the Sunday Mirror headline on 12 July 1964. In its story, the newspaper broke the news of an investigation into the alleged homosexual relationship between a peer who was a household name, and a leading villain in the London underworld. When he saw the article, Bernard Black hot footed it to the offices of the Sunday Mirror, where he offered them for sale his roll of film. He wanted to make himself a little extra cash by selling the Ron Kray/Lord Boothby photographs to the newspaper. He left them with the roll of film until they had made up their minds how much to pay him.

Within hours Black was back at the Sunday Mirror offices in Fleet Street. Could he have the photographs back, please, at once? They didn't belong to him, and he had had no right to try to sell them. His predicament became acutely embarrassing, not to say life-threatening, when the Mirror denied his request.

On Tuesday, 14 July, a statement appeared in The Times, secreted away on page ten. It had been issued on behalf of Sir Joseph Simpson of Scotland Yard:

'I have today asked senior officers for some enlightenment on newspaper reports that:

1. I have ordered an investigation into, among other things, allegations of a homosexual relationship between a peer and a man with a criminal record.

2. I shall give the Home Secretary details of reports submitted by members of the Metropolitan Police resulting from this investigation.

3. An investigation embracing relationships that exist between gangsters, a peer and a number of clergymen has taken place and that blackmail is alleged.

None of these statements is true and beyond this fact it is not my intention to make any report to the Home Secretary.

My duty as Commissioner of Police in serious criminal cases is to put the facts before the Director of Public Prosecutions, for him to decide whether prosecutions should take place.

In saying that, I hope it will be understood in the press that I am not going to disclose information about the many inquiries being conducted into various aspects of underworld life. Inquiries of this kind are in fact going on almost continuously.'

The *Mirror* group, having sold a lot of newspapers on the strength of their 'exposé' on 12 July, now felt themselves to be in a powerful position. After all, they had the photographs of Ron Kray and Lord Boothby in their possession — and they couldn't resist exploiting their advantage. On Thursday, 16 July, they blazed the headline THE PICTURE WE DARE NOT PRINT on the front pages of all editions of the *Daily Mirror*. And followed with a story about the photos of the peer and a gangster who was deeply involved in the protection rackets in London.

On 22 July, the German magazine *Stern* went even further. LORD BOBBY IN TROUBLE was their headline. They went on to name Lord Boothby as the peer in the *Mirror* articles and Ron Kray as the gangster. They even published photographs of both men, although not taken together.

When Lord Boothby returned from his holidays in the south of France on 17 July, he decided that the time had come to take some definite action. He phoned his old friend, the MP Tom Driberg, who was also a regular at Ron Kray's orgies at Cedra Court, and Driberg took the matter to his boss, the leader of the labour Party, Harold Wilson. With the advice of lawyer Arnold Goodman, then Harold Wilson's personal solicitor, at the time when Wilson was about to become Britain's new Labour prime minister, and Gerald Gardiner QC, who later became Lord Chancellor, Lord Boothby wrote a letter to the *Times*. It was published on Saturday, 1 August.

> 'Sir,
> On July 17 I returned to London from France and found, to my amazement, that Parliament, Fleet Street and other informed quarters in London were seething with rumours that I have a homosexual relationship with a leading thug in the London underworld involved in a West End protection racket; that I have been to 'all male' Mayfair parties with him; that I have been photographed with him in a compromising position on a sofa; that a homosexual

relationship exists between me, some East End gangsters and a number of clergymen in Brighton; that some people that know of these relationships are being blackmailed; and that Scotland Yard have for months been watching meetings between me and the underworld thug and have investigated all these matters and reported on them to the Commissioner of the Metropolitan Police.

I have, for many years, appeared on radio and television programmes; and for this reason alone, my name might reasonably be described as 'a household name', as it has been in the Sunday Mirror. On many occasions I have been photographed, at their request, with people who have claimed to be 'fans' of mine; and on one occasion I was photographed, with my full consent, in my flat (which is also my office) with a gentleman who came to see me, accompanied by two friends, in order to ask me to take an active part in a business venture, which seemed to me to be of interest and importance. After careful consideration I turned down his request, on the grounds that my existing commitments prevented me from taking on anything more; and my letter of refusal is in his possession.

I have since been told that some years ago the person concerned was convicted of a criminal offence, but I knew then and know now nothing of this. So far as I am concerned, anyone is welcome to see or to publish any photographs that have ever been taken of me.

I am satisfied that the source of all sinister rumours is the Sunday Mirror and the Daily Mirror I am not homosexual. I have not been to a Mayfair party of any kind for more than 20 years. I have met the man *alleged to be a 'king of the under-world' only three times, on business matters, and then by appointment in my flat, at his request and in the company of other people.*

I have never been to a party in Brighton with gangsters, still less clergymen. No one has ever tried to blackmail me. The police say that they have not watched any meetings, or conducted any investigations, or made any report to the Home Secretary, connected with me. In short, the whole affair is a tissue of atrocious lies.

I am not by nature thin-skinned; but this sort of thing makes a mockery of any decent kind of life, public or private, in what is still supposed to be a civilised country. It is, in my submission, intolerable that any man should be put into the cruel dilemma of having either to remain silent while such rumours spread, or considerably to increase the circulation of certain newspapers by publicly denying them. If either the Sunday Mirror, *or the* Daily Mirror, *is in possession of a shred of evidence — documentary or photographic — against me, let them print it and take the consequences. I am sending a copy of this letter to both.*

Your obedient servant,
Boothby
House of Lords, July 31

It was a storm in a teacup, which Lord Boothby handled with grace and intelligence. So much so, that he got away with it and no-one mentioned his homosexuality again —not in public, that is. Some days later, when the

Daily Mirror published their unqualified apology, they also agreed to pay Lord Boothby £40,000 in compensation. Ron, though, received nothing. Except a photograph of himself and Lord Boothby, one of the batch taken by Bernard Black, which he sold to the *Daily Express* for the princely sum of £100.

A few important facts emerged from this eventually comic episode. First, since Sir Joseph Simpson was forced to deny that any particular investigation against the Krays existed, contrary to the view expressed by the *Sunday Mirror*, then all the facts uncovered by Nipper Read and his team to date were no longer valid as evidence against the Krays in future trials.

Second, after Lord Boothby had written his letter to the *Times*, in which he refuted all the allegations made by the *Mirror* group, Ron Kray decided to confirm to the world at large that he was indeed the London villain to which the *Mirror* group's articles referred. He specially selected the photograph of himself, sitting beside Lord Boothby on his sofa in Belgravia, for exposure and publication in the *Daily Express* on 6 August. The press would handle the Krays with kid gloves for a while from then on.

Third, although Lord Boothby had received £40,000 from the *Sunday Mirror* as part of his libel settlement, Ron Kray had got nothing. Except, that is, an enormous amount of publicity. He was now a household name, and Ron quickly learned to turn this to his advantage. He adored the publicity. He was famous, at last.

Fame was something Scotland Yard wanted to avoid like the plague at this stage. They obviously had a leak, an unintentional one that had severely impeded Nipper Read's investigation. They had their own internal inquiry to deal with — and fast.

But other people were asking questions too. The Krays, for example, wondered about the real reason behind the investigation into their activities, particularly in relation to Lord Boothby. Was there a political edge to the investigative sword?

Later, it became well-known that Boothby had had a long-running affair with Dorothy Macmillan, wife of the Tory prime minister who had resigned over his mishandling of the Profumo call-girl scandal. And recent revelations have shown that Lady Dorothy even managed to conceive a son, sired by the AC/DC Boothby. Macmillan admitted later that the lengthy relationship between his wife and Lord Boothby had had a major effect on his health. Boothby may well have been under investigation for these reasons, and Ron Kray, for once, only an innocent victim of political intrigue.

With hindsight, the Boothby incident was a bout of summer madness, whose ripples spread across the twin ponds of the Kray empire and Scotland Yard, disguising what was really going on in the murky waters below.

The construction site was now ready, and the building due to start. The time had come for a Kray contingent to visit Enugu and organize the initial stages of the work. Charlie Kray, Leslie Payne, Freddie Gore and a Canadian businessman, Gordon Andersen, received a reception at the President Hotel in Enugu that was far from warm.

After the newspaper articles in July and August 1964, the Krays knew that getting investors for the Enugu project was going to be more difficult than they had anticipated. And the trouble was that although the township enterprise was now basically sound, they still needed long-term finance to make it viable.

This was an on-going problem that faced the Krays, over which Charlie had mulled on his flight to Nigeria this time. But he realized that the lukewarm welcome at the President had nothing to do with this. On previous occasions, Nigerian government ministers would have been present to greet them, and the staff were always cordial and respectful with them. This time, it was different. Charlie had to find out what had happened. Something had gone badly wrong.

It was in the bar the following lunchtime that Charlie got to the bottom of it. A dispute between Leslie Payne and the Nigerian builder, who had paid the initial £5000 to them a few months earlier, was holding up the building work.

With the monsoons over and the weather much better by October 1964, there was no reason why the construction should not have started. Only that Payne would not agree with the local builder about where the construction should start. When approached by Charlie about this later that day, Payne said that he was taking care of business, that Charlie shouldn't worry his head about some local Nigerian contractor. He'd take care of him. Charlie was not convinced.

His fears were confirmed the next day when he chanced upon a furious row taking place in the hotel lobby between Leslie Payne and the Nigerian contractor. Payne, who was a big man and towered over the Nigerian, was wagging his finger and shouting at the top of his voice, a voice normally so understatedly refined that had momentarily adopted a common touch.

Charlie barged in and tried to separate the two men. To some avail, but it took a while for them to calm down. Then the Nigerian said very slowly and almost inaudibly, 'I want my money back.'

Payne just laughed at the man, dismissively, while Charlie continued to pour oil on troubled waters and use every ounce of his innate tact and diplomacy.

'No,' the man repeated firmly, 'I just want my money back.' As he turned to leave the lobby of the hotel, he stopped and turned to them. In a throwaway remark, he dropped his bombshell, 'My cousin is the chief of police.'

All Charlie could think about at that moment was Ron Kray's description of the local jail. Dartmoor's a holiday camp in comparison, echoed round and round his head, until his anger towards Leslie Payne brought him back to earth. Had the glamour and grandeur of being the great white hunter — God knows he dressed the part — finally made Payne flip? Why had he been so intransigent with the Nigerian contractor about the start site? Could he not bear anyone ever telling him what to do?

As these thoughts and feelings fought for order in Charlie's head, they were suddenly accompanied by the shrill notes of police sirens. The Nigerian contractor had been as good as his word — the local police had just pulled up outside the hotel in their droves. Seconds later three armed officers accompanied the contractor into the hotel.

As no one could come up with his £5000, the chief of police ordered that everyone be taken into custody. Everyone, that is, who was a part of GAS — which Charlie was not.

Leslie Payne, Freddie Gore and the English surveyor from the construction site, all represented the Carston Group's Great African Safari, and as such were kept in custody at Enugu jail. Charlie and Gordon Andersen were not officially on the GAS payroll, or even part of the GAS outfit. In Charlie's case it was odd that his brothers had been so reluctant to allow him a position in the company. Maybe they didn't trust him, or perhaps they envied his natural business ability. Whatever the reason, it was Charlie's salvation then. And ultimately of the three imprisoned men. With Charlie on the outside, they had some chance of getting released.

This was just as well. Enugu jail was in the worst part of town and operated like something out of a bad Western. Being in the tropics, it was infested with bugs and looked like it hadn't had a fresh coat of paint since its construction, years earlier. Leslie Payne made things more uncomfortable for himself by his endless whingeing, despite Charlie's assurances that he would cable the twins and get the money to Enugu immediately. They would soon be free.

Or, at least, this was what Charlie hoped for. As he left the jail in the middle of the night to return to the comfort of the President, he noticed a small blackboard. On the board was a chalked list of prisoners currently held under detention. Against each name was a description of the man's crime and details of his sentence.

Some of the names had been scratched off. Not because the men had been set free, but to indicate that they had died in Enugu jail.

Back in London, the twins realized that however angry they felt with Leslie Payne, they could not afford to let him rot in jail. He controlled a large part of the Carston Group and even some of their bank accounts. But it was for these reasons rather than friendship, loyalty and compassion that they set about raising the £5000 that would ensure his release.

It had been hard for Charlie to find a means of getting in touch with his brothers. Communications from Enugu were primitive, at best, but he had located a field telephone that transmitted through a relay station to Lagos, then on to England. As luck would have it, Charlie also met up again with young Jai, the boy he had helped with his stolen wage packet on an earlier trip. Charlie had a plan, and Jai could help him.

Charlie was sharp enough to realize that if the twins couldn't come up with the money, he would have to leave Enugu quickly — and quietly. He was too well-known at the local airport to make a discreet getaway, so a car out of town and on to Port Harcourt, 150 miles away, where he could board a ship for England, was probably his best way out. Jai was to buy Charlie a car with money that he entrusted to him then and there. He would hide the car behind the hotel, just in case Charlie needed to use it urgently.

It took hours to get hold of Ron and Reg at Vallance Road. Ron's first reaction was direct — and disastrous. He, Reg and all the firm would take the next flight out, they'd come down to Enugu to sort them out.

When Charlie explained that this course of action would only bring out the army, Ron gave up and handed the phone to Reg. Reg, thank God, proved more reasonable. He understood at once that the money would have to be dispatched immediately.

But how to raise £5000 overnight? First things first. A quick call to the Nigerian High Commissioner in London confirmed Charlie's story. He also added that if the money wasn't forthcoming Charlie could be imprisoned in

Nigeria as an accessory. With family now so tied up in the Nigerian fiasco, there was no alternative but to raise £5000 — that night. This would have been difficult at the best of times, but it was a Saturday evening and members of the firm were scattered all over London, enjoying themselves, probably just about to embark on a breezy drinking spree.

Ron and Reg felt that the first source to tap had to be Charlie's missus, Dolly, who they didn't get along with anyway, and Leslie Payne's wife. But they got nothing out of either of them. Ron had already sent out his spies to try and track down the firm members, and Reg decided to join them. Anything was better than that awful hanging about, waiting.

One by one the firm gathered at the Crown pub, just around the corner from Vallance Road. Ron was in charge, in full Colonel mode. He had already made out a list of names and addresses, against which entry he wrote a sum of money — anything from £100 up. Some as much as £500. All the names came from the pension list, the nipping list had too many small fry. It would have taken for ever to collect from it anything near the five grand they needed that night.

The firm members went out with clear orders. Get the money from these people and don't come back without it. No excuses. And the members of the gang knew that they'd be expected to dip into their own pockets too. If there were any problems with a collection, then Ron was on the end of the telephone at the Crown. One call to him, and he'd sort out any stragglers, iron out their creases. The phone never rang once.

With Ron as co-ordinator and controller, Reg had taken on the duties as chief collector and had gone off to visit the big fish on Ron's list. Over the course of the evening, the money kept pouring in — first £1000, then £2000, soon £3000 and eventually £3400. It was late by this time and all the gang had come back. They'd raised all they could, but it wasn't enough. Where was Reg? they worried. He'd been expected back an hour or so earlier.

Triumphantly on cue, Reg pushed his way into the Crown, emptying money like snow from his pockets. With his collection, they'd reached the £5000 target. Just in time. It was a hell of a lot of money to have raised in an evening, soon transferred as a bank draft to Nigeria. Now, in London, all they had to do was to wait.

It took two days for the money to arrive from England. When it did, Charlie had to pay it to the Nigerian government through the intermediary of a judge.

Charlie's solicitor, a local man, went with him to the judge's house, where the transaction was to take place. The road to the house was a narrow track, which had been hacked through dense jungle. For a while on that journey Charlie got scared. It was a convenient place to get rid of a man, any man, who was carrying £5000. Even if he'd managed to beat off any attackers, he'd still have thick jungle between him and safety. As it happened, everything went well and according to plan. The drop was made, and it was time to visit Enugu jail.

During the past few days Nigerian prison life had made its mark on Payne, Gore and the unfortunate surveyor. Their morale was shattered, and they were in tears when Charlie came to release them. Leslie Payne was chronically depressed, on the verge of a breakdown.

The subdued group of men left Enugu under police escort, which sounded its sirens all the way to the airport. It was a sound that they'd never forget all their lives — a shrill humiliation. The plane stood on the runway ready to go, its departure delayed by the chief of police who stopped all the airport traffic and drove right out, on to the runway. He had the British men bundled unceremoniously on to the plane, their dignity in shreds.

None of the men spoke as the aircraft flew first to Onitsha, then on to Benin City and finally Lagos, from where there was a direct flight to England. There was no cheerful imbibing of champagne or whisky this time. It had been three days since the arrests, and no one wanted ever to live through three days like that again.

Eventually, Leslie Payne and Freddie Gore would be given their marching orders by the twins. Later someone even tried to kill Payne.

But it was not until much later that the truth about Leslie Payne finally revealed him as the con man he surely was. He had said he was a major in the army, but he was only a sergeant. He had bragged about his big business exploits, prior to his association with the Krays, but in reality he had only financed the sale of used cars and nothing else.

The Krays' power and access to wealth had turned Payne's head. In the end he had neglected his own talents, his basic, sound business sense, and had lived, instead, off the Krays' influence. He had run up an internal debt, and Payne the brain had become Payne the pain — to himself and others.

His sidekick Gore was lost from the start — Laurel was no good without Hardy. And the Krays, for their part, never took up their option to buy a fleet of ferries to ply the river Niger. And they never completed a lucrative deal to market the country's palm oil.

Without the aspirations and delusions of one man, Leslie Payne, who had proved such an asset in the past, the Enugu township scheme could have been beneficial — for Nigeria and the Kray empire alike. But business, like life, is a learning curve, and the Krays would never again get involved in a business project overseas. Except, that is, for the Mafia franchise. Which was almost Leslie Payne's last chance.

8

THE KENNEDYS V. THE MOB

ANGELO BRUNO WAS A VERY POWERFUL MAN in organised crime, a top mafioso. He was a member of the Mafia's own *commissione*, headed by Vito Genovese, probably the most notorious Mafia boss in the world. When Bruno had visited London in 1962, he had met Ron and Reg Kray. Impressed by them and the Kray empire, Bruno had taken the Firm seriously and saw them as one of the closest contenders for a Mafia-like structure in Britain.

The twins, especially Ron, had blustered and charmed their way through their first direct, albeit congenial, encounter with Bruno at the London Hilton. Bruno was no fool. He could see for himself that the

Krays were a force with which to be reckoned, a London gang with an international reputation. He had the Kray name on the tip of his tongue when it came to organised crime in the United Kingdom. And in this case, when it came to disposing of a $2 million stockpile of stolen bonds which were furring things up.

The rest of Bruno's syndicate realised that if Bruno gave the Krays the thumbs-up, then they were undoubtedly worth more than a second glance. The three Kray brothers were about to become involved in the sale of bonds and securities supplied by the American Mafia. In the bluff of the gangster marketplace they pretended it was just another way of doing the business, but privately they were only too well aware that they had moved into international, big-time crime.

During the Krays' first meeting with Angelo Bruno, they had talked about his various business interests in London, which included several clubs and casinos that he had asked them to protect — for a fee of course. Taking care of this kind of business was second nature to the Krays, no matter what problems would arise. Their duties covered minding Bruno's establishments and protecting his wealthy clients, many of whom came over to London on gambling trips or junkets, from all over the USA.

Americans had always enjoyed a trip to London, where now, in the mid-sixties, gambling had just been legalised. This had led to a mushrooming of gaming venues, of which the Krays had made sure that they got their piece of the action. There were rich pickings to be made in the capital city, in the West End in particular, and this was all in sharp contrast to what was going on over the water.

Robert Kennedy, as Attorney General, was trying to wipe out organised crime — and this included gambling. But the Mafia were more than just a society of gambling freaks, they were involved in every criminal activity possible from political corruption to 'Murder Incorporated'. There were many in the United States, however — apart from the FBI — that also considered this aggressive action by the Attorney General to be a complete waste of time. The links between government and organised crime were so strong that each had too much at stake to risk exposure. Some even said that the CIA and the American Mafia were a mirror image of each other.

Joseph Kennedy, the father of both the President and the Attorney General, was no stranger to political corruption. In the early days of Jack's career he had purchased the assistance of a Massachusetts newspaper in the fight to get Jack elected to the Senate in 1952; this was achieved by making a $500,000 loan available to the publisher. He had already funded and organised five failed campaigns before learning that money talks louder than a publisher's ideology. It was this attitude that directed him in his later fight to get his son Jack elected to the presidency.

John F Kennedy was good at electioneering and put in a good performance at the 1960 Democratic National Convention at the Los Angeles Coliseum on 26th September, and it was here that the whole Kennedy clan realised the importance of image and of the emergence of television as a vital tool in campaigning. But Jack Kennedy was a catholic and no catholic had ever been elected President of the United States of America. So Joseph Kennedy, who as

Ambassador to Great Britain during the 1939-45 Great War had urged the USA to remain neutral and to let Germany and the other Europeans fight it out, decided that he needed extra help. So when Jack Kennedy visited Chicago for a live televised debate with Richard Nixon, father Joe accompanied his son and kept a private meeting of his own.

The Mob, or Outfit as they are called in Chicago, had always ruled the city. Al Capone had earlier continued a great tradition of corruption and now it was the turn of the current head of the Mafia, Sam 'Mooney' Giancana, to run the slaughterhouse of America. Giancana had reached the top by literally killing off all the competition, but by the late fifties the Outfit were being put under a lot of pressure by the local FBI, who harassed Sam Giancana and his right hand man Murray 'The Camel' Humphries. So Giancana was somewhat surprised when he received a message from Robert McDonnell, a local lawyer who had represented organised crime on many occasions, asking him to meet with Joseph Kennedy. So while Jack was discussing world events with Nixon on television, Joseph Kennedy was keeping his appointment with Sam Giancana at the Chicago Courthouse, in the private offices of a friendly judge.

The televised debate was a deciding factor in the election. Not because of the content or of the decisive campaign style of Jack Kennedy, but because of the importance of image and the nature of the extensive media attention. Joe Kennedy knew that he would need the help of the Chicago Outfit, who both controlled the labour unions and Hollywood, if his son was to be successful. So he made a deal with Sam Giancana, telling him that he would arrange to take the FBI off his back, if he in turn arranged for Humphries to organise the unions to support John F Kennedy in his bid for election to the presidency. Giancana already had the able assistance of J Edgar Hoover, but he could see the possibilities of being in bed with the Kennedys so he agreed to the deal.

Murray Humphries didn't trust Kennedy, an old bootlegger from the days of prohibition and one of America's wealthiest men — he even owned the world's largest shopping mall, The Merchandise Mart in downtown Chicago. But he was persuaded by Sam Giancana to mobilise the unions on behalf of Kennedy, so in October of 1960 he set up a meeting at the Chicago Hilton to speak to delegates from as far afield as Kansas and New Orleans. It was no surprise that the labour leaders were baffled, since both Jack and Bobby Kennedy were only recently on television as part of a Senate Committee, investigating organised crime. Jimmy Hoffa, in particular, had been given a tough ride by the brothers. But they set to work to provide the votes so desperately needed by Joseph Kennedy.

By the spring of 1960, Joe Kennedy had already had his focus of attention firmly switched on to the movie capital of the world, Hollywood. He had previously had a well publicised affair with the Hollywood legend Gloria Swanson, so he knew his way around in the city of angels. But even here he needed help, so he turned to one of Jack's best friends for advice and assistance — that man was Frank Sinatra.

Sinatra, aided by Peter Lawford, Dean Martin and Sammy Davis Junior, staged fund raisers for Jack Kennedy during the early part of 1960 and it was at one of these celebrity events that the future President of the United

States met the most famous movie actress of all time, Marilyn Monroe.

Marilyn Monroe, was one of the most glamorous, sexy and desirable women in the world. Unfortunately for her she was also a close friend of the Chicago Mafia boss and required to socialise with certain people when requested. So she became a glittering prize, awarded to Jack Kennedy by Sam Giancana's social network. When Jack tired of his new plaything, he simply handed her over to his kid brother, Bobby, trying to keep all the secrets well hidden within the control of the family, but Marilyn became a problem.

When it came to popping pills and knocking back the booze, Marilyn was an expert. So when she started phoning at all hours of the day and night trying to talk to Jack, Bobby Kennedy tried to control her by sending friends to talk to her, to try to persuade her to be cautious. For a while it worked.

But Jack Kennedy had already moved on to pastures new, in the shapely form of Judith Campbell. She had been introduced to him at a party given by Frank Sinatra and she at once fell in love with the Senator from Massachusetts. So when Sam Giancana asked Frank Sinatra to supply a go-between between the Kennedys and the Chicago Outfit, Judith Campbell's name came readily to mind. It was at this time that Judith Campbell was asked to take the first delivery of ready cash to Chicago, directly to the safe hands of Sam 'Mooney' Giancana. The deal was on and soon millions were to flow through Chicago, all aimed at getting Jack Kennedy elected to the presidency.

Joseph Kennedy had kept his word, so far, and the Outfit did the rest. When Kennedy won by the smallest of margins, 118,000 votes, it was the victories in Illinois, Missouri and Nevada that had swung the election — all states controlled from Chicago. John F Kennedy was now President of the United States and Sam Giancana thought he had a foot in the door at the White House itself.

The first appointment made by Jack Kennedy was to make his brother Robert, Attorney General, but all the talk at the time was about the new first lady, Jacqueline Kennedy. She brought a new kind of glamour to Washington, a spirit of gladness and kindness. But behind the scenes things hadn't changed in the Kennedy household.

The Secret Service were kept busy trying to protect their new President, but the President was more intent on bedding every woman in sight, even having prostitutes brought in from outside for his rampant pleasure. This continued on tour, where the evenings would all end the same, with women being paraded into his bedroom for pleasurable entertainment. The Secret Service were forced to turn a blind eye to these episodes, but since prostitution was both illegal and immoral, it was hard for them to take. They had a problem and they knew it only too well. When Jacqueline Kennedy was away, her husband would get all the sexual pleasures he needed upstairs at the White House.

Even when Jack Kennedy ventured over to the West Coast, things remained the same. When Peter Lawford, who was married to Jack's sister Pat, was asked to lay on entertainment at his Los Angeles home for the President, he knew that Jack wanted to see Marilyn Monroe. Marilyn always complained to her close friends about the 'quickies' she had with Jack, a quick fuck was all he wanted. He was apparently such a busy man that foreplay was out of the question, so when his plane landed in LA he rushed secretly and anonymously over to the Lawford house, where he wanted it here and now with a big bang! While the other guests were drinking downstairs, Jack Kennedy, the President of the United States, was upstairs fucking one of the most famous women in the world, Marilyn Monroe — and no-one, apart from the two love-birds and their friends, the Lawfords, knew anything about it.

Frank Sinatra was really worried about Marilyn, who was making regular phone calls to Washington, trying to talk to Jack Kennedy. But Jack was still carrying on an affair with Judith Campbell, the Mafia go-between. And to make things even worse Marilyn was hospitalised for her addiction to both drugs and drink. Jack Kennedy didn't want any trouble; neither did his brother the Attorney General. Again Bobby Kennedy sent someone to talk to Marilyn, but she didn't appear to understand about the dangerous and precarious position that had arisen.

On the 19th March 1962, Marilyn Monroe performed at Madison Square Garden in New York, at a gala celebration honouring the birthday of Jack Kennedy. Her sexy version of 'Happy Birthday to You' was aimed directly at the President, who was obviously moved by her performance, but her days were numbered. When she yet again began asking for visits to the White House, she had to be stopped. Bobby Kennedy was afraid of a sex scandal, so too was father Joe. In the course of her relationships with the Kennedy brothers, pillow talk had made Marilyn too knowing, too well informed about wheeling and dealing that went on between the CIA, the American Mafia, the FBI and international world leaders. She knew too much — she had to die. And the task of her execution was handed over to the Chicago Mafia boss, Sam Giancana, directly on orders from the CIA.

After Marilyn's death, the FBI had a job on their hands clearing up the mess. Robert Kennedy had been there at the house just an hour before, accompanied by a doctor, and the FBI felt almost sure that it was Kennedy who had killed her. It was a tricky situation, extremely convoluted, and it was complicated even further by the Kennedy connection with organised crime. Bobby Kennedy had almost found himself set up as the killer of Marilyn Monroe, the most glamorous of all Hollywood stars. There was only one thing to do — to go all out for retribution. The fire of hatred burned ever deeper in the heart of Bobby Kennedy. The flames were fanned throughout his brief life.

But again Jack Kennedy could not stop his womanising. His affair with Judith Campbell continued, even after she began sleeping with Sam Giancana, and the Secret Service were all too aware of the numbers of women entering the White House, just to satisfy the needs of the President. There were spies everywhere at this time, due to the problems with the Soviets over Cuba. Blackmail would have been difficult to deal with, if not impossible, and there was the chance of a woman entering the building with a camera, or drugs or tape recorder, all aimed at getting the President into a compromising position. Everyone was on tenter-hooks, including Bobby Kennedy.

By the autumn of 1962 The Cuban Missile Crisis was on every front page around the world. The Kennedys hated Castro, who seized power in 1959, and they were determined to use every effort to overthrow the new communist dictator. But Jack Kennedy, by this time, was not a well man and he had to have vitamin shots on a regular basis. Brother Bobby even had the dosage analysed and he found to his horror that besides vitamins there were huge amounts of amphetamines. But Jack Kennedy was persistent that Dr Jacobson should continue the treatment — he became dependent on the drugs.

Kennedy had made a secret deal with Kruschev to get the missiles out of Cuba, in return for the dismantling of US missiles in Turkey, but the press hadn't been made privy to this information. So when Jack Kennedy gave Kruschev his ultimatum, he already knew the answer. Jack Kennedy was a hero to the people of the United States, but secretly he persisted in his efforts to overthrow Castro. The CIA wanted Castro dead, so to the Mob who had lost control of all their casinos on Cuba. So Sam Giancana was asked to help get rid of Castro.

Giancana was still trying to get the Kennedys to honour their deal over the 1960 election, so he used Judith Campbell, the President's lover, to once again act as go-between. She passed secret messages to the Outfit and Giancana used his connection with Mob boss Santo Trafficante in Miami to organise the Cubans. At first they tried to poison Castro, then they tried to shoot him, but they found him more elusive than any normal pigeon. So when the USA, led by Cuban exiles, landed at the Bay of Pigs, Cuba, on April 17th, 1961, they met with massive resistance and Castro in good health and fighting fit. 114 of the mercenaries were killed and another 1000 captured. It was a complete failure and Jack Kennedy was forced to go on television to apologise to the American people. But the struggle against Castro continued.

Meanwhile, Frank Sinatra was trying to get the Kennedys to patch up their disagreements with the Chicago boss, a good friend and golf partner. Sinatra travelled to Chicago to have meetings with Sam Giancana, but he was not helped by the attitude of the Kennedys. Giancana felt betrayed and Sinatra was devastated at his treatment by Jack Kennedy, who refused to talk to him.

The whole situation was getting very serious, since J Edgar Hoover had received news and evidence concerning the relationship between Jack Kennedy and Judith Campbell. He also knew that she was sleeping with the enemy, in the form of Sam Giancana. So he took his files to Washington and confronted the Kennedys, who had little to say for themselves.

On the 22nd March 1962 J.Edgar Hoover laid his cards on the table, along with some of the most incriminating evidence against Jack Kennedy. The President was horrified that the FBI chief would try to intimidate him, but for a while it worked and the White House became a quieter and more lonely place. But that had to change, since there was no way of suppressing the sexual urges of the President.

Bill Thomson, a man who worked at the White House and who knew of his President's thirst for women, met an old friend, Bobby Baker, at the Quorum Club in Washington some weeks later. Baker was a regular at the club and so he introduced a friend of his, known as Ellen, to Bill Thomson telling him that she had enjoyed sexual relations with many of his good friends and that all reports of her were very favourable, she would do anything that turned them on. Bill Thomson asked if she was interested in meeting the President. The answer was in the affirmative.

Their first of about ten get-togethers was in the summer of 1963, but by July 3rd the FBI had managed to find out about the affair and had uncovered disturbing information about Ellen. She was a registered communist from East Germany and news of the intimacy between the President and a communist was dangerous water indeed. It was enough to provoke Bobby Kennedy into direct action. Immediately he sent Laverne Duffy to see her and soon she was on her way back to East Germany, with only a heavy shopping bag for company — full of his best wishes for a bright future. When it came to money, the Kennedys knew all the tricks.

But on November 22nd, 1963, the name of the East German woman, 27 years old and a communist, was on every front page. And on the same day, in Paris, the CIA were again attempting to overthrow the Castro government.

But something else was happening on this tragic day of 22nd November, 1963 — someone, in Dallas, Texas, was plotting to assassinate the President of the United States, John Fitzgerald Kennedy.

Bobby Kennedy had made it known on several occasions exactly what his feelings were concerning the Mafia. He felt that 'If we do not on a national scale attack organised crime with weapons and techniques as effective as their own, they will destroy us.' Powerful words that he was not strong enough to turn into action. Why, asked some of the politicians of the day, put so much effort into such a minor problem? His reply was that organised crime 'corrupts government, preys on the weak of our society and contributes to our climate of lawlessness', which is why, in 1965, the American government assembled a strikeforce to deal with corruption.

THE KENNEDYS V. THE MOB

In the early 1960s the FBI would not even acknowledge that the Mafia existed at all in America. That all changed with the appointment of Robert Kennedy as Attorney General. His investigations had started as early as 1961, instigated by his father Joseph Kennedy, who was trying to get out of his deal made with the Chicago Outfit. Even the FBI hadn't been of any help, although Hoover had his own problems to worry about and was trying to work for both sides. Hoover would never have wanted to share glory or power with anyone and certainly not with a young Kennedy, but he, like so many others in power at that time in the USA, had other more disturbing motives. It is now well-known and substantiated from many varying sources that J Edgar Hoover was a flamboyant homosexual who liked to flaunt his somewhat feminine charms in the company of other like-minded men of the time. The gay community was hidden away behind the outward facade of masculinity, but the Mob had trapped the head of the FBI on both film and photographic print, where his homosexuality was plain and obvious for everyone to see. This left Hoover between a rock and a hard place, trying to do his job while trying to appease the Kennedys and simultaneously satisfy the Chicago Outfit. Hoover had always denied the existence of the Mafia in the USA and never went up against them; now we know why! And it was this secret connection between the FBI and the Mob that kept Sam Giancana one step ahead of Bobby Kennedy.

When Sam Giancana, with a little help from his friends at the CIA and the Naval Intelligence Service, had Jack Kennedy killed in Dallas he was, in reality, taking reprisals for the broken Kennedy promises that had helped elect Kennedy to the presidency back in 1961. Giancana had even visited the Kennedys in The White House, on Pennsylvania Avenue in Washington DC, urging them to keep their bargain with him. He wanted them to allow him to take over crime in the USA, as agreed.

Father Joe and son Jack answered the Chicago boss by giving brother Bobby orders to nail the Mob once and for all. But the killing of Jack Kennedy gave everyone something new to think about — not least Sam Giancana.

It wasn't that he was worried about public opinion or about further threats or repercussions at the hands of the US government — after all, he had the FBI to help him sort that out if his own knowledge was not enough to overcome any difficulties. The main problem for Giancana was the fact that Oswald was still alive and well; and that meant that he could talk.

When Lee Harvey Oswald was taken by the police, shortly after the assassination of President John F Kennedy the plans had to be changed and Jack Ruby, who worked for the Chicago boss in Dallas, was brought in to solve the problem.

Ruby, who had managed to build up good relations with the Dallas police through his club business, was the only one who could get into a position to kill Oswald, a man he knew well. He had met him on many occasions and knew him to be in the employ of the CIA. Lee Harvey Oswald was to be the fall guy — the lone assassin, set up by the Mob/CIA conspiracy, but they hadn't expected him to be taken by the police. The plan was to have him shot by other accomplices, but even a well planned execution can go wrong; even those worked out in such meticulous detail by such experts as the CIA, the Mafia and the Naval Intelligence Service.

Sam Giancana gave Jack Ruby orders to kill Oswald and like the honourable man he was he carried out his duties to the best of his ability. He shot Lee Harvey Oswald at close range at the Dallas Police Headquarters and it was all shown live on prime time television.

Oswald was another who just had to die, fingered by the Mob. He was dangerous, since he had life long connections with the CIA and other intelligence services which had only a short time prior to the assassination worked closely with the Mafia on and during the Bay of Pigs disaster, when the USA invaded Cuba. Even his well publicised trip to the USSR had been set up by the CIA — and all the time he thought he was doing it for his country. But Giancana knew that even he would figure it out eventually and no-one wanted to risk their wealth, their security, their lives for the sake of Lee Harvey Oswald.

Only one year after the death of his brother, Bobby Kennedy was on the trail of the Mob — his plan was working. In 1960 there had been only 19 indictments for organised crime; in 1964 there were 687. The squeeze was on and since there were only some 4000 Mafia members in the entire United States at the time, then Robert Kennedy soon made inroads into their ranks. The Mob responded by simply reorganising their countrywide operations and this included looking overseas. To the Krays, in fact, in the East End of London.

Mafia activities in America included straightforward thieving, safe-cracking, armed robbery, smuggling, and rackets such as gambling and prostitution. It had not been easy to liaise and cohere the Mob network across the USA, but it had been achieved in such an organised way, whereby they could operate across state lines. This had been a great advantage prior to 1965, but thereafter the strikeforce, brought in by Bobby Kennedy, would be able to cross state lines too — in search of the evil Mob.

It was getting harder to make a dishonest living.

Robert Kennedy had invited teams from the Federal Bureau of Narcotics and Dangerous Drugs, the IRS Intelligence Division, Customs, the Secret Service, the labour Department, the Alcohol and Tobacco Tax Division of the Treasury and the Postal Inspection Department to pool their resources. Police departments throughout the USA would support these groups. This way they could operate together nationally, on a basis that would cross all internal borders. Now, if crime knew no boundaries, neither did the law.

Crime as export, an age-old commodity. It took a while to establish a bond of trust between the criminal fraternities separated by the Atlantic ocean, but it was a firm handshake that sealed it. The Krays would not be expected to pay up on delivery, since this was new business and no one knew for sure what kind of a deal they could expect to get in Europe. The bonds were to be assigned to the Krays, and the American Mafia would just have to cool its heels at the profit margins.

The syndicate set up by the Mafia to deal with this aspect of its business had to explain this to its bosses, a number of individually powerful Mafia families. The role of the syndicate was very important to the smooth running of daily Mafia business. It kept the peace and combined the efforts of individual families when large-scale enterprises were undertaken. Syndicates had begun back in the early 1930s, started by one Lucky Luciano, mainly to keep law and order within Mafia ranks, but they gradually infiltrated external Mafia business.

The commissione is the ruling syndicate. In the mid-sixties it was made up of nine of the most powerful and influential American Mafia bosses. These included Vito Genovese, then serving fifteen years imprisonment in Leavenworth Penitentiary, Carlo Gambino, Joseph 'Joe Bananas' Bonanno and Joseph Colombo, all from New York; John Scalish from Cleveland; Joseph Zerillo of Detroit; Salvatore 'Sam' Giancana, Chicago; Stefan Magaddino, Buffalo; and Angelo Bruno, Philadelphia.

For the Krays to have Angelo Bruno as a friend and business associate was prestige indeed. They were in auspicious company. Bruno remained one of the most powerful of all Mafia leaders for three decades. Even if they'd wanted to, the Krays could not have afforded to ignore his approaches.

A clandestine meeting had been set up to talk about it among themselves. You could never be too careful. Someone might notice the out-of-town number plates on the cars, which were hardly discreet in themselves, black and sleek motors that reeked of up to no good, a cheeky statement that crime can pay. Back in 1957, the Mafia had had their fingers badly burned by a police rout at a safe house in Apalachin, New York. The Mafia heads had had to flee through the woods. They'd learned the hard way that sometimes it is better to keep a low profile.

In England, the Krays couldn't be bothered with all that. They didn't give a toss about secret meetings. They operated in full view of everyone, including the police, who had by then started to take them very seriously.

Nipper Read was most definitely on their case, knew lots about them. And when the American Mafia came to call, he knew about that too. About how the twins minded the Yanks' casinos and clubs. What he couldn't have known about at that point was the proposed deal in instantly negotiable bearer bonds.

The time had come for the Kray empire to spread its net of activities even wider, and the bonds deal would do just that. They hadn't wanted to get involved in drugs, which could have been the next step, but they chose to wait, confident that something would turn up. Their meetings over the years with Bruno had reassured them that he would put some other kind of business their way, sometime, somehow.

The twins were increasingly in favour of Angelo Bruno, though never awestruck by him. Ron used to repeat one of Bruno's favourite sayings, 'If you kick the dog, you kick the master;' it touched the right spot for Ron. Tough but fair and remember where you've come from, don't ever forget the family. Bruno himself was hard and aggressive in company but always a gentleman with the Krays.

In the United States the Mafia had made up its mind after lengthy discussions among the six men who comprised the syndicate. They'd talked it through the ranks, from the capos downwards, to the subcapos, the lieutenants and soldiers. Everyone had been consulted and involved. An agreement had been drawn up, to put to the Krays, but nothing was ever written down.

It was a 50:50 deal and quite straightforward. If they sold the bonds for $2 million, then half of that would go to the Americans, the rest was the Krays to keep. It looked like all their Christmases had come at once. The only snag was that they didn't have a clue about financial transactions involving bearer bonds. This was out of their league. There was only one man they knew who could play in that class: Leslie Payne. It was his golden opportunity to redeem himself after the Nigerian fiasco, and, incidentally, to make a lot of money.

'It's all very simple,' a self-assured Payne announced to Ron and Reg. 'I can easily arrange for the sale of instantly negotiable bearer bonds. I have friends in the City.'

The twins still had enormous faith in Leslie Payne. He had steered them through the shark-filled waters of the murky rivers that had run their course through Esmeralda's Barn and the Kentucky Club in the early days, carrying away with them all sorts of treasures. He had dammed their flow and used the accumulated wealth to increase Kray power tenfold. Although the Enugu township project had tarnished Payne's image, they still saw every reason to entrust him with the American Mafia's proposition. He contacted his friends in the City with this in mind. He got the nod from them. It was OK to proceed.

After three years of doing business with Angelo Bruno, the Krays were ripe for their first Mafia deal, precipitated by Robert Kennedy's strikeforce. The date for the handover was set for the middle of July 1965, but both sides agreed that a trial run was in order. All the Krays had to do was to send someone over to pick up £20,000 worth of bearer bonds, fly back to England with them and arrange for the sale.

The collection point was to be Montreal. Don Ceville, the head of the Mafia there, would meet the Kray contact and deliver the bearer bonds into their hands. But in London the question remained: Who would go to Canada to fetch them? Neither Ron nor Reg were able to risk being caught for smuggling, at the very best, besides they might not even be allowed into Canada with their police records. Their courier had to be someone they could trust with their mother's life, who knew what was at stake, spoke the financial language and would create the right impression on Don Ceville in Montreal. The Kray empire needs you — Leslie Payne.

It was a Catch 22 for Payne. If he went to Montreal and got caught as a smuggler, he was in trouble. If he refused the twins' request and declined to go to Montreal, he was in even bigger trouble. He made the only decision he could.

9

THE CANADIAN CONNECTION

IT WAS MID-AFTERNOON, and the sun was shining, when the Boeing 707 carrying Leslie Payne touched down at Montreal Airport. Payne took a cab for the five-minute journey to the motel where he was to meet Don Ceville. It was an anonymous place — just one of many hotels and motels around the airport — which made it perfect for their rendezvous.

Leslie Payne checked into the motel in his own name and was given a room overlooking the swimming pool. It was very quiet that afternoon: there was no one in the pool and only a few vehicles were parked outside the rooms. Payne knew that he must wait for the Mafia to make contact, so he couldn't leave his room. Instead, he turned on the television and rested on the bed for a while.

Time passed. After a while Payne started feeling nervous. Worries began to flood in: was it a set-up; were the Mafia really coming; would the police turn up instead? He drank some of his duty-free whisky to steady his nerves, and peered out at the empty swimming pool. It would soon be getting dark, and still no one had arrived.

Then there was a quiet tap on his door, followed by a second, much louder tap. This was it, Payne thought. Nervously, he walked to the door and slowly turned the handle.

In front of him stood two well-dressed young men. They could have been bank clerks, except that no bank clerk could afford the suits they were wearing.

'Mr Leslie Payne, from England?' asked one of them softly.

'That's right,' said Payne, his heart galloping. It was beating so loud he felt sure they could hear it.

'Mr Ceville is here to see you.'

One young man walked over to a limousine that was parked just outside Payne's door. As he reached the vehicle he nodded to someone inside and opened the rear door. A well-built man of average height got out. It was Don Ceville, the Mafia boss.

Leslie Payne stood in his doorway, holding out his hand.

'Mr Ceville, I presume,' he said, trying to smile. He was remembering Ron Kray's words about the importance of creating a good impression.

'Mr Payne.' Don Ceville shook hands and the four men entered the motel room.

Leslie Payne's first impression of the Montreal Mafia

capo was a favourable one. Don Ceville was immaculately groomed. He wore a beautiful dark grey suit and a trilby hat, which he took off as soon as he came in. Leslie Payne could always appreciate a good suit. Yes, he thought, this was a man of substance.

They got down to business immediately. Don Ceville may have taken off his hat, but he obviously did not intend to stay long. One of his bodyguards handed him a large, sealed envelope.

'Here you are, Mr Payne,' said Don Ceville. 'Let's see what you can do with these.' He gave Leslie Payne the heavy brown envelope.

'I'm sure we can handle these, Mr Ceville,' said Payne. 'Ron and Reg Kray are very pleased to be doing business with you.'

'I look forward to seeing them soon, when I come to London. Can you tell them that?'

'Of course. I'd be delighted.'

Don Ceville stood up. His bodyguards, who had been keeping watch out of the window, moved to join him. 'I'm afraid I have some business to attend to this evening, otherwise I would have shown you around my city,' he said. 'Would you like my friends here to take you out instead?'

Leslie Payne looked at the two men, noticed the slight bulges of the handguns under their jackets, and decided to decline the offer as politely as possible. 'Thank you, Mr Ceville, but I have a few phone calls to make, then I'd better get an early night. I'm flying straight back to London tomorrow morning.'

Now he had the bonds, he was in a hurry to get rid of his illustrious guest. Although he had looked forward to this meeting, somehow he felt very much out of his depth. These men made him nervous. Though he didn't want to upset anyone, he knew that only being left alone could calm his racing heartbeat.

'Then give my regards to Ron and Reg Kray — and please remember, take good care of the merchandise.'

'I certainly will,' said Leslie Payne fervently.

A brief handshake and the men were gone. Payne took a deep breath, and looked down at the envelope in his hands. It was very large — he began to wonder if it would fit into his briefcase, the only luggage he had brought with him for this short trip. A quick check reassured him that it would. Thank God for that, he thought. Now all he had to do was get the bonds back to England.

After a restless night, Leslie Payne was beginning to wonder whether or not he was really suited to this kind of venture. The envelope contained £20,000 worth of negotiable bearer bonds, complete with all the necessary certification. Anyone could sell these bonds, so he couldn't let them out of his sight for a moment. Already, the nervous strain of babysitting them had robbed him of most of his sleep.

Fortunately, the trip back to England was uneventful. The BOAC flight left Montreal at 9 a.m., and touched down at Heathrow Airport at nine in the evening, local time. A very weary Leslie Payne made his way across the tarmac and into the passenger hall of Number 3 building. With no luggage to collect, he was the first passenger to reach passport control, and was quickly through. Then came the moment he had dreaded: the bearer bonds were safely stowed in his briefcase, but if the customs officers decided to look inside he was going to have a lot of explaining to do.

In the event, he needn't have worried, because customs was completely empty. He had arrived so far in advance of the other passengers that no one was yet in position to check the arrivals on the Montreal flight. Leslie Payne strode swiftly past the vacant desks of the customs and excise men, into the arrivals hall and out to freedom. He felt as elated as if he had been an East Berliner who had succeeded in getting through Checkpoint Charlie to the West. It was great to be home; all he had to do now was to sell the bonds, which would not be difficult with all their documentation complete.

The Kray twins made nearly £10,000 from the sale of the bonds. By any standards, this was a very good haul for forty-eight hours' work, and Ron and Reg began to feel that bonds were a sure route to superwealth.

The following month, Leslie Payne was contacted by Gordon Andersen, an old associate from the Nigerian project. Andersen, a Canadian, knew Don Ceville and had already arranged for the transfer of the Mafia capo's share of the previous bond sale. Now he had received word from Don Ceville that there were more bonds awaiting collection in Montreal, and that a date should be set up for another meeting.

Gordon Andersen was a man with an unusual business. He sold insurance to US military bases in Europe, specializing in cover against bomb damage. He was a fair man with a pleasant manner who lived in London, drove a big American car and also had his own light aircraft. He was someone whom Leslie Payne thought he could trust.

The batch of bearer bonds awaiting collection in Montreal came with a problem attached. They had no certification which meant that all the paperwork, apart from the bonds themselves, would have to be forged. This was tricky for Leslie Payne, who was no forger. He couldn't even keep the books very well, which was why he employed Freddie Gore. Someone else would have to be involved. This meant setting up an urgent meeting with Ron and Reg Kray to discuss the problem.

The Krays had already realized that sooner or later they would need a friendly banker who could 'handle' paperwork like this for them. They had been given the name of someone who might be able to help, but meanwhile Ron suggested that they go ahead and arrange the meeting in Montreal anyway.

Leslie Payne assumed that he would again be the one to pick up the bonds, but the twins were beginning to wonder if they were becoming a little too dependent on him. They suggested that he should go, but accompanied by their brother, Charlie. This didn't please Payne at all, as Charlie had been a witness to his humiliation in Nigeria, but he had to agree.

During the following week, the proposed Canadian party grew even larger. Ron and Reg decided to send a whole deputation to Montreal for in-depth discussions of potential Anglo-Canadian business ventures. As well as Leslie Payne and Charlie, the members chosen were Charlie Mitchell, a bookmaker and moneylender; Bobby McKew, a printer and one of Charlie's closest friends; and Gordon Andersen himself. Charlie had become friendly with Gordon Andersen when they were in Nigeria together, so he was pleased to work with him again.

Leslie Payne's main comfort was that at least someone

else would have to carry the bearer bonds back through UK customs. He realized now that his future involvement with the bonds would be limited, as the twins were now definitely making arrangements to bring in someone with banking knowledge who could supply the necessary certificates and sell the bonds on to the European market.

Charlie Kray was glad that Bobby McKew was going with them. He had known Bobby for a very long time: his main claim to fame was his marriage to Ana Gerber, the world waterskiing champion. She was the daughter of Jack Gerber, a South African millionaire, and her brother Robin worked for Charlie Kray at Raynors, the club he ran in Leicester. Though his father was a millionaire, Robin was always short of cash and Charlie had taken him on as a croupier, a job the ex-public schoolboy did very well.

Bobby McKew had many friends amongst the celebrities of the time. Later, he became a celebrity in his own right when he wrote the book *Death List* about international terrorism, in collaboration with Reed de Roun, a former Battle of Britain pilot.

The fifth member of the party, Charlie Mitchell, was the fly in the ointment as far as Charlie Kray was concerned. He just could not get on with Mitchell, nor did he trust him. Mitchell was a small, broad-shouldered man with a fresh face and a full set of sparkling white teeth; he was also completely bald. He ran his bookmaking and moneylending business from Fulham's North End Road.

Mitchell was coming along to talk money matters with Don Ceville, but Charlie was sceptical about his inclusion: he suspected that Mitchell could use this opportunity to take business away from Ron and Reg. Still, his brothers had given him the OK, so he was not going to argue with them.

The deal with Don Ceville over the bonds would be the same as before. The Krays would get 50 percent of the proceeds, with the other half going to the Montreal capo. The date for the trip was set for September. Just beforehand, Ron and Reg had a last meeting with their brother, at which they asked him to take personal charge of the bearer bonds. They also wished him a pleasant journey.

The five men made their separate ways to Victoria Coach Station, where they were to board the coach for Heathrow. Since they were to be away for a week on this trip, they all had luggage with them, which they checked in at Victoria. They would not see it again until they reached Montreal. Then they took their seats in the coach, and were soon headed out along the M4 motorway to the airport.

All of them were smartly dressed in dark suits and ties. They looked like bankers or accountants. No one would have guessed that they were any different from the other international business travellers disembarking for their flights at Heathrow's Terminal 3. Certainly no one would have supposed that they were on their way to do business with the Mafia.

As they walked across the tarmac to the waiting BOAC Boeing 707, a pack of photographers ran past them towards the aircraft.

'What the hell's going on?' asked Bobby McKew.

'I don't know,' said Charlie. 'They can't be here for us, can they?' Suddenly he could visualize the newspaper headlines: KRAYS VISIT THE MAFIA IN CANADA,

THE KRAYS AND THE MAFIA, KRAYS CANADIAN MAFIA CONNECTION.

But the photographers weren't taking any notice of Charlie and his companions. They were interested only in the group of beautiful young ladies who were standing on the steps leading up to the aircraft. Along with all the other passengers, the five men stood and stared at the eight lovelies in mink coats.

'Thank God for that,' said Charlie, almost to himself.

'But who are they?' asked Gordon Andersen. 'Does anyone know?'

The photographers crowded round the steps, while a man talked to newspaper reporters. Suddenly he signalled to the girls.

'Will you look at that!' exclaimed Bobby McKew, as the girls let their mink coats fall to the ground.

A smile spread across Charlie Kray's face. 'So that's what it's all about.'

The eight girls were all dressed in Playboy Bunny costumes. Hugh Hefner was about to open his new Playboy Club in London's Park Lane, and these were the first ever English 'Bunny Girls', on their way to be trained at Playboy headquarters in Chicago.

Charlie and his companions laughed with relief, their apprehension melting away.

'This should be a good trip,' said Charlie to Gordon Andersen.

'It looks that way,' replied the Canadian. 'Do you think we can get to sit near them?'

The flight was only part-full, and with plenty of spare seats, the five men were able to move closer to the Playboy party once they were airborne. There were twelve of them in all: the eight Bunny Girls, two women chaperons and two men. They didn't take much persuading to join Charlie and the others in a drink. It was a long way to Chicago via Montreal, so they might as well enjoy the trip.

The plane headed west towards Ireland, then out across the North Atlantic. The sun was shining, the drink was flowing, and soon the party was well under way.

By the time the plane was over the mid-Atlantic, Charlie was deep in conversation with one of the BOAC air hostesses. He had always wanted to see the cockpit of a large aircraft such as the Boeing, and when he mentioned this she readily agreed to ask the captain. A few minutes later, Charlie was on the flight deck, looking in fascination at the huge instrument panel. The captain, a likeable man, patiently answered all his questions and Charlie's admiration grew as he listened. It was no easy task to fly a plane like this, but how he would have enjoyed the captain's job, he thought.

When he at last returned to his seat the party was still in full swing. Someone was even suggesting to the Bunny Girls that they join them in Montreal. But this, as it turned out, would not have been a good idea.

The plane made a beautifully smooth landing at Montreal airport, and the five men were all in high spirits as they made their way to the terminal building. The air was clean and crisp; they were happy to be back on terra firma and looking forward to their stay in Canada.

They joined the queue for passport control. As a Canadian citizen, Gordon Andersen could have gone through a separate channel, but as there was such a small queue he elected to remain with the rest of the group.

When they arrived at the immigration desk, the five men were asked, very politely, to wait for a moment. The other passengers walked on through. While they waited, Gordon Andersen spotted Don Ceville on the other side of the barriers, and pointed him out to Charlie Kray.

At last, Leslie Payne was called forward, but soon he was back with his associates, having been asked to wait once again. By now they were all beginning to worry.

'It's taking too long,' said Charlie Kray to Bobby McKew. 'Something's not right. We should have been through by now.'

Time passed, and their agitation grew. Charlie was right: something was definitely up.

Suddenly they were joined by two men. Although they were not in uniform, they spoke with an air of authority.

'Would you come with us, please?'

They were shown into a large room which seemed to be full of men. Most of them wore the famous red jackets of the uniform of the Royal Canadian Mounted Police, and all of them carried guns. Some even carried machine guns.

A very nasty feeling crept over Charlie Kray. 'What's all this about?' he asked one of the plainclothes men who had brought them there.

'We'll ask the questions,' said the man. He looked from Charlie to his companions. 'Are any of you gentlemen carrying firearms?'

'Look here,' said Gordon Andersen indignantly. 'I'm a Canadian citizen, and I demand to know what's going on.'

'I said we'll ask the questions, Mr . . . Andersen.' The

man gave him a hard stare. 'Now will you please face the wall and put your hands out.'

The five men were frisked, one after the other. No firearms were found. After this the tension in the room eased a little. The five turned back to face their captors.

Once again, Charlie spoke. 'I don't know what you're after, but would someone please tell us what's going on?'

Another plainclothes man stepped forward. 'What are you here for?'

'We're here on holiday,' said Bobby McKew.

There was a long silence. The first plainclothes man had been quietly talking to his associates. Now he turned and said, 'You'll be held in the tombs until tomorrow morning. Then you'll go before the immigration board.' He turned to one of the uniformed police. 'Take them to the tombs — in separate vehicles.'

Leslie Payne had almost fainted at the word 'tombs', but he was too frightened to say a word. Charlie Mitchell showed no signs of worry, but then he never did. Gordon Andersen was convinced there must be a big mistake: he was a Canadian citizen and he had never committed any crimes in Canada — or anywhere else.

'I thought we'd be safe once our feet were back on the ground,' said Bobby McKew ruefully.

Charlie Kray just looked at his friend. He knew there was no point in saying anything, and he suddenly felt very tired.

When Charlie and his associates emerged from the terminal with their escorts, they were greeted by an astonishing sight: the whole building was surrounded by red-coated policemen. Some were in cars, some on horseback, some on foot; all were heavily armed. Five big Canadian police cars were also waiting for them.

Each man was hustled in to a separate car, accompanied by two plainclothes policemen. The cavalcade sped away towards the city.

Charlie Kray was in the last car. 'Just what are the tombs?' he asked his escorts.

'The main Montreal police station. It's about a ten minute drive.'

'From the air, Montreal looked a nice place,' commented Charlie. 'Any chance of us going through the centre, just in case I don't have time to do any sightseeing.'

The other man gave a muffled laugh. 'No chance at all. We just follow the others.'

Ten minutes later, they arrived outside a heavy steel gate, set in the middle of a gigantic, slab-like wall. It was the only opening of any kind in the wall — there wasn't even the smallest of windows. An electric motor began to whine, and slowly the gate began to rise. One by one the cars passed through the gap into a big yard.

When Charlie got out of his car, the others were standing waiting for him, surrounded by policemen. As he walked towards them he heard the electric motor start up again. He glanced back towards the gate and saw that it was closing, slowly and deliberately.

The five men were herded towards an outside elevator. It looked like the goods elevator for a warehouse. The policemen who were pushing and shoving them along spoke only French — something which Charlie later discovered was standard practice in the Montreal police.

In the elevator, the five stood huddled together, with the policemen crowding round them. There must have been twenty people in that confined space, crammed together like sardines. No one said anything. Then the elevator began to move.

Charlie had no idea whether they were going up or down. It was very dark, and there were no buttons or lights that he could see to give him a clue. All he knew was that it was taking a long time, and that wherever they were going, he would rather be somewhere else.

The automatic doors opened. They had arrived. As they stepped out into the wide open spaces of the detention area, all they could see were iron bars, stretching as far as the eye could see. It was not a welcome sight.

Just beyond the elevator was a solitary desk and standing behind it was a giant of a man dressed in a sergeant's uniform. He stepped forward to meet them.

'Empty your pockets.'

Charlie Kray was closest to him, and it was not an order he was about to disobey. He emptied his pockets: wallet, full of Canadian dollars, plane tickets, cigarettes, gold lighter.

'Take off your rings.'

Charlie stripped the gold rings from his fingers.

'And your tie.'

'I'm not about to hang myself, you know.' Charlie couldn't help showing his irritation now.

The sergeant placed all his belongings in a large envelope, but first he took a few dollars from the wallet and gave them back to Charlie. Surprised, Charlie stuffed them into his trouser pocket. Then his armed guards took him through a door in the outer wall of iron bars and showed him to a group of six cells — three on either side of a gangway, with a toilet at the end. It had only a half stable door — there would be no privacy here.

All the cell doors were open. Charlie was told to take

whichever he liked. The outer door was closed behind him and he was left to wait for the others.

Bobby McKew was next through the door. He looked worried.

'What the hell's going on, Charlie? This is way over the top.'

'I know,' said Charlie. 'Someone's been talking.'

'Telling porkies, more like,' exclaimed McKew.

'Keep it quiet, Bobby.' Charlie tried to calm him. 'We don't want any trouble.'

'But trouble, Charlie is what we've got.'

Gordon Andersen was next through the gate, then Charlie Mitchell, and last of all a very tired and despondent Leslie Payne.

'At least we've all got beds.' Gordon Andersen looked around at the six empty cells. each with its own bunk.

Why had this happened? What exactly were the police at Montreal airport expecting? Who had informed the authorities about their visit? What had they told them? They were all asking the same questions, but no one had any answers. There was only one thing to do in a situation like this: try and relax.

Charlie Kray told them all to take a bunk and get some rest. They were going to be taken back to the airport immigration offices the following day, so with any luck their stay here would be a short one.

As the others dispersed, he looked through the bars. The police were moving away; some were chatting and laughing. But Charlie Kray was not in a laughing mood. He went into his cell, took off his jacket and sat down on the bunk. As he did so, his mind went back to the Nigerian fiasco. He had managed to get Leslie Payne out of Enugu Jail on that occasion, but now that he too was imprisoned, who was going to get them out of Canada?

Suddenly, he remembered the few dollars that the sergeant had given him back from his wallet. He took the notes out of his pocket and looked at them. There were plenty more dollars in his wallet, but would he ever see them again? And what were these notes for, anyway?

There were no other prisoners in the cells, apart from the five of them. There were no windows, and he had left his watch with the sergeant, so he had no idea what time it was. Days and nights could come and go in a place like this, and no one would know the difference.

He was trying to settle down to sleep when there was a rattling noise outside, and a man appeared wheeling a trolley full of snacks and drinks. This, it appeared was what his small change was for. In Montreal Police Station, prisoners had to buy their own food.

He chose a pack of fruit pies, and wedged it between the bars of his cell, telling the others to help themselves if they felt hungry during the night. Charlie Mitchell had a sandwich. He was the only one of them who felt like eating at that moment.

Then Charlie Kray lay down on his bunk again, hands behind his head. He knew he had to get some sleep, but sleep would not come easily in an oppressive place like this.

'Rise and shine,' shouted the sergeant, clattering his truncheon along the outer wall of bars.

Charlie opened his eyes and slowly moved his aching body. No, he hadn't been dreaming. He was really here, in the Montreal tombs, being held by the Canadian police.

He got up and looked out at the others' cells. They were all showing signs of life; no suicides in the night.

'The quicker we get ready, the quicker we get out of here,' he croaked. His voice was always rough and harsh in the mornings. He had had problems with his vocal chords and nasal passages since his boxing days.

They were able to wash, but not to shave, and of course there was no change of clothing as their luggage was still at the airport — or so they presumed. During the night, the pies had mysteriously disappeared, so there was no breakfast either.

'Charles Kray.' The sergeant had unlocked the outer cell door, and was beckoning him forward. Charlie followed him back to the desk. There were several other policemen waiting, but not nearly as many as the night before, and Charlie noticed that the sergeant hadn't bothered to lock the cell door behind him. The whole atmosphere was subtly different — the sergeant was even trying to be polite.

'Is it all there, Mr Kray?' he asked, as Charlie checked the contents of his envelope. 'You can smoke if you like,' he added, when Charlie put his cigarettes and lighter back in his pocket.

The others followed Charlie out in quick succession, and soon all five were standing round the sergeant's desk, wearing their ties once again and smoking cigarettes.

'Let's go,' said one of the policemen. They all crowded into the elevator. Once more, Charlie couldn't tell whether they were going up or down. But this time, as long as they were going out, he couldn't have cared less. The policemen were chatting to one another in French. This time, there were no machine guns to be seen.

They stepped out into the daylight. 'Fresh air at least,' said Gordon Andersen with a smile.

'At least we're still alive,' said Charlie, taking in deep breaths of the early morning Montreal air. It tasted very good to him.

Down the path they walked, towards the waiting cars. There was no pushing or prodding this time. It was just like a morning stroll. They got into the cars, each in a separate one as before. Charlie could see the heavy steel gate opening; he couldn't wait to get under it and out on to the open road. As they passed through the thick walls, he hoped that he would never, ever, come back here again.

At the airport the cars pulled up outside a large, anonymous building which Charlie Kray assumed was the headquarters of the immigration department. The five men were hurried through a narrow entrance and into a smallish waiting room. It wasn't big enough to hold all the policemen so most of them waited outside, standing guard.

After a short while, an official appeared. 'You will be going in for your interview one at a time,' he said, 'but first there's someone here to see you.'

He turned to one of the policemen. 'Show them into room three.'

As they made their way to the room, Charlie Kray wondered who on earth wanted to see them. Was it another police official, or perhaps someone from the embassy?

The small room into which they were shown was empty. It had five chairs positioned round the walls. At the end of the room, under a window, was a desk, and behind this was another chair.

The five men sat down, and the escorting policemen closed the door behind them, leaving them alone. Then the door opened again. A young woman came in, and sat down behind the desk. She was very attractive, smartly dressed, and carried a briefcase.

'Good morning, gentlemen,' she said. 'Which one of you is Charles Kray?'

'I am,' said Charlie. 'And who are you?'

'My name doesn't matter, but I'm a solicitor, and I'm here on behalf of Mr Don Ceville,' she said briskly, opening her briefcase. 'Here is confirmation.'

She handed Charlie a letter from Don Ceville. It explained that Don Ceville had seen them being taken away at the airport, but had been unable to arrange for anyone to see them before now. It also asked them to put complete trust in his representative.

'How do we know that is all on the level?' asked Charlie.

'I'm just here to help. If you'd rather I went . . .'

'No, no,' said Charlie quickly, as the young woman half-rose from her seat. He looked round at the others.

'It looks OK to me,' said Gordon Andersen.

'I reckon she's telling the truth,' added Charles Mitchell.

'Then, we're agreed.' Charlie Kray turned back to the solicitor. 'What do we do, then?'

'You have two options. I am sure we can get you into Canada — after all you've done nothing wrong here — but it will take a week or two. Otherwise, you could take the plane back to London this evening.'

This time, Charlie did not ask his associates for their

opinions. 'Let's get home as fast as possible. I don't want to spend another day in the tombs!'

The others nodded agreement.

'Right, then this is what you must do. When you go in to your interview, they'll be waiting to question you. You will see that they have your passport in front of them. Whatever they ask, you must give only one reply.' Their attractive solicitor looked at them all closely to see if they understood. 'First give your name, then say, "There's my passport, together with my passport number. I refuse to answer any questions since I have done nothing wrong in this country. I wish to return to England on the first available flight." You must answer in exactly the same way to every question you are asked.'

The men sat for a while, making sure that they had memorized these words. By the end of the day, they would remember them for the rest of their lives.

The solicitor left, after having shaken hands with her clients and wished them a pleasant flight back to England. Then the five were taken back to the waiting room.

'I'll go first,' said Charlie Kray, 'then I can tell the rest of you what will happen.'

The policemen ushered him into an adjoining room, where the three men who made up the immigration board awaited him. They began their questioning, and Charlie replied exactly as the solicitor had instructed. After the first few questions, he put forward a suggestion. 'Can't we skip the rest of the questions. I'm going to reply to each one the same way. You must know that by now.'

'I'm sorry, Mr Kray. The law states quite clearly that we must ask a number of previously established questions and that you must provide an answer to every one, for our records.'

The inquisition continued for thirty weary minutes. At the end of it, Charles Kray was told that he would indeed be returned to England on the first available flight.

He felt a huge sense of relief as he returned to the waiting room. 'Just remember your speeches,' he told the others. 'Say exactly what the solicitor told you and you'll be all right.'

When they had all been interviewed, they were shown into another room to wait for their flight, which would be at nine that evening. There were still about fifteen policemen with them, mostly in plain clothes. The room had no carpets and was sparsely decorated, but there was a desk in one corner with some papers and books on it.

Bobby McKew made his way over to the desk. No one noticed him pick up the books, but they all heard the resounding crash as he dropped them.

In a flash, every policeman in the room had pulled out his gun and aimed it at Bobby.

'Not now, Bobby,' snapped Charlie Kray angrily. He knew Bobby was a great practical joker, but seeing all those guns pointed at his pal wasn't amusing at all. Fortunately the policemen saw the funny side of the incident. They laughed and put their guns away, and the atmosphere in the room thawed several degrees. Soon the five men from England were chatting and joking with their Canadian police escorts, who a little later on took them to the main transit hall. They were still under guard, but they were allowed to do whatever they wanted, within reason.

Together with their escorts, they had a good meal in

the airport restaurant, a few drinks, and a look round the shops. At last, a call for the 9 p.m. flight to London rang out over the loudspeakers in the transit lounge.

Even Leslie Payne had a smile on his face as they walked back across the tarmac to the waiting Boeing 707. When they reached the steps leading up to the aircraft, their police guard formed a line. Their former prisoners walked past, smiling, and shook hands with every one of them. It was all a far cry from their reception just 24 hours earlier.

'We've enjoyed your visit,' said one plainclothes policeman. 'Do come again.'

'Someone got something very wrong,' said another.

'Have a good trip back,' said a third cheerfully.

Yes, thought Charlie Kray, someone did get something very wrong. But at least they were on their way home now.

Though they were allowed to board the plane first, like celebrities, there were no Bunny girls on the return trip. There was no party and no visit up front to the flight deck. It reminded Charlie uncomfortably of his last flight back from Lagos, Nigeria. That had been another trip to forget.

When the plane took off, the five men slept. They didn't even wake to see the inflight movie. When they arrived at Heathrow Airport, they were still tired, they were dirty, and their clothes were grubby and dishevelled, but they were too relieved to care. This was their home territory. They were safe now.

They walked slowly across the tarmac to the luggage collection point. As they waited for their luggage to arrive, Charlie Kray thought that there was a comical side to what had happened. Here they were, back in

England, and they hadn't even opened their suitcases. Indeed, they hadn't even seen their suitcases.

When they reached customs, Charlie was the last of the five in the queue. The others went through without being stopped, but as Charlie walked past the desk one of the customs officers stepped forward.

'Do you have anything to declare, sir?'

'No,' said Charlie firmly.

'Are there any purchases in your suitcase?' persisted the official.

'No,' said Charlie again. He was only too well aware that there were not. He was also irritated at being stopped.

'Are you one of the men deported from Canada?' asked the customs officer suddenly.

Charlie glared at him. He had had enough of being questioned. 'Yes, and so what?'

His anger must have been obvious. The customs officer took a step back. 'Nothing. Nothing at all,' he said timidly.

Charlie picked up his suitcase and the plastic bag containing his duty frees — a bottle of whisky and a pack of Players — and walked on. The customs man did nothing to stop him. He joined the others in the arrivals hall and they headed for the nearest taxi rank.

Though the Canada trip was a failure, the Krays learned a number of invaluable lessons from it. First of all, they knew that someone had talked. The Canadian authorities had been too well informed — the army of police waiting at the airport knew exactly when the group would be arriving. This was information which couldn't come about just by rumours — someone must have given it to the police in London before they left. They would have to be far more discreet and secretive about any future trips.

Secondly, they decided it was a bad idea to invite outsiders on a trip like this. In future, the bonds would be collected and that would be that. No other business would be discussed. Whoever went would be quickly in and quickly out, in 48 hours at most.

Thirdly, Ron and Reg Kray decided they would have to take a greater personal interest in the acquisition and sale of the negotiable bearer bonds. Leslie Payne would not be making the arrangements for future deals. They had been hearing more and more stories about Payne since the disastrous outcome of the Nigeria business, and had decided to have a good look at the business arrangements he had set up for running their firm. They were not satisfied with what they found. In future they would be controlling business arrangements and business accounts themselves.

In October 1965, Don Ceville himself came over to England to see Ron and Reg Kray. He had no difficulty getting into the United Kingdom and he brought the bearer bonds with him. He discussed future business with Ron, Reg and Charlie. Leslie Payne was not present. After this, Don Ceville came to England on a number of occasions and was never refused entry — unlike his friend, the actor George Raft.

The police never learned about the twins' dealings with the bearer bonds, and it proved a highly successful venture. The Canadian connection became well established.

Gordon Andersen continued to help the twins in their business dealings with the Montreal Mafia capo, but he never travelled on their behalf again. He later moved to Rome, where he continued his business of selling bomb insurance. Later in the 1970s, Charlie Kray was serving his ten-year prison sentence when he read an amusing newspaper story about a Canadian businessman. The man had parked his big American car next to his private plane, intending to retrieve a briefcase from the plane. Unfortunately he failed to leave the car in gear or put the brake on properly. The car started to move, and he was still walking towards the plane when it rolled past him and crunched straight into the aircraft. He had managed to crash his car and seriously damage his plane without being in either of them at the time! That man was Gordon Andersen.

Charlie Mitchell ended up eventually in southern Spain where, faced with a possible criminal prosecution, he began fabricating stories about his association with the Krays. He had never been known as a 'grass' and his actions surprised the criminal communities of the Costa del Sol and London's East End. Later he was shot dead at his Costa del Sol villa — the killer or killers were never found.

No one ever discovered who had informed the police about the Montreal trip, and none of the Krays ever visited Canada again. Instead, the bonds were brought to Europe. The US Mafia had safe routes into Paris, Hamburg, Geneva, Amsterdam and Frankfurt — all the Krays had to do was collect the bonds from these cities and bring them safely back to the UK. Charlie Kray was given the job of organizing this, together with an American banker named A B Cooper, who was to forge the necessary certification for the bonds.

Leslie Payne's role dwindled to nothing. In 1967 there was an unsuccessful attempt on his life, but by this time his days with Ron and Reg Kray were well and truly over.

DOING THE BUSINESS

Bobby McKew and his wife Ana inherited her family fortune. They now live in South Africa, together with Ana's brother, Robin.

Don Ceville met an untimely end some years ago. He was shot in the head and his body dumped in a peat bog outside Montreal. It was a typical Mob killing — nothing personal, just business. Montreal has always been a violent city, with the Mafia families of New York and Buffalo disputing ownership of Mob business there.

10
ONE NIGHT IN PARIS

'GOOD MORNING, MUM,' said Charlie Kray.

'Hello, Charlie,' said Violet. 'What are you doing here?'

'I'd like to borrow your dustbin, please, mum. I've got some old accounts I want to burn.'

'That's OK, Charlie. Would you like a cup of tea?'

'I'd love one. I'll be round the back.'

Charlie made his way through to the back yard, carrying a large cardboard box. It contained petrol, matches, old news-papers and a plastic bag with a large brown envelope inside.

The dustbin was empty. 'All nice and clean,' said Charlie to himself as he peered inside.

He started tearing up the newspapers and throwing them, piece by crumpled piece, into the dustbin. When he had torn up two or three, he pulled the brown envelope from its protective plastic bag, opened it, and took out the contents.

He definitely didn't want to do the next bit, but orders were orders, and the phone call had been quite explicit: 'They're too hot to handle. Just get rid of them.'

He had only glanced at the envelope's contents before; now he took a good look. They were impressive, but so they should be — not accounts, as he had told his mother, but securities that would bring instant wealth to anyone who held them.

With a sigh, he started to tear up the first document. Then he threw the pieces in the dustbin. The second document went the same way, and the third. He continued until the envelope was empty.

As he tore up the pieces of paper he added up their value. He had just destroyed $250,000 worth of negotiable bearer bonds which he had collected, in Paris, from the representatives of the Mafia.

The rest was like following a recipe. Just add petrol and light. It was all over very quickly. Charlie stood and watched as the bonds turned to smoke and ash.

'Well that's it,' he thought, looking at the burnt remains in the bottom of the dustbin. Small flakes of blackened paper were still floating around the yard, but that didn't matter. No one could identify these minute scraps.

It had taken him about two minutes to get rid of a fortune.

Charlie Kray was not a happy man. He took a packet of cigarettes from his pocket and lit one. Bearer bonds or cigarettes, he thought resignedly, they all went up in smoke in the end.

His thoughts went back to the events leading up to his trip to Paris. What a pity it had to end like this, when it had started so well.

'Hello, Reg, what's happening?' said Charlie, answering the telephone.

'You're going to Paris, Charlie. Let's meet at mum's and I'll give you the whole story.'

'Fine. I'll see you there in an hour.'

As Charlie hung up he was feeling pleased. He loved going to Paris, and he was already looking forward to his trip. He didn't yet know what his brothers wanted him to do, but he was always, in principle, prepared to take part in any of their business deals. And Ron and Reg were always pleased to involve their older brother, whenever possible. He was the only person they could absolutely rely on — if you couldn't trust your own family, then who could you trust?

Charlie knew that Ron and Reg would not involve him directly in any criminal activity. If violence was necessary in business matters, they would take care of that themselves. They were well aware that Charlie would not be a party to it.

But they also knew that Charlie was always as good as his word. If he agreed to take care of their business in Paris, he would do just that. He had run the clubs exceptionally well and never let them down. The twins knew they could always trust Charlie.

Charlie drove over to 178 Vallance Road to find that Ron had already arrived. Reg soon joined them. Violet made them some tea, then left her boys alone in the front room. She knew there would be a reason for their little get together and that it was best for her to stay out of it. When she had gone, Ron and Reg got down to business — the acquisition of more bearer bonds from the US Mafia.

It was November 1965. Since Leslie Payne's first trip to Montreal in July of that year, the twins had already made a lot of money from the bonds. They had taken on AB Cooper, an American banker, to handle the forgeries necessary for the sale of the bonds, and he had also established contacts in the various European bond markets. His forgeries had been readily accepted by banks and brokers alike.

After the problems encountered on Charlie's trip to Montreal, the Mafia had arranged for the bond deliveries to be made to Europe. The bonds brought into the UK by Don Ceville had been sold by AB Cooper in Hamburg, and Charlie himself had visited Geneva to collect bonds there. These too had been sold off in Germany, and the proceeds brought back to the UK through the established international banking structure. The system had worked well.

Now another batch of bonds needed collection in Paris.

Charlie's pick-up point was to be the Claridge Hotel at 74 Champs-Elysées. It would only be a quick trip — out one day and back the next — but Charlie didn't mind. Any stay at the Claridge Hotel was all right with him.

The twins had decided that Leslie Payne and the accountant, Freddie Gore, would accompany Charlie. They had also decided that it would be Freddie Gore who carried the bonds back through customs. They were always keen on their employees getting involved in this way, as it gave them more control over them.

When the three met at Victoria Coach Station at the start of their trip, it was Freddie Gore who was the new boy. Like Payne, he had been freed from the clutches of the Nigerian police by Charlie Kray in the summer of 1964. He had also heard what happened in Canada. So, understandably, he was just a little nervous. But Charlie and Leslie were able to reassure him that so far the European collection of bearer bonds had passed off without incident.

Their journey from London to Paris was uneventful. They might have been any three executives flying to France on business. By early afternoon they were seated in an old yellow taxi, speeding north up the N7 from Orly Airport into the heart of Paris. Charlie remembered his many trips to France when he had run his own travel company, transporting tourists to the South. He had made many a memorable stopover in Paris on his way to Provence, and knew the city well.

Now they were in the city centre, passing the Elysée Palace and the Tuileries and on round the Place de la Concorde. Then up the Champs-Elysées, where the taxi stopped outside the Claridge Hotel.

The three paid the driver and got out. If they looked up the Champs-Elysées they could see the Arc de Triomphe; if they looked down, they saw the fountains of the Place de la Concorde. It was, and is, one of the great views of the world.

'So this is the Claridge,' said Leslie Payne, looking as if he was about to devour the hotel in one bite.

'This looks nice, Charlie,' added Freddie Gore as they made their way through the glass doors and into the hotel lobby.

As the three waited for their reservations to be

checked, they admired their surroundings. 'Nice' was an understatement. There were deep lush red carpets, gold-framed mirrors, huge glass chandeliers and deep brown wooden panelling on the walls. It all spelt luxury in big, glorious, capital letters.

It didn't take them long to check into their rooms, which were as elegant as one would expect from one of the finest hotels in Paris. Time for a quick freshen up and then they were back out on the street. It was still only two in the afternoon and their meeting with the Mafia was not until six. They had four hours in which to enjoy Paris, and they weren't going to waste any time.

They walked up the Champs-Elysées towards the Arc de Triomphe, past the cafes with their tables and chairs still outside in November, past the striped awnings and wooden tubs planted with evergreens, past the sophisticated young women in dark glasses and the young men in tight short leather jackets sipping their tiny cups of black coffee and watching the world go by.

They reached the Renault showrooms, which seemed unusually crowded for a car dealership with masses of people going in and out.

Charlie stopped. 'Come and have a look inside,' he said to his companions.

They followed him to the rear of the showroom, where cars were lined up, bumper to bumper.

'Well, which do you fancy?' Charlie asked. 'A Renault, a Citroën, a Mercedes, or maybe a Rolls-Royce?'

'A Citroën,' said Leslie Payne. 'After all we are in Paris.'

Charlie found them a Citroën and opened the door. 'Sit down, and make yourselves comfortable.'

The Citroën contained two bench seats with a table between them. This wasn't a car showroom at all, but a very popular restaurant, with separate cars instead of separate tables.

When a waiter came to take their order, Charlie whispered something to him. 'It's a surprise,' he said, grinning at the others.

'You've been here before, haven't you?' said Freddie Gore.

'Lots of times,' Charlie replied. 'I used to bring busloads of tourists here.'

Soon the waiter was back with Charlie's order. He put three tall glasses on the table, piled high with multicoloured scoops of ice-cream, layered with chocolate, cherries and cream. These glorious ice-creams were a speciality of the Renault Bar. The three men dug in and all was quiet in the Citroën as they savoured their delicious treat.

'I can't eat another thing,' said Leslie Payne as they came out on to the street again. 'I've never had an ice-cream like that before.'

'We won't be eating again until we've finished our business with our American friends,' Charlie reminded him.

All three thought about the forthcoming meeting as they continued up the Champs-Elysées to the Arc de Triomphe. They admired the huge monument for a while, then Freddie Gore said, 'Let's have a closer look.'

They descended the steps to the underpass which led to the tomb of the unknown soldier with its eternal flame. Then they stood admiring the view down the Champs-Elysées towards the Place de la Concorde. It was a great feeling being there, but they knew they had to get back to the hotel. Although the meeting was not scheduled until six, in their business anything could happen, so they had decided to go back early.

'Do you know what we're collecting, Charlie?' asked Freddie Gore, sounding nervous. He was thinking about his job of taking the package through customs.

'Bonds,' said Charlie, with a slight smile.

'I know that.' Freddie Gore was whispering in case a passer-by happened to be listening. 'But what's their value?'

'A lot,' said Charlie. 'It could be as much as $100,000, I suppose.' He watched Freddie's face. 'Or it could be more.'

Freddie turned pale. Suddenly, he didn't feel like a tourist any more.

They made their way back down the opposite side of the Champs-Elysées. There were a lot of restaurants and all of them seemed to be busy. Many of the customers were American tourists.

'Have you ever noticed how you can always hear the Americans?' asked Leslie Payne. 'They always seem to have louder voices than the rest, don't they?'

Neither of the others replied. They were thinking about the Americans that they were about to meet.

It was almost dark when they returned to their hotel. They found a table in the bar and ordered coffee. Trying to relax, they talked about their initial impressions of Paris.

'Do you know,' said Charlie suddenly, leaning forward and speaking very quietly, 'we haven't seen a gendarme all day.'

'They must have known we were coming.' Leslie Payne tried to sound unconcerned. Then he looked around the bar. 'Charlie,' he went on, 'there are so many Americans here. How will you recognize the two we're supposed to meet?'

'They'll ask for us. I've left a message in reception to say we're in here. When they arrive, I'll give them the password so they'll know we're kosher.' He paused, then added, 'They'll be wearing trenchcoats, by the way.'

The three sat in silence for a while, drinking their coffee and keeping a watchful eye on everyone entering the bar. After a few minutes, Freddie Gore whispered, 'But Charlie, they're all wearing trenchcoats.'

Charlie smiled. 'Don't worry, Freddie. They'll find us all right.'

At five minutes past six two men, both wearing trenchcoats, walked into the bar.

'We've got company,' said Charlie, rising from his seat. He walked over to the men. 'Are you looking for me, gentlemen?' he asked.

'If you're Charlie Kray, then we are,' said the elder of the two, who looked about 50. His companion was probably ten years younger.

'I am,' said Charlie. 'Which one of you is Artie?'

The older man smiled. 'I'm Artie and this is Tony.'

'It's good to see you.' Charlie shook hands with them both. 'Now come and meet my associates.'

The three walked casually over to the table where the others had risen to greet their Mafia contacts. Charlie made the introductions, the Americans took off their coats, and everyone sat down. They ordered more coffee and chatted about their flights to Paris. It was like the beginning of any ordinary business meeting.

After a while, Charlie decided it was time to get to the point. 'Do you have anything for us?' he asked Artie.

'We have a little package for you back at our hotel. But first we wanted to be sure you had made it here OK.'

'What do you have in mind?' Charlie could well understand that these men didn't want to roam the streets of Paris carrying the stolen bearer bonds.

'We'll come back in two hours,' said Artie, finishing his coffee. 'We'll see you here again, if that's OK with you.'

Charlie looked at his associates and they nodded. The meeting was agreed. They shook hands all round again, and the two Americans left the bar. The others settled back into their comfortably padded seats.

'I could do with a drink,' said Leslie Payne.

'Me too,' said Freddie Gore. He was starting to look quite cheerful, perhaps because Artie had said that the package to be handed over was a little one. That would probably mean that the bonds had only a low value, rather than the $100,000 or so that Charlie expected. It didn't occur to Freddie that whatever the value of the bonds, smuggling them into the UK was still a criminal act.

Charlie ordered their drinks — a bottle of French beer for Freddie, a gin and tonic for Leslie Payne and a Pernod for himself. They were in no hurry to leave the bar. They were enjoying the luxurious surroundings and they had plenty of francs in their pockets, even though at the prices they were paying here, they could be drinking at the Ritz or the Savoy in London. But then this was one of the best hotels in town, thought Charlie. And anyway, it wouldn't cost them a penny personally, because it would all go down as expenses. None of the three men would be expected to cover any part of this Paris trip out of their own pockets. It was all a very enjoyable part of doing the business.

When the men from the US Mafia returned to the bar just before eight o'clock, the three Englishmen were still there. The Americans joined them at their table and started talking about their impressions of Paris. It was their first trip to the French capital and for both of them it was love at first sight. It was the sights to be seen by night that interested them most, and they suggested that the five of them should go out on the town together. Charlie had the most experience of the city, so they would leave it to him to plan their itinerary.

'But first of all,' said Charlie, 'we have some unfinished business to attend to.'

Artie handed him a plastic bag with a little something inside.

'I see you've been shopping at Macy's,' remarked Charlie with a smile, 'and you've got a parcel for me.'

'The deal is the same as before,' said Artie. 'Fifty-fifty.' He looked round at them all. 'Well, how about this evening?'

Charlie was happy to fall in with the Americans' wishes. He wanted to impress them and he knew it was important to keep them happy. Anyway, Leslie Payne and Freddie Gore were keen to sample the local nightlife too. But first he had to find somewhere to leave his package safely.

'Just give me a few minutes to take care of these, gentlemen.'

'OK,' said Artie. 'We'll see you outside in five minutes. How does that sound?'

'Fine,' said Charlie. 'It's all the time I need.'

The lights were shining brightly along the Champs-Elysées as the two Mafia men waited outside the Claridge Hotel. Meanwhile, Charlie Kray was standing in the middle of his luxurious room with a raincoat in one hand and a Macy's plastic bag containing a quantity of negotiable bearer bonds in the other. He was looking round to see if he could spot a suitable hiding place. There was always the hotel safe, of course, but that wouldn't do in this case.

His five minutes were rapidly running out. He had already rejected the bathroom and the bed. Only the wardrobe was left. His few clothes would not hide the bag inside the wardrobe, but there was a space behind it. It was not the safest hiding place in the world, but it was the best he could find. The maid had already turned down the bed, so no one else would be entering the room that evening. Besides, who would think of looking behind a wardrobe, or expect to find a package of bearer bonds there.

He stuffed the plastic bag into the space. That should be safe enough for a few hours, he thought. Then he hurried downstairs to join the others.

They were all gathered in front of the hotel, waiting for him.

'Ready,' said Charlie. 'Then let's go.'

They walked up the north side of the Champs-Elysées, and as they walked they talked. But not about business matters. That was over and done with now and they wanted to enjoy themselves.

'Was there anything special you wanted to do while you were here?' Charlie asked his American companions.

'Now that you ask, Charlie,' said Artie. 'I've always wanted to eat real French escargots.'

Charlie smiled. 'That shouldn't be a problem. We're just about to pass one of the best places for escargots in the whole of Paris.'

'Well then,' said Artie, 'let's go in and try some.'

The café/restaurant was called La Pergola. It was already quite full, but they managed to find a well-positioned table. In the end, all five of them decided to have snails. Freddie Gore was doubtful at first, but Charlie persuaded him to give them a try. They ordered a bottle of

Chablis to go with their escargots, and there was plenty of crusty French bread on the table to mop up the garlic butter. They ate, drank and talked. Before long, they were ordering another bottle of Chablis.

'What a treat,' said Artie, looking at his empty plate.

'Now I've really got something to tell the folks back home,' added Tony.

They all agreed it had been a fine meal, even Freddie Gore. 'I didn't think I could eat snails, he said. 'I suppose it's all the garlic and butter that does it.'

'Good food and good wine,' said Charlie. 'It'll make better men of us!'

He asked the waiter for the bill, which was speedily brought to them. It was expensive, but Charlie didn't mind. The meal had been worth every franc of the twins' money.

Once out on the street again, they stood discussing the rest of the evening's entertainment. While they did so, Charlie bought a copy of the Evening News from one of the newspaper sellers who wander up and down the Champs-Elysées every day of the year.

'English newspapers?' asked Freddie Gore, peering over Charlie's shoulder.

'That's right. I just wanted to make sure we weren't in the headlines back home.'

His remark brought a laugh from the others, but Charlie's words were not intended to be funny. The Kray name had a habit of appearing in the newspapers, and Charlie didn't want any attention drawn to it when they went back through UK customs the following day.

'Nothing there,' he said with relief, stuffing the newspaper into one of his raincoat pockets. 'Next stop, Pigalle.'

In fact, Pigalle came several stops later. First they visited Harry's Bar, a favourite with Americans since the days when Scott Fitzgerald and Ernest Hemingway had drunk there. Then they went on to the Moulin Rouge, or was it the Folies Bergère? It was a long and arduous evening, so it was hardly surprising that the details became a bit blurred.

In the early hours of the morning, the three Englishmen finally said goodbye to their new Mafia pals. All were by now the very best of friends. It had been a very enjoyable night out, but now it was time for a well-earned rest.

Just before Charlie Kray got into bed, he removed the plastic bag containing the stolen bonds from behind the wardrobe and put it under his pillow. There would be no chance of losing them now, he thought sleepily. His head was going to be firmly on that pillow for the rest of the night and most of the coming morning. He would dream about the new bonds of friendship that were now becoming well established between the Mafia in New York and the Krays in London. This is one time, he thought, that sleeping on the job will pay off.

As he slept, Charlie smiled, and he was still smiling when he woke up the following morning. A quick right hook under his pillow told him that the bearer bonds were safe. A slower glance at the clock told him that it was nearly 10 a.m.

Their flight back to London didn't leave Orly until five that afternoon, so there was plenty of time. Charlie was pleased that he had remembered to put the 'Do Not Disturb' sign on his door before he went to bed. He had a leisurely bath and shave. Neither of the others had called his room, so he assumed they were still asleep.

By the time he was dressed it was nearly eleven. He picked up the phone. 'Bonjour, Leslie.'

Leslie Payne yawned. 'Morning, old boy. What are you up to?'

'I'm ready for some breakfast. How about you?'

'I'll be ready in about fifteen minutes. I've just spoken to Freddie, and we'll see you downstairs in the restaurant.'

'OK.' Charlie put the phone down and considered what to do next. He could phone his brothers and let them know how he'd got on, but he decided not to. Eyeing the Macy's bag sticking out from under his pillow, he decided instead that it was time to check the bonds. He had not so much as glanced at them yet, so he had no idea of their value.

The bonds were well wrapped in crisp brown paper. Charlie took his time opening the package, knowing that he would have to re-seal it when he had finished. Then he carefully pulled out the contents. He looked at the first of the bonds. Very satisfactory, he thought. The second was also for a tidy sum, and so was the third. But how much was it altogether? Taking out his pen, Charlie wrote down the value of each bond, then he quickly added up the figures.

The total made him sit back with a startled expression on his face. Had he got his sums wrong? He counted again, and there was no mistake. Ron and Reg would be very pleased with the results of their brother's errand — he had in front of him negotiable bearer bonds to the value of $250,000. And to think he had left them behind the wardrobe the previous night.

Charlie took his luggage downstairs with him. He had stowed the bonds away in his black pilot's bag, feeling safer if he carried them with him.

The hotel restaurant was completely empty when he entered. It was well past breakfast time and still too early for lunch. However, a waiter soon appeared and brought him a lunch menu, together with a pot of hot coffee. It wasn't long before Charlie was joined by Leslie Payne and Freddie Gore, who also had their luggage with them.

As they ordered their meal, it soon became obvious that while Charlie and Leslie were in good humour, Freddie was not. He was very quiet; it didn't look as if he had slept very well. Charlie knew that sooner or later Freddie would ask about the bonds, but he was not about to offer any information himself. Freddie would have to sweat until he had plucked up enough courage to raise the subject.

Their omelettes and salads arrived and Charlie and Leslie ate with relish. When they had finished, Freddie at last raised the subject which had been on his mind for so long.

'Have you had a look at the bonds, Charlie?' he muttered, staring at his plate.

'Yes I have,' Charlie replied in an off-hand manner. He beckoned to the waiter. 'Could we have some more coffee, please?'

Then he looked round the restaurant, which was now filling up with a well-dressed clientele. 'I wonder if Georges Charpentier has ever eaten here,' he mused, as if he were completely ignorant of the implications of Freddie's question. 'Did I tell you that I met him in London not long ago?'

Freddie did not want to hear about Charlie's encounter with the famous French boxer. 'Charlie,' he said in an irritated tone. 'How much are they worth?'

Charlie did not answer immediately. Then, with a hint

of a smile, he said, 'In my bag I have bonds to the value of $250,000.'

'Marvellous.' Leslie Payne was obviously delighted with the news.

But there was no reaction from Freddie Gore. He did not say how pleased he was to be taking $250,000 worth of stolen bonds back to England. Instead he went very quiet, staring into his coffee cup.

'Are you all right, Freddie?' asked Charlie at last.

There was a short pause. 'I didn't think it would be that much, Charlie,' the accountant said at last. He had gone very pale.

'Ron and Reg will be pleased,' said Leslie Payne, trying to cheer him up. 'Anyway, it'll all be over soon.'

Leslie felt very privileged to think that he was part of such a big operation. With so much cash floating around, surely some of it would stick to his fingers. And he was even happier to know that he wouldn't be the one who had to smuggle the bonds back into England.

'It's after one,' said Charlie suddenly. 'Let's do some sightseeing on the way back to Orly.'

'Good idea,' said Leslie. 'What about the hotel bill?'

'I'll settle that; you two go and get a cab. And try to get a driver who speaks English.'

Charlie was sorry to leave the luxury of the Claridge Hotel, but it was time to get back to England now. Their cab headed towards the Seine and the Eiffel Tower. Charlie and Leslie were in high spirits, but Freddie had the look of a man about to go to the guillotine. His body may have been in the cab, but his mind was certainly not.

'Look,' said Charlie, 'there's the Eiffel Tower across the river.' Freddie ignored him.

The cab driver took them over the Pont d'Iéna and

stopped for a minute or two by the Eiffel Tower. Then he drove them along the south bank of the Seine, pointing out well-known landmarks along the way, towards the Boulevard Périphérique and the turn-off for Orly Airport. It was a pleasant journey on a pleasant day. The whole trip had gone so well up to this point.

Once they were on the road to Orly, Charlie decided that it was time to give Freddie the bonds. He opened his bag and took them out.

'Here you are, Freddie. Keep them safe.'

Freddie stared at the package, but made no move to take it. He was frozen with fright.

'Come on,' Charlie urged. 'This is what you're here for.'

Still Freddie did not move.

'It was all agreed, old boy,' said Leslie Payne. 'There's no problem — it'll be a piece of cake.'

'If it's so easy, then you do it.' Freddie forced the words from his mouth.

Charlie was getting angry. 'We all agreed back home that you would take the bonds.' He raised his voice, 'So take the bloody things!'

'I can't do it,' whispered Freddie. 'I can't, I can't.'

Charlie looked at Leslie. 'Then you'll have to do it.'

'I'm not doing it,' pleaded Leslie. 'That wasn't the agreement.'

Charlie looked at his companions in disbelief. 'You've got no bottle,' he said dispassionately. 'Neither of you. I'll do it myself.' He put the bonds back in his bag.

No one spoke during the rest of the trip to Orly. Charlie sat by himself in the transit lounge as they waited for their flight to Heathrow. He didn't feel like talking; instead he bought a newspaper and sat quietly reading it.

Leslie Payne and Freddie Gore sat together; they were also very quiet, though they did exchange a few words.

The British European Airways flight back to London was uneventful. But once the aircraft was safely on the tarmac at Heathrow, Charlie faced the problem of getting the bonds through UK customs. He was still disgusted at the actions of his two associates, but he decided that they had better go through customs as a group. He would be less conspicuous that way.

The three men entered the customs hall and walked slowly but resolutely past the desk. Don't look at the officers, thought Charlie. Just look straight ahead.

'Anything to declare, sir?' said one of the customs men.

'Do you mean me?' asked Leslie Payne.

'No, the other gentleman.'

Freddie Gore stepped forward.

'No,' said the customs man again. 'The other gentleman.'

Reluctantly, Charlie Kray approached the desk. 'It's always the same,' he said. 'Why do you always pick on me?'

The customs officer smiled. 'Have you anything to declare, sir?'

'Nothing,' said Charlie firmly.

'And what do you have in the bag?'

'Just paperwork,' replied Charlie. 'Here, have a look.' He put his pilot's bag on to the desk in front of the customs man and opened it wide.

'Help yourself.' He turned away, as if unconcerned.

'No cigarettes, sir?' The uniformed man peered into the bag.

'I didn't bother,' said Charlie, turning to face him again. They looked each other in the eyes, and to Charlie that stare lasted an eternity.

'I don't think we want any of your paperwork, sir,' said the officer at last. 'Have a safe journey home.'

'Thank you, I will.' Charlie quickly closed the bag, before he could change his mind, then hurried on to join the others. They had gone on when he was stopped and were both waiting for him outside. If Charlie had been caught, they were not going to be caught with him.

As Charlie approached, they watched him closely.

'What happened?' asked Leslie Payne.

'Nothing,' snapped Charlie, walking past them.

Leslie Payne was laughing, and even Freddie Gore was able to raise a smile. But Charlie was furious with the pair of them.

'I'm going home,' he said. 'Alone!' And with that he got into a taxi and left them to it. It was a long trip back to his home in Poplar, but a long trip alone was better than one with those two. On the way he did some hard thinking. He decided that any future trips to collect bonds would be done without the assistance of any so-called friends or members of the firm.

When he arrived home, Charlie took his flight bag up to his bedroom and removed the bonds in their plastic carrier. He was not going out that evening — he wanted a peaceful night at home — but even so he couldn't just leave the bonds lying about the house. He thought about the various hiding places available to him.

They're in a plastic bag, he said to himself, so they won't get wet. 'That's it. I've got it!' he exclaimed out loud.

He took the carrier into the bathroom and knelt down by the bath. At the tap end he had had a panel built in to the side of the bath surround. It could easily be levered off using a screwdriver or coin, and he proceeded to remove it. Then he pushed the plastic bag inside and under the bath itself. It was a good hiding place, if a little damp, but the bonds wouldn't be there for very long.

Charlie slept well that night, secure in the knowledge that he had done his job.

He woke to the insistent sound of the telephone bell. He waited for a while to see if anyone else would answer, then sleepily lifted the receiver. 'Hello.'

'Hi, Charlie, it's Artie here,' came the voice over the wire. 'That is you, Charlie, isn't it?'

'Yes, it's me. Who is that again?'

'It's Artie. The guy you met in Paris.'

'How are you? All right?'

'I'm fine,' said the American, 'but there's a little problem with the package I gave you. I'm afraid you'll have to get rid of them — they're just too hot.'

'What do you mean, get rid of them?' Charlie was wide awake now. 'You don't mean destroy them, do you?'

'I know, I know,' came the dejected reply, 'but we daren't risk our source of supply. There's a lot more to come, so we'll make it up to you. But for now, just get rid of them somehow. Can you do that for me?'

'I'll take care of it,' said Charlie Kray gloomily. As he hung up the receiver, he felt despondent. After all that I've been through, he thought. But he knew that Artie was right. If there was likely to be trouble, it was better to ditch these bonds and continue the business in safety rather than risk being exposed.

It didn't take long to shave, shower and dress. He knew that Artie wouldn't have phoned him if there weren't serious problems, so it was obvious that the bonds had to be disposed of immediately. He retrieved the package of bonds from under the bath, grabbed his coat, and made his way out to his car. On the way he picked up a can of petrol and some old newspapers, which he put in a cardboard box in the boot. Then he drove to 178 Vallance Road.

'Your tea's cold, Charlie,' called Violet from the kitchen. 'I'll make you a fresh one.'

'OK, mum, I'm finished now.'

Charlie turned and walked back into the house. That was it. The bonds had gone forever. But as Artie had said, there would be plenty more where they came from.

And Artie was as good as his word. The stolen bonds continued to flow from the US Mafia in New York to the Krays in London. It was a highly successful operation. For now, though, Charlie couldn't help being depressed at the thought of all that money going up in smoke.

'Don't forget your petrol can,' said his mother, as he made his way to the front door.

'I'll pick it up tomorrow,' said Charlie dejectedly.

'But you might need it tonight,' Violet persisted.

'Why?' Charlie asked. He watched the smile on his mother's face broaden.

'Because it's November the fifth, Charlie,' she laughed. 'It's bonfire night!'

11

HE DID IT HIS WAY

THE SHOW HAD BEEN A TREMENDOUS SUCCESS and Sinatra's performance was supreme. It was everything the Kray family had expected and more. The Apollo Theatre on Wilton Road, London SW1, had seen one of its best nights ever — a complete sell-out. As Frank Sinatra left the stage, the whole audience was standing up to applaud him. He certainly hadn't let his numerous British fans down.

'Oh, Reg,' sighed Violet Kray, settling back into her seat. 'This really has been a night to remember.'

'It hasn't ended yet, Mum,' said her son. 'We've been invited to a party after the show — at Frank's suite in the Mayfair Hotel.'

Violet heard what he was saying, but at first she didn't fully understand what the words meant. Ron had told her that she was in for a treat, but she hadn't expected anything like this. Would she really be meeting Frank Sinatra in his own hotel suite that very same evening? It was all too much for her to take in. Perhaps it was just a dream, but if so she hoped very much it would continue.

'We have to stay seated for a while, Ron,' said Reg to his brother.

Ron Kray slowly lowered himself into his comfortable front-row seat again. He always enjoyed a special occasion, and this one was very special indeed. He would be meeting a man who was a legend in his own lifetime, and Frank Sinatra would have the pleasure of meeting Ron Kray, a man who had his own claims to fame. It would in Ron's eyes be a very significant meeting indeed, and one he expected to remember for the rest of his life.

The Krays' seats that evening were the best in the house, and why not? They were the leaders of London's underworld, with contacts throughout the British criminal fraternity. They were also good friends of the US Mafia and known on both sides of the Atlantic as important and influential 'businessmen'. When the top Mafia bosses came over to London, they always paid the Krays a courtesy visit at least. Yes, the Krays had reached the top in their society, and this evening they were all gathered to pay their respects to a man who had also established himself as the best in his own chosen sphere. The fact that they had mutual friends just made things a little easier.

'What a wonderful show,' said Charlie Kray to his father, lighting up a cigarette.

'We've had a lovely time,' said old man Charlie. 'Just look at your mother — she's really got stars in her eyes.'

Violet was sitting quietly, trying to stay calm in this moment of ecstasy.

'Look,' said Reg to Ron. 'There's Eddie!'

Approaching them was the huge, powerfully built figure of Eddie Pucci, Frank Sinatra's bodyguard. Prior to taking up a career in showbusiness, Eddie had been an American football star. He knew everyone who was anyone in the US entertainment world, and everyone knew Eddie. It was difficult not to notice him and the nineteen stone he carried around wherever he went.

'Eddie,' said Reg. 'It's good to see you.'

'I'd like a word, Reg,' said Eddie, beckoning him to one side. Reg rose from his seat and joined him, quickly followed by Ron and Charlie. The brothers could tell from Eddie's expression that something was most definitely wrong.

'What is it?' said Reg.

'I'm afraid the party is cancelled.' The amiable giant's manner was deadly serious — a far cry from his normal jovial self. 'We've just had some bad news and we're taking the first flight home.' He paused, then added, 'It looks as though Frank Junior has been kidnapped again!'

Kidnapping, unfortunately, was nothing new to Frank Sinatra. He had always lived with the fear that sooner or later someone would try to take his son from him and three years earlier, back in 1963, his fears had become a reality. On 8 December, Frank Sinatra Junior was taken at gunpoint from the lodge where he was staying at Lake Tahoe, on the California-Nevada boundary. He had been appearing at the Harrahs Casino with the Tommy

Dorsey Band, something his father had also done on many occasions. He was only nineteen years old.

The following day the FBI and the local sheriff's department arrested six men in connection with the kidnapping. They were taken from a cabin some twenty miles from where Frank Junior had been kidnapped. A friend of Frank Junior's had been staying with him at the lodge, and had been left bound and gagged by the kidnappers. However, he was unable to identify any of the six men as his assailants, and the police were forced to let them go free.

No ransom demand had been received, and the police were becoming increasingly concerned for Frank Junior's safety. On FBI advice, Frank Sinatra was waiting in a hotel in Reno, Nevada. The newspapers publicized this fact, following police instructions, in the hope that the kidnappers would contact him there.

Then, on 11 December, Frank Junior was released in Los Angeles. He was found in the early hours of the morning, walking along a road in the Bel-Air district of Hollywood, a blindfold still dangling round his neck. The local police took him to his mother's home, which was nearby.

Frank Sinatra issued a statement saying that he had received a phone call the previous evening demanding $240,000 for his son's release. After he had collected the money — all in used notes of small denominations — from several banks, he had received another call giving the time and place for the drop. The ransom had been left, as arranged, in a piece of luggage near the US Veterans' Hospital.

When Sinatra was questioned as to whether any deal had been made with the kidnappers about what would happen afterwards, he replied, 'They're on their own now.' No immunity from prosecution had been promised, he confirmed. He added that he thought the gang could have had as many as nine members. An 'associate' of Sinatra's predicted that the kidnappers would be caught within 24 hours.

It is still not known whether any pressure for Frank Junior's return was exerted by any of Sinatra's Mob pals. It seems quite probable that Sam Giancana, the Chicago mafia boss, had been contacted for help, as he ran Tinseltown as far as Mob business was concerned and was a close personal friend of Sinatra's. The two had worked together on the John F. Kennedy presidential campaign, which benefited greatly from Sam Giancana's money and Frank Sinatra's well-organized fundraising activities with his celebrity pals.

Another man Sinatra might have called on was his old Mafia pal from the Sands Hotel in Las Vegas, Meyer Lansky.

Back in the early fifties, Frank Sinatra had been joint owner of the Sands with Lansky, Lansky's fellow New York Mob boss Frank Costello, and his old Hollywood pal George Raft.

On 15 December, just three days after Sinatra's 46th birthday celebrations, he was able to celebrate the safe return of most of the ransom money, as well as of his son. Three men had been arrested the previous evening, and all but $6145 of the money had been found. The three — John William Irwin, a 42-year-old house painter; Barry Keenan, a 23-year-old unemployed son of a local stockbroker; and John Clyde Amsler, also 23 and a former boxer, were all charged with kidnapping and faced possible life sentences.

So 1963 ended on a good note for Sinatra after all,

but the early sixties had been a turbulent time for him and his Mob associates. When the celebrations of Jack Kennedy's presidential election victory were over, Sinatra was given the cold shoulder by the Kennedy clan. It is not difficult to understand why this should have happened, but it was a great blow to the singer after all his efforts on Jack Kennedy's behalf.

The trouble was that Sinatra knew too much about the Kennedys. He knew all about their womanising from pre-election parties held throughout California and Nevada, including two he had arranged himself at the Sands Hotel in Las Vegas in January and February of 1960, well before his old pal Sam Giancana became directly involved in the election campaign. He knew all about the deal made between Joe Kennedy and Sam Giancana, his close friend, and even at one time acted as go-between, passing information and money to the Chicago Outfit. And he knew why Marilyn Monroe had to be silenced.

Just a few weeks before her death on August 4th 1962, Marilyn was staying with Sinatra at his house in Palm Springs. Sinatra knew of the danger she was in and was even considering marrying her to keep her from the bloodied hands of his old pal Giancana. But Marilyn never suspected the plot and a short time after being Sinatra's house guest, she was found dead at her home, apparently having popped too many of her favourite pills. Sinatra knew the truth about her death, but kept it quiet in the hope that he could renew his friendship with JFK — it never happened.

Back in 1960 Sam Giancana had attended most of the pre-election parties himself, just to make sure the

Kennedys had a good time. But he also made sure that tape recordings were made of bedroom conversations and events: the Chicago capo liked to keep track of what was going on. During this time, Sinatra was a great favourite of the Kennedys. One of his Hollywood pals, Peter Lawford, even married into the Kennedy family itself. The family was known as the Kennedy Clan, but Sinatra too had his own 'clan' including his close friends Dean Martin and Sammy Davis Junior. This connection to the Chicago Outfit through Sinatra became very handy for Sammy Davis Junior in particular, who was continually in debt due to his constant, addictive gambling, but Giancana treated him kindly since he was a good friend of a good friend. Undoubtedly the Kennedys needed Frank Sinatra more than he needed them — all the hard work he put in on Jack's behalf was because he sincerely believed that he would make a good President.

The rift between Sinatra and the Kennedys came after the election. Sam Giancana had met Joe Kennedy in the September of 1960 at the Chicago Courthouse, and arrangements were made between the two men, behind closed doors, to get Jack elected to President. Joe would have made a pact with the devil to secure Jack's victory in the presidential elections, but the devil was unavailable so instead he made a deal with the Chicago Mafia capo. He promised Sam Giancana a foot in the door at the White House if he would mobilize his forces to help with Jack's presidential campaign, and it was the votes gathered throughout the mid west that secured victory — all supplied by the labour unions, ordered to do so by Murray 'The Camel' Humphries, on behalf of Sam Giancana.

But once Jack Kennedy was successfully installed in

the White House, the Mafia connection became something of an embarrassment. Bobby Kennedy, Jack's younger brother, became Attorney General with a strict brief to crack down on organised crime — and especially the Chicago Outfit. This he did with a vengeance, especially after Jack was killed in Dallas, Texas, on 22nd November 1963. This is the reason why the Mob were forced to expand their operations into other territories, such as the United Kingdom. Sam Giancana, however, was too powerful — even the Attorney General could not get rid of him. Giancana even had the audacity to visit the President in the White House in early 1963, to try to enforce the deal he thought he had made in 1960.

Sinatra too, did all he could to patch up the bad feelings between Chicago and Washington, DC, even acting — once again — as a go-between. But Giancana held on to the deal made with Joe Kennedy and nothing could persuade him otherwise. Soon Sam Giancana would be plotting revenge.

Frank Sinatra was one of the best friends that Jack Kennedy ever had, only Jack didn't appreciate it. He believed in the man, totally. Even so, after the election campaign his friendship with Giancana told against him. In the summer of 1962 he was banned from the White House and Jack Kennedy cancelled a planned stay at Sinatra's Palm Springs home. The excuse given referred to an FBI report on Sinatra's Mob connections — a report which had been instigated by Bobby Kennedy himself.

After the 1963 kidnapping, Frank Sinatra tightened security around his son. In 1965, Frank Junior visited England for a series of concerts, and with him came big

Eddie Pucci. Eddie already knew Ron and Reg Kray — he had acted as Angelo Bruno's bodyguard when the Philadelphia Mafia capo visited England — and he asked them to supply 24-hour protection for Frank Junior. He knew protection was something the Krays were very good at.

Angelo Bruno had first come over to England by boat, disguised as an officer on a cargo ship. He had no difficulties landing at Southampton and getting admitted to the UK, something that amazed him at the time. Bruno met the Krays at the Park Lane Hilton — the meeting had been arranged by Pucci. After the meeting, Bruno returned to New York by a direct flight from Heathrow. On future visits to the UK, he was always to arrive at Heathrow travelling under his own name and with his own passport.

The Krays looked after Sinatra's son very well. In fact they did such a good job that Eddie began asking them to look after other American entertainers when they visited the UK. Soon the Krays were mixing with some of the top names in international showbusiness. And they were even being paid for doing it.

When Eddie asked Ron and Reg to look after a visiting celebrity they would put on their best suits, turn on the charm, and have a whale of a time. Ron Kray, in particular, loved meeting the visiting stars: artists such as Judy Garland, Billy Daniels, Tony Bennett and Johnny Ray.

On one occasion, Eddie Pucci phoned Ron from New York and asked him to look after the wife of Nat King Cole, who was coming to London to do some shopping for a few days. Her husband wasn't well enough to accompany her, so Eddie asked Ron to see that she was well looked after. Ron spent two days showing her the pay-sights of London and accompanying her on shopping trips to Harrods and other top London stores. He didn't think of it as a chore — it was a privilege, and he loved every minute of it.

When the American visitors returned home they were full of praise for their English protectors and the way they carried out their assignments. The Krays were pleased — they were becoming celebrities in their own right. The Mafia were also pleased — they could now guarantee their celebrity friends complete protection when in the UK.

The Mafia 'owned' many film stars and entertainers. This 'ownership' came about in different ways. Sometimes it was because they were owed money in the form of a loan or a gambling or other debt. Sometimes the artists had Mafia bodyguards forced upon them. Sometimes the Hollywood unions, all controlled by the Mob, made demands on the stars.

Most film stars, entertainers and television celebrities are insecure people by nature. This makes them easy prey for the Mafia. There were not many actors whom the Mafia genuinely respected — most were only tolerated because of the income they could inject into Mob-controlled business activities. The exception was Frank Sinatra, who was respected by all the top Mafia bosses for both his wealth and his personality. The only other Hollywood star who even approached Sinatra's status was his old friend George Raft.

Sinatra had been known to have Mafia connections for many years, long before the Sicilian-American Eddie Pucci joined him in 1960. But in Tinseltown it is difficult not to have some kind of connection with organized crime. After all, the Mob run the unions, they run the gambling rackets, and they even run some of the Hollywood studios. Anyway, Sinatra had never hidden his involvement, together with George Raft, in the Sands Hotel in Las Vegas. The city had been established by Bugsy Siegal on behalf of Meyer Lansky of New York, and Lansky himself was a partner in the Sands, so Sinatra's connections were the very best.

The Krays left the Apollo Theatre extremely disappointed at not having met Frank Sinatra in person. Violet was especially sad. They learned afterwards from Eddie Pucci that the second kidnapping of Frank Junior was a false alarm — just a prank by a group of college kids. Ron Kray never got to see Sinatra again, but Reg did encounter him briefly in early 1967 at George Raft's Colony and Sporting Club in Berkeley Square. However, on that occasion Sinatra was exhausted by a gruelling touring schedule, and there was no opportunity for a proper meeting. When Sinatra next came to London in the spring of 1968, the Kray brothers were already behind bars awaiting trial.

On 5 May 1967, Frank Sinatra became chairman of the American-Italian Anti-Defamation League — a society which worked to remove discrimination against Americans of Italian descent. One of the first things he did was write to authors and film and television writers asking them to cut down references to the 'mafia' or 'cosa nostra'. His action was perfectly legal and above board, but to some writers, especially those in Hollywood, the letter could have been construed as a threat.

When Paul Anka appeared on the Des O'Connor show on UK television in 1992, he was asked about the background of the best-known song he has ever written — 'My Way'. 'When Sinatra asks you to write a song for him, you write a song for him,' said Anka. Had he felt privileged by Sinatra's request, Des O'Connor asked him. Anka's reply was unexpected. 'Well, I didn't want to wake up with a horse's head beside me in my bed,' he said.

This, of course, was a reference to the famous scene in Francis Ford Coppola's first Godfather film where a Hollywood producer wakes up one morning to find the head of his favourite racehorse in his bed. The producer has turned down the young Italian-American actor Johnny Fontane for an important movie role, and this is the Mafia's way of telling him to think again.

When the film came out it was widely speculated that the character of Johnny Fontane was based on Frank Sinatra. In the film, Johnny Fontane got the movie role that he so desperately wanted. In real life, Frank Sinatra received an Oscar in 1953 for his part in the film, From Here to Eternity. Any similarity, of course, is pure speculation.

Ron and Reg Kray have often talked about the stars they met through Eddie Pucci in the mid-sixties, but, perhaps because of their sporting background, it is the boxers they remember even better. One of them was the great heavyweight, Rocky Marciano, who visited London with Angelo Bruno, the Philadelphia Mafia capo. The UK authorities were informed that Bruno was in London to look after Rocky Marciano's business interests, but in reality it was Marciano who had come to look after Bruno, as his bodyguard. Rocky Marciano became a good friend to the Krays, and he travelled all over the country with them when they were looking after the singer, Johnny Ray.

Then there was Sonny Liston, whom Reg once drove back to central London from the Cambridge Rooms, a club the Krays owned in Kingston-on-Thames. It was early in the morning, and Reg had drunk a huge amount during the night. His driving was never good at the best of times, and this particular trip was just an alcoholic blur to him. Sonny Liston must have wished he felt the same, because he couldn't get out of the car fast enough. 'I'd rather fight anyone than get in there again!' he remarked, once he was safely on two feet again. Part of the trouble was that although Reg was shortsighted, he wouldn't wear spectacles. Even when he wasn't drunk, his passengers had a rough time.

The boxer who made the greatest impression on Ron, Reg and Charlie Kray was the man whom many boxing fans still regard as the greatest heavyweight champion of all time: Joe Louis. Once again it was Eddie Pucci who arranged for Joe Louis to visit London. Louis had fallen on hard times and Eddie asked the Kray twins to see if they could fix up a little business for the ex-champion in England. Through their contacts, the Krays set up some promotional events throughout the UK for the great boxer. Joe Louis was well paid for his participation and the events were a great success. Charlie Kray once said of Joe Louis: 'He was so big. Everything about him was immense. He had big hands, big feet, everything was big!'

Though the giant Joe Louis made a big impression on the Krays, none of the celebrities they met, in boxing or showbusiness, meant more to them than Judy Garland. Naturally, it was Eddie Pucci who introduced them to the star. Judy Garland was a frequent visitor to London throughout the 1960s, and Ron and Reg Kray had the pleasure of being in her company on many occasions.

There were always parties when Judy was in town — sometimes at a popular West End nightclub, sometimes at an East End public house, sometimes in private houses. Wherever she went, Judy Garland was welcome, and it was often Reg Kray who accompanied her.

Reg took Judy wherever she wanted to go. Once he even took her to a birthday party held in a small terraced house near his old home at Vallance Road, Bethnal Green. Everyone knew in advance that Judy Garland would be there — it was a treat for the whole neighbourhood. Reg had made everyone promise that they would treat her like any other friend or neighbour, and that they would definitely not ask her to sing — it was to be a relaxing evening for Judy after a strenuous performance. The occasion was a huge success — everyone loved Judy and she loved her evening out in London's East End.

On one occasion, Reg Kray and his wife Frances visited Judy backstage after a London concert, along with a number of other friends. Judy was so pleased to see Reg that she forced her way through the throng and put her arms round him. Reg was embarrassed; he didn't want to make his wife jealous. He needn't have worried, because Frances understood, but the scene shows how highly Judy regarded him. When Frances committed suicide at the age of 23, Judy Garland was one of the first to offer sympathy. She even tried to persuade Reg to go away for a while to help get over his loss, offering him her home in Hawaii to use at any time.

Reg Kray still recalls one particular evening in the mid-sixties when he took Judy to the Establishment Club in London's West End. Here they met a group of youngsters who were starting to make a big name for themselves in the music business. They thought it was just fabulous to meet Judy Garland, and Judy was just as pleased to meet John, Paul, George and Ringo otherwise known as the Beatles.

All three Kray brothers carried very fond memories of the Hollywood star, Judy Garland. 'I believe she truly loved Reg,' said Charlie Kray recently. 'I could see it in her eyes. You know,' he added, 'Reggie could have married Judy Garland!'

In 1972, Eddie Pucci, the jovial giant who introduced the Krays to Judy Garland and so many other stars, was shot and killed while he was playing golf in Chicago, Sam Giancana's home town. He wasn't robbed or mugged it was another straightforward Mob killing. The Krays were all saddened by his death, since Eddie had been a real friend to them and a key player in the celebrity game. But happenings like this are never really unexpected where the Mafia are concerned. Angelo Bruno, too, was shot and killed in his car in his home town of Philadelphia — there was no Eddie Pucci around to protect him any more, and with their deaths an era had come to an end.

Frank Sinatra is now dead and residing somewhere in 'Tinseltown Heaven' along with his old buddies Dean Martin and Sammy Davis Jnr. They all perished due to the overindulgence and extravagant lifestyle of their days and nights full of wine, women and song — but what a way to go! Sinatra was, and always will be, the ultimate

American entertainer. Though everyone has heard about his involvement with the Mafia, no one seems to mind any more.

12

THE GEORGE RAFT STORY

'HI THERE, CHARLIE,' said George Raft, holding out his
hand. Charlie Kray walked swiftly towards him across the
plush red carpet of the George Raft Colony and Sporting
Club, one of London's most famous establishments.

'Hello, George,' said Charlie to the famous actor.
'You're looking well this evening.'

'It's just the good living, Charlie,' George Raft
replied. 'If you really want to know the secret of staying
young then I'll tell you. You must socialise! Forget
television, just get out and meet people.'

It was early September in 1966 and George Raft was
almost 71 years of age, but he didn't look it. He was
always immaculately dressed and beautifully groomed —

his suits and everything else that he wore were the best that money could buy. His smartness had always been one of his trademarks, even way back in his boxing days in his home town of New York.

George Raft's remark about socialising wasn't just a joke — as a man who had always been dedicated to the pursuit of a good life he meant what he said. 'Well we've got a good bunch in tonight, Charlie,' he continued. 'There's plenty of people to socialise with here.'

The two men stood together in the centre of the Colony Club, as it was usually called, and surveyed the guests enjoying their evening out in Mayfair. They were all well dressed. They had to be or they wouldn't have been allowed in to this prestigious gaming club. It was all a question of style — the club had it, the host had it in abundance, and the guests had to have it too.

George Raft's Colony Club had been a success from day one. It had quickly become the place to be seen, and the place to see all the well-known faces of the day. This evening was no exception. The gaming tables were crowded with customers with plenty of cash in their pockets — some were winning but most were losing. The losers, however, didn't seem to mind. They were probably used to it.

'Let's mingle, said George Raft.

'That's fine by me,' replied Charlie, 'but I could use a drink. Shall we start with the bar?'

The two men made their way through the double doors which divided the casino from the bar. Charlie ordered a gin and tonic, then leant on the gleaming mahogany of the bar while George Raft got busy saying hello to the evening's clientele. No matter where he went, George Raft always took time to talk to people. It didn't matter if they were rich or poor, known or unknown, they were all important to the ex-boxer, ex-dancer, ex-film star, and the Colony Club's guests were no exception. He just loved socialising.

On this particular evening, George Raft was chatting to some people sitting at an oval table near the bar. He turned and beckoned to Charlie Kray. 'Come and meet a friend of mine.'

Charlie picked up his drink, which he didn't bother paying for, and made his way over to the table. The man's face was already familiar to Charlie. 'Good to meet you,' he said, shaking hands with the American actor, Charles Bronson, whom he had seen in supporting roles in a number of films and television series.

Bronson said that he had only just arrived in London to work on a new film. 'He'll be a real star one day,' commented George Raft as they left the actor and made their way into the main casino.

In the casino, Raft stopped by one of the gaming tables. 'Here are some more Hollywood pals, Charlie. I'd like you to meet Telly Savalas, Donald Sutherland and Richard Jaekel.'

It was an impressive line-up. And Lee Marvin and Robert Ryan would be coming in to join them later, Raft said.

'What's going on, George?' asked Charlie. 'All these Americans — it's an invasion, just like the war.'

'MGM are making a war film here. What did you say it was called, Telly?'

Telly Savalas looked at Charlie Kray. 'It's based on a book,' he growled. 'I believe they're gonna call it The Dirty Dozen.'

DOING THE BUSINESS

George Raft was born on 27 September 1895 in New York. In his younger days he was a very good bantamweight boxer, but his interests gradually turned to the world of nightclubs, where he became recognized as a virtuoso dancer. He was very graceful on the dance floor and his slicked-back dark hair made him look like a suave Latin Romeo.

In his mid-twenties, at the height of his success as a dancer, he travelled the whole of the USA and even journeyed to London, where he made a number of well-received appearances during the early 1920s.

But it was the movie industry which brought him real fame. He made his debut as a bit player in 1929, and he was soon in demand in Hollywood both as a dancer and an actor. The highly successful gangster film, Scarface, with Paul Muni made a star of him in 1932. By the following year he was the highest paid actor in Hollywood.

George Raft could choose any parts he wanted, but unfortunately he was not always very good at selecting them. He turned down roles in both The Maltese Falcon and Casablanca, roles that made Humphrey Bogart a huge international star. He did make several highly rated movies such as Fritz Lang's You and Me and the film called Broadway, in which he played himself, but he failed to develop himself as an actor as he grew older, and his career began to decline.

By the 1950s, George Raft was ready to work anywhere. He spent a few years living in London and made some mainly second rate films there, but returned to his home in Hollywood when he realised he was not progressing in England either. From then on, he played only guest roles in movies that belonged to other people. George Raft also tried his hand at writing. In 1950 he

Top: The plush Kentucky Club was the Kray way of doing business. Pictured here with Charlie, third from right, are his three sons: Ron, far right, young Charlie, next to Ron, and Reg, second from left.

Bottom: Leslie Payne, far left, second row, hedged in by Ron, above, Reg, right, and a distant Charlie in profile, top right. Payne the Brain was the financial man behind many Kray enterprises. He became Payne the Pain in the end.

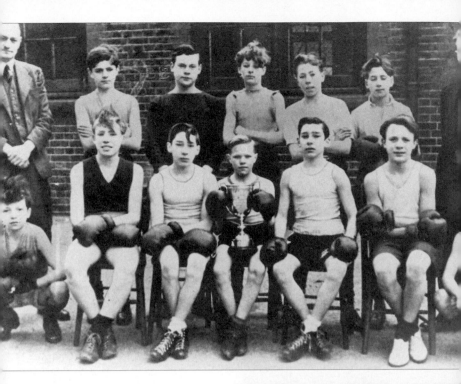

Top: The twins at school, seated either side of the trophy holder in the front row: Reg, left Ron, right. They'd been sparring since they were so small that they had to stand on a chair to reach the punchbag.

Right: Ron and Reg fought their first fight in public at a funfair boxing booth in the East End's Victoria Park.

Reg in the ring at his double R Club in 1957. With Ron inside, he'd gone into business alone with his brother Charlie. The gymnasium at the club was Reg's pride and joy, frequented by boxing legends such as Henry Cooper and Tommy McGovern.

Above: Never ones to miss a good photo opportunity, the twins host a prestigious première party for Joan Littlewood's film *Sparrows Can't Sing*, co-starring Barbara Windsor, James Booth and George Sewell.

Right: Eddie Pucci, Frank Sinatra's body-guard, holds hands with Shirley Bassey, surrounded by his friends, including the Krays. Through him they minded and met wealthy American showbiz personalities in London.

Above: During the 1960s Judy Garland was a frequent visitor to London, when Reg often accompanied her to celebrity parties.

Above: Ron, clubbing with heart-throb singer Johnny Ray, who shared his tastes.

Right: Reg and his adored wife, Frances, flank Barbara Windsor and the former world heavyweight champion, Rocky Marciano. Reg, unlike Ron, enjoyed the company of women, especially glamorous ones.

Above: Ron, centre, with Lord Boothby, left, and Leslie Holt, right, who had set up the meeting. Ron's association with Boothby caused a furore in the press and government circles during the summer of 1964.

Above: After his performance at the London Palladium, Billy Daniels croons at the Kentucky Club. The Kentucky, like all other Kray clubs, was always a star attraction.

Right: Frank Sinatra's son Frank junior, left, in deep discussion with Ron. In Tinseltown, organised crime and entertainment were strongly linked.

published his memoirs, in which he claimed to have associated with leading New York gangsters during the Prohibition era.

By now, George Raft was lending his name to business ventures organized by Meyer Lansky of New York. As mentioned in the previous chapter, he co-owned the Sands Hotel Casino in Las Vegas with Lansky, Frank Sinatra and Frank Costello, the New York Mafia boss; he also fronted the Riviera in Las Vegas, part-owned by Lansky, and in the late fifties and early sixties he ran a successful casino in Havana, Cuba, on Lansky's behalf.

The Mob treated him well, but it was good business to do so because George Raft was an excellent host and a very good front man. It is important to note that the casinos with which Raft was associated were always legally operated. Everything was above board and done entirely correctly; Raft enjoyed his job and took a real pride in his work.

The film of George Raft's life story came out in the early sixties, with Ray Danton putting in a good solid performance as Raft. The movie was entitled *Spin of a Coin* after the famous coin spinning sequence in *Scarface*. It was very successful in England, and the publicity it generated made Raft a natural choice when the subject of a host for the new Colony and Sporting Club came up in New York.

The club's founder was Meyer Lansky. He was a perfectionist when it came to casinos, and so he hired the best man in the business to set the club up — Dino Cellini. Cellini travelled the world opening casinos. To him the Colony Club was just one of many, but his approach was never less than professional — in this case he even set up a croupier school in Mayfair to ensure the standard of the club's gaming personnel.

The Colony Club was to be London's newest and best casino. The setting was perfect — Berkeley Square, right in the heart of Mayfair, one of the capital's prime residential areas. No expense was spared on fitting out the club's premises, and the latest equipment was shipped over from the USA. Even the bar and the chandeliers were American imports.

As refurbishment neared completion, Dino Cellini set about hiring staff for the club. He was already awaiting the arrival of George Raft, who had been appointed chairman of the management company and given the task of hosting this prestigious establishment. Raft was given an apartment in Mayfair and a chauffeured Rolls-Royce — the trappings of success required to maintain the position of a man who would have made a creditable board member of any city conglomerate.

Alfred Salkin, who had already worked with Dino Cellini in London, was taken on as manager of the Colony Club and two former Scotland Yard CID men were hired to handle house security. But that was not enough for the owners of the Colony Club. Their investors had to be absolutely certain that adequate protection was available at all times, which was where Eddie Pucci came in.

Knowing the London scene as he did, Frank Sinatra's bodyguard was the obvious man to ask for advice, and Eddie was only too happy to help his employer's old business associate, George Raft. When it came to protection for the club, he knew the best people in London — the Krays. So at the end of February 1966 he invited them to a meeting in Mayfair.

'Settle the cabby, will you, Charlie?' asked Reg Kray as he joined his twin under the red and white striped canopy of the new George Raft's Colony and Sporting Club.

Ron Kray looked in through the club's glass doors. 'Eddie should be here soon,' he said.

There were still a few days to go until the club's official opening, but the whole place was already lit up like a Christmas tree. There was even a great neon sign high above the canopy announcing to the world that they were ready for business — well, almost.

Charlie paid the cab driver and joined his brothers. 'Berkeley Square,' he sighed. 'Trust the Americans.'

Ron and Reg smiled. This was another good chance to get a foothold in London's West End and they didn't want to miss their opportunity. If the club meant money, the Krays were definitely interested.

'There's Eddie now,' said Reg.

The giant American was approaching the huge glass doors with a key in his hand. He unlocked them with a flourish.

'Welcome to George Raft's Colony and Sporting Club, gentlemen.'

The Krays stepped inside.

'Is George Raft here this evening?' asked Ron eagerly. He was keen to meet the famous actor.

'He's here, Ron,' said Eddie. 'Don't worry, you'll be meeting him soon.'

The brothers took off their coats and prepared to follow Eddie down the stairs which led to the casino.

'Just a few words before we go down,' said Eddie, pausing by the wrought-iron railing at the top of the stairway. 'The club is opening soon and we want your services. In return, you'll be getting a share of the takings.' He smiled at Reg, then looked across to Ron and Charlie. 'We want you with us. What do you say?'

No discussion was needed. The Krays knew it was an honour to be offered a share in an important club like this.

'That's fine by me,' said Ron impatiently, heading past Eddie Pucci and down the stairs. 'Now let's meet George Raft.'

The other three quickly followed him.

'What a lovely place you've got here, Eddie,' said Reg as they entered the casino. Everything was new: the red carpets, the soft velvet wallpaper, the shining paintwork, the flowered curtains. There were gold-framed paintings on the walls and highly polished gaming tables in the casino.

A tall, thin man approached them. 'Good evening, gentlemen, may I take your coats?'

Eddie introduced him as Alfred Salkin, the club manager. As they shook hands, Ron Kray was busy looking round the room. He still couldn't see George Raft. Reg and Charlie were also looking forward to meeting the American, whom they had seen in so many gangster films.

'Now let's go and see George.' Eddie led the way into the bar, which was furnished with fine dark wood tables and chairs. There, at a huge oval table on the left-hand side of the bar, sat the 70-year-old actor.

He rose as they approached. The Krays were all known for being well dressed and they were wearing their smartest suits for this important meeting, but George Raft's elegance put them to shame.

As Eddie introduced them, the three brothers shook

hands vehemently with the host of the Colony Club and made their well rehearsed little speeches. They were all impressed with him, especially Ron, and in 1966 it was no small achievement to impress the Krays.

'I believe you'll be working with us,' said George Raft. 'Is that right?'

The three Kray brothers looked at their giant American friend.

'That's right,' said Eddie Pucci, smiling. He knew the Krays well, and he knew that they would not refuse this offer. It would be a very lucrative deal indeed.

George Raft smiled too. 'Then let's have a drink to celebrate.'

Although the club was not officially open, it was full of people getting things ready for the opening night. It took a lot of people to run a club of this size — by its opening night there were 140 on the payroll. The Krays were made to feel very much at home and they stayed at the club until the early hours of the morning, enjoying the company of their new-found American friend and business partner, George Raft. This was really what they called doing the business.

When the club opened at the beginning of March, the Krays were there to keep an eye on things. The two CID men were mainly concerned with internal security problems like croupiers becoming involved in crooked dealings or barmen fiddling the drink sales. It was the Krays' job to deal with potential troublemakers and keep them off the premises. And the Krays knew a lot of troublemakers.

Business at the club was good from the start. The customers had a good time and membership soon rose to over 2500 people, most of whom became regular visitors. But then it was the best club and casino that Sicilian-American dollars could buy. George Raft became a popular figure in and around London, and was soon a close personal friend of the Kray brothers. They took him everywhere — Ron, in particular, loved to be seen with the famous actor.

When George Raft told the Krays of his early boxing days in New York, they decided to introduce him to the Repton Club, a boxing club in the East End. His visit was well-publicized. As it happened, Rocky Marciano was over in London on a visit with Angelo Bruno, and the Krays brought him along as well.

George Raft and Rocky Marciano caused quite a stir at the Repton Club. It was normally exciting enough for the club members when the Krays appeared, but these American celebrities had an air of glamour that not even they could achieve. The visitors took their time talking to everyone at the club, and Rocky Marciano was able to give the young boxers some good sound advice. Both men were great ambassadors for the sport of boxing.

When George Raft left the Repton Club, he asked the manager if the youngsters at the club would like a jukebox, so that they could train to music. He said that this was something he had always found beneficial.

The manager accepted his offer with gratitude, but he did not really expect anything to come of it. After all, a man like George Raft had far more important things to attend to. Just his presence — and that of Rocky Marciano — at the Repton Club that day had been far more than any of the youngsters could have hoped for. But a few days later the manager was opening up the club when a man in a chauffeur's uniform appeared and asked for his help. The puzzled manager followed him outside to a gleaming black limousine.

'Where do you want it?' asked the chauffeur, pointing to the boot. The manager looked at the huge machine which was sticking out of it. It was the latest Wurlitzer jukebox — George Raft had been as good as his word.

During his stay in London, George Raft became a familiar face at many clubs and restaurants throughout the capital. One evening, Reg Kray took him to the Starlight Club, one of the establishments run by the Krays. It was just off Oxford Street, on the edge of Soho. In those days it was quite a sleazy area, but the clientele didn't seem to mind — it gave the club some extra character, and it was a popular place for gambling money away.

When Reg Kray walked in with George Raft, an air of excitement filled the club. People were whispering and sneaking looks at the American film star. 'Reg,' said one delightful young lady, a good friend of Reg's, 'please introduce me to George Raft.'

She didn't seem to be interested in Reg himself any more.

'He's so cuddly,' she went on, 'I just want to put my arms around him and give him a hug.'

Why did this never happen to him, Reg wondered.

'All the women were crazy about him,' he said to Charlie later that evening. 'Next time, you can give it a try.'

This was just one of many similar incidents. Wherever he went, George Raft was always the centre of attention.

Taking George Raft around town was fun, but back at the Colony Club, the Krays had a job to do. Reg Kray vividly recalls the time when he was sitting in the Colony

Club bar having a quiet drink with the American film star, Robert Ryan. The actor had become a regular visitor to the club while he was in England filming *The Dirty Dozen*.

While they were chatting together, Don Ceville, the Canadian Mafia boss, came over to their table. He was in town to discuss business with AB Cooper, the American banker whom the Krays had taken on to dispose of the stolen bearer bonds.

The Montreal Mafia capo had obviously been drinking, and was looking for trouble. 'You're not as tough as you look,' he sneered at Robert Ryan. It was an awkward moment for Reg. He didn't want any trouble with Don Ceville — he was doing a lot of business with him. And he didn't want Robert Ryan annoyed — he was a good friend of George Raft's.

Fortunately, Ryan was equal to the situation. He did not say anything to the Mafia man, but simply stared him straight in the eye. It was the icy stare which he was famous for in his movies, and it had a startling effect in real life too. Reg Kray had never seen Don Ceville back down before — he always came over as a very tough character indeed — but faced with Ryan's stone cold eyes he slowly turned away and disappeared into the crowd. Ryan continued talking to Reg as if nothing had happened.

Throughout the summer and autumn of 1966, the whole Kray family would often gather at the Colony Club for a get together. Sometimes they would just have a drink at the bar and gamble a little at the tables. Sometimes Violet and old man Charlie would put on their best clothes and have dinner with George Raft. The actor always had a charming companion with him — he was never short of female company. Although he had separated from his wife, Grace, way back in the twenties, he had never actually divorced. But then, he had never felt the need to marry again.

As the club's reputation spread, more and more celebrities came there. One was the well known British actor, Richard Harris. He was also well known for his heavy drinking, which caused a number of problems. On one occasion he insulted both Ron and Reg Kray, and it was fortunate for him that the twins were in a benevolent mood at the time. They did, however, ask one of the firm to have a quiet word with him when he was sober — it was the last time they had any trouble with Richard Harris, and he later became a good friend of Charlie's.

Eddie Pucci, of course, visited the club regularly when he was over in London on business. On one occasion he brought Rocky Marciano and Frank Sinatra Junior with him. Frank Junior was performing at the Rainbow in the Seven Sisters Road, and Pucci and Marciano were both keeping an eye on him.

Those were good times at George Raft's Colony and Sporting Club. Everything ran smoothly, thanks to Alfred Salkin and his excellent staff, the customers were happy, and the club was becoming more and more popular. But as Charlie Kray has always said, when things are going well, something always comes along to spoil it. And in February 1967 something did spoil it — George Raft was refused permission to re-enter the UK.

On 24 February, the famous Hollywood actor returned from a short vacation at his Beverly Hills home. He had been chairman and host of the Colony Club since March 1966, having been granted a twelve-month stay in

Britain under part of the Alien Order of 1953. This states that an alien may be admitted to Britain for an extended stay if he is in a position to support himself. When the end of the allotted stay is reached, it is quite normal for permission to be granted for a further twelve months, as long as the person concerned has committed no crime and continues to be able to support himself.

George Raft had not committed any crime while in the UK, and with his luxury apartment in Mayfair and his chauffeured Rolls-Royce he could certainly show that he was in a position to support himself. Nevertheless, when he flew into Heathrow after his holiday, the immigration authorities refused to let him enter the UK.

The decision made headline news at the time, and surprised a great many people. George Raft's papers showed no irregularities, his passport had been renewed at the US Embassy in London shortly before Christmas, and he even had a work permit, obtained when he supplied the commentary on the Clay fight for American television. There had never been any complaints about the running of the Colony Club, as was verified by Eric Morley, the chairman of the 400-strong British Gaming Association.

Questions were even raised in Parliament. Gordon Bagier, the Labour MP for Sunderland, asked, 'How many American citizens have been made prohibited immigrants in the last twelve months?' The Home Secretary of the time, Roy Jenkins, could not supply a convincing answer. The Home Office had told George Raft that 'his continued presence in the UK would not be conducive to the public good,' but no justification for this was given. Joel Tarlo, Raft's solicitor, tried to argue his case, but the Home Office simply stated that its decision was final.

George Raft himself was astonished at the Home Secretary's action. Having returned to the United States, he said from his Beverly Hills home, 'I am at a loss to understand why I have been refused permission to return to Britain.' In this, he was not alone. He continued, 'I regard London as my second home. I pay taxes there and here too. I have no idea what this is all about.' And nor did most people in Britain.

It is still unclear what was behind the refusal to let George Raft re-enter the UK. If the police had any adverse information which they passed on to Roy Jenkins, no one has ever discovered what it was. The Colony Club was run completely legally, and in any case the authorities were not closing the club, simply stopping its host from entering the country.

Did the police think they could halt Mafia activities in the UK by getting rid of a 71-year-old American actor? If Raft's Mafia connections did tell against him, it is surprising that the authorities didn't stop Angelo Bruno, or Don Ceville, or Sam Giancana, or Dino Cellini. They didn't stop Tony 'Ducks' Corallo of the Lucchese family, either, when he came to London to discuss gambling arrangements with the Krays. And they certainly didn't stop Frank Sinatra, who possibly had better Mob connections than George Raft.

Perhaps it had something to do with the increasing media attention the Krays were getting — maybe someone didn't like the glamour being created around them by people like George Raft. But in this most secretive of societies, the truth will probably never be known. What is certain is that when the Colony Club closed in 1969, a new venture was soon started up by the same people. It was called the Victoria Sporting Club, and though there was no George Raft this time, the business was the same, and run in the same way. The police knew all about it, but Scotland Yard did not appear to mind and no action was taken.

Meanwhile, George Raft was clearly not wanted in the UK. He tried to enter the country again in 1971 and 1974, but without success. Back in the United States, however, he continued to make news. Shortly after being snubbed by the UK authorities, a huge birthday celebration was held for him in Las Vegas, a town where he had many friends. Many of the top US stars of the day were present at the party at Caesar's Palace, and tributes came pouring in from friends such as future President Ronald Reagan and his wife Nancy, and Frank Sinatra, his partner of years gone by.

The star had gone home, and there he stayed until his death on 24 November 1980. He died in a Los Angeles hospital after having been in a coma for a week. Though his life had to some degree reflected the tough guy roles he played on screen, his death came not from a bullet, but from leukaemia.

The Krays always remembered George Raft as a true gentleman and a good friend, who did not deserve his shabby treatment by the Home Office. Meanwhile, the Mafia continued to flourish, right under the noses of Scotland Yard and the Home Office. The only change that occurred was the arrival of the Sicilian Mafia and their world-wide drugs operation.

By the early seventies, the Caruana-Cuntrera syndicate had built up a network of companies in the UK, with English front men, most of which had been originally set up in the Virgin Islands and the Bahamas. These companies were busy trading in London, just like any of the city's legitimate businesses, The only difference was that they dealt in death, selling hard drugs all over the world.

For a long time, the police seemed to be doing nothing at all about them. The first case brought against the Sicilians in the UK was not until 1985, a good ten years after they had brought their heroin trafficking to the country. Even then, the police seemed to treat it as an isolated incident.

Now, in the 1990s, the UK has many top Sicilian Mafia bosses in its prisons, but the Mafia has always had a way of continuing its business. Just think of the amount of business carried out by Vito Genovese from his prison cell at Leavenworth. If the reader would like to know whether or not the Mafia are still operating in Britain, it might be worth asking Scotland Yard, or maybe the Home Office. Of course, there is no guarantee that you will get an answer — and if you do, it needn't necessarily be correct.

13

NEW YORK, NEW YORK

'I DON'T BELIEVE IT,' Reg Kray exclaimed.

'Well, I don't care,' said Ron Kray, not even bothering to look in the direction of his twin brother. He continued drinking his tea as Reg got up and walked towards Alan Cooper, who was sitting across the lounge in the flat in Braithwaite House, Shoreditch.

'Prove it,' said Reg, staring hard at the American banker.

'There's ab-absolutely no problem.' AB Cooper stuttered slightly as he replied. Reg was looking worryingly aggressive — Cooper knew that he had to choose his words well. 'I have friends in Paris who can arrange all the details for us,' he continued, trying to reassure the Kray twins and possibly himself as well. Though AB Cooper certainly had many friends and contacts around the world, it was less certain if they could be trusted.

Reg Kray didn't trust Cooper himself, and neither did brother Charlie. But Ron had listened intently to what Cooper had told him, and it all made perfect sense to him. After all, they had nothing to lose, so it wasn't worth considering the matter any more. Ron Kray had made up his mind.

'I think it's a good idea,' he said firmly.

Even Cooper was taken aback. There was silence for a moment, a silence which held a hint of menace.

'I have to go to the bank,' said Cooper, getting up and shutting his briefcase. 'I'll see you both later.' As he left the room he breathed a sigh of relief.

Ron and Reg said nothing until they heard the front door close behind him. Then Reg could contain himself no longer. 'I've never heard such bullshit! Don't tell me you really believed him.' Ron continued to drink his tea placidly. 'I've never trusted him. He's up to something. It's a bloody stupid idea.' There was much more that Reg wanted to say, but he was trying to contain himself. He knew that the worst thing to do was to lose control — he couldn't win an argument with Ron that way.

'How about another cup?' said Ron. He had asked Cooper to visit them at the flat to discuss Mafia business. He wanted a greater involvement with the New York families over clubs and gambling in particular. Cooper had become used to these early morning conferences since joining the twins in 1965 and had already been to this flat a number of times. Sometimes he bore good news, sometimes bad.

On this occasion he had said that if the mountain would not go to Mohammed, then Mohammed should go to the mountain. Ron Kray saw himself as Mohammed and the mountain he had to climb led to the Mafia in New York.

Reg handed the tea to his brother. 'That's the last.'

Ron was waiting for the argument to begin. It was common knowledge amongst the other members of the firm that if Ron said 'Yes' then Reg would most likely say 'No' and vice versa. But on this occasion Reg didn't want to clash with his brother, so he decided to change his tactics. Choosing his words with care, he said almost casually, 'I'd love to go, if only to see Read's face when he found out.'

Ron laughed.

'But it's impossible,' Reg went on. 'I can't see the American Embassy, even the Paris one, giving us visas to go to the States.'

Once again silence prevailed on the ninth floor of the council house block. Number 43, Braithwaite House, had been the home of Violet and Charlie Kray for only a short time, and they had not yet settled in properly. They were already missing their friends in Vallance Road, and they were also spending as much time as they could at the lodge of The Brooks, Ron's new country home in Suffolk. While they were away, they let Ron and Reg use the flat whenever they liked.

'If Cooper says he can do it, then he can,' remarked Ron calmly after a while. 'But if he can't, then we just come home.'

Reg sat down next to Ron. 'There's no way,' he said, speaking slowly and deliberately, 'that the embassy is going to give either of us a visa to America. Not with our prison records.'

Ron smiled at his brother. 'That's why we're going to Paris.'

'But they'll check up!' Reg tried to restrain his exasperation.

'So we don't go,' said Ron simply. 'But if they don't check, and we do get one, we can go and do the business.'

He smiled at Reg again. Reg knew that smile. It meant that he would not win the discussion this way. The time for diplomacy was over.

'You've got a prison record as long as your arm, you've got a dishonourable discharge from the army, and half of London know you walked into the Blind Beggar and shot Cornell!' he shouted.

'And the other half know you did for McVitie!' screamed Ron.

The brothers glared at each other in silence. They had suddenly realized that people in the other flats might be able to hear their words. Though they knew the telephone was tapped, the flat itself was not bugged — both the twins themselves and specialists from the firm had carried out enough searches to be sure of that. But they both knew that their private feelings should not have been aired at the tops of their voices.

Ron Kray got up and left the room without a word. Reg waited in the lounge and thought some more about Cooper's suggestion of the trip to America. He knew that if Ron was determined to go, he couldn't stop him. Maybe, just maybe, it was not such a bad idea after all, but they certainly should not go together. There was no knowing what might happen if both of the twins were out of the country at the same time. Someone might even take it into their heads to talk to Nipper Read of Scotland Yard about the murders. Or the Americans might lock them up, just as the Canadians had arrested Charlie in Montreal. That would really put the cat amongst the pigeons.

By the time Ron came back into the lounge with his raincoat over his arm, Reg had made up his mind. Ron could go to America if he wanted, but he would stay here and take care of business.

'I'm not going,' he said. 'I still think it's a trap.'

'Then you stay home,' said Ron as he walked to the front door. He stopped with his hand on the door handle and said in a voice that was loud but more or less controlled, 'But if I want to go to New York, then I'll fucking well go to New York!'

It was all agreed. Reg would stay in London and try and keep out of Nipper's reach, whilst maintaining the pressure on friends and associates and anyone else who needed a little encouragement to keep their mouths shut. Ron would go to Paris with AB Cooper and Ron's old school friend and long-firm companion, Dickie Morgan. Morgan was always fooling around and Ron enjoyed his light-hearted conversation.

If Cooper could get them the visas for the USA, then they would go directly from Paris to New York. If not, then they would return home to England after a few days in Paris.

Ron certainly knew the dangers of such a trip and was well aware that Cooper's arrangements and intentions might be suspect, but if he could use the American to secure passage to New York and access to the Mafia in their own back yard then he would do so. And he would call it a success, no matter what reason Cooper might have for getting him there, because he would have beaten the system.

AB Cooper had helped the Krays in their dealings with the stolen bearer bonds, but he had also tried to help them in other, more deadly, ways. Early in 1966 he had supplied the Krays with two Browning machine guns when the twins were stockpiling arms ready for a clash with the rival Richardson gang. The Richardsons were arrested and sent to prison before the gang war materialized, but the guns were the real thing and helped to establish Cooper's credentials with the Krays.

Only a few months prior to the proposed New York trip, Cooper had helped Ron Kray plan a killing at the Old Bailey law courts. Ron wanted to kill a man as a favour to another London gang, but the only place he could be sure of locating the intended victim was at the Old Bailey, where he was due to testify.

Faced with the problem, Cooper said he had an idea. A few days later he produced a smart briefcase with a hypodermic syringe full of cyanide concealed within the casing. He showed a delighted Ron Kray how it worked. Pulling a small lever made the needle protrude from the case, then the briefcase could be swung against the victim's leg, jabbing the needle into him and releasing the cyanide. Death would follow within minutes. Cooper even said that he had the right man for the job — a known killer named Elvey. The tall young man was sent to the Old Bailey armed with the briefcase and enough cyanide to kill an army. Unfortunately he could not, or so he claimed, get near enough to his target to make use of it.

Everyone was disappointed, but Cooper soon came

up with another clever idea. When the target's next visit to the Old Bailey was due, he armed Elvey with a crossbow and sent him off again. This time, however, the victim never showed. Elvey the killer had failed again.

It was curious that whatever AB Cooper suggested to the twins, something often seemed to go wrong. Even his trip to Tangier was a failure. He had gone there to do a deal with representatives of Moise Tsombe of the Congo, who was under house arrest at the time. The deal was that the Krays would organize an army to go to the Congo and free Tsombe. Cooper had originally put the idea to Ron Kray, saying that it came from one of his good contacts in the arms trade. He promised the twins a good share of the money to be handed over in Tangier to secure the deal. No one had any real idea of sending an army to Africa, but the money would certainly be welcome. Cooper, however, returned empty-handed.

The main effect of these failures on the twins was to increase their curiosity about Cooper. Was he really what he said he was? Was he a gold smuggler, a gun runner, as he sometimes claimed? Was he even really a banker?

He was unquestionably a wealthy man. He lived in a large house in North London, drove a Rolls-Royce and had all the trappings of success. His wife seemed very pleasant on the few occasions the Krays met her and they had as a family lived in the UK for many years, although Cooper had kept his American citizenship.

Surprisingly enough, neither Ron nor Reg had ever visited Cooper's 'bank', which was in central London near Wigmore Street. Not even Charlie had seen the inside of the bank, which was in fact only an office dealing with the purchase and sale of securities. This is very odd, considering the amount of negotiable bearer bonds that Charlie had passed over to AB Cooper to sell on the foreign securities exchange market. But somehow Cooper had managed to take on Leslie Payne's former role as adviser, consultant and manager of Ron Kray's business operations.

Leslie Payne had long since left the 'firm'. A failed attempted on his life by Jack 'The Hat' McVitie had led to contact between Payne and Nipper Read, who was now extremely busy trying to persuade Payne to come clean about his association with the Krays. In his absence, Ron Kray still needed someone to look after his affairs and tell him how great he was, or could become. AB Cooper seemed to fit the bill.

At this time, Cooper was about 38. He may have been something of a man of mystery, but he was not impressive to look at — a thin, smallish Jewish–American with a moustache, but almost no hair, who liked to smoke large cigars. The most memorable thing about him was the slow stutter with which he spoke.

Ron might have suspected that Cooper was playing games with him about the New York trip, but if the banker was up to something he didn't want to warn him in advance about his suspicions. He promised Reg that he would keep in touch by telephone every day in case of trouble at home, and told his brother that he would be staying at the Frontenac Hotel in Paris.

'Keep a good eye on Nipper for me,' was his last remark to Reg as he left Braithwaite House for Heathrow. He was not referring to Nipper Read of Scotland Yard, currently on the prowl after the two of them, but to his pet snake, a python which he had named Nipper.

'And you watch out for the Yank,' said Reg. 'He's up to something.'

It was the beginning of April, when Ron Kray, AB Cooper and Dickie Morgan arrived in Paris. Since it was late afternoon when they reached the Frontenac Hotel, just off the Champs-Elysées, it was too late to visit the US Embassy. Instead, Cooper suggested that they meet one of his good French contacts to discuss possible European business arrangements.

There was nothing Ron Kray liked better than talking business. He really enjoyed the process of setting up a deal. Once it was worked out in detail, with jobs allocated and everyone primed to make sure that his instructions were carried out exactly, Ron would lose interest in a project and move on to the next idea or venture. Getting there was the interesting part.

Cooper made a phone call and then told Ron and Dickie that he had set up dinner with an associate who knew all the top men in Europe. 'He's really looking forward to seeing you. He wants to talk serious business,' Cooper said.

This was fine with Ron Kray, but he couldn't help his thoughts straying to the visas. If Cooper was able to arrange them, then he either had extremely good contacts at the embassy — because issuing a visa to Ron Kray would be strictly illegal — or he had to be on the payroll of the US authorities. Either way, he knew he would have to be a little more wary of Mr AB Cooper in future.

The evening went well. They had a good meal with Cooper's French contact, who had spent some time in New York and spoke excellent English. He was an entertaining talker and there was never a pause in the conversation as they discussed crime in all its aspects in both the UK and Europe. Even so, though they discussed and argued about everything under the sun, nothing concrete was decided. AB Cooper seemed very keen on the Frenchman and Ron collaborating in some way, but the shape or form of the collaboration was never quite spelled out. No further meetings were arranged and the Frenchman merely said that he would be in contact with the banker again.

Ron and his two companions spent a peaceful night at the Frontenac, but next morning there was a certain excitement in the air. It reminded Ron of the nervous tension he used to feel before a boxing match — it wasn't what he was about to do that disturbed him, but the unknown outcome. Ron Kray had never been afraid of anything or anyone and that wasn't about to change, but he couldn't help remembering his brother's parting words: 'He's up to something.' He knew that he would have to take extra care about everything he said and did while he was at the embassy.

They took a taxi to the embassy, an imposing building on Avenue Gabriel with a huge Stars and Stripes wafting in the breeze above the entrance. On either side of the main doors were heavily armed US marines, who looked as if they could handle themselves very well in any situation. Guarding the United States Embassy in Paris was a prestige job for a marine, and only the best were chosen.

'They look impressive, don't they?' said Cooper. 'And every one has seen service in Vietnam.' The three men walked up the steps past the guards in their immaculate uniforms. Ron even stopped to look at the shining sabres which the marines wore attached to their white belts. He was impressed — he liked swords. 'Let me do the talking,' said Cooper, leading them along a maze of corridors. There were no signs to guide them, but he seemed to know his way. He stopped outside a door. 'Now remember, leave it all to me.'

Ron Kray couldn't help wondering how Cooper knew they had reached the correct department. There was not even a sign on the door to indicate that this was the visa section. There were some desks and a few chairs in the office but only one person, a woman. It was as deserted as if it had been lunchtime instead of first thing in the morning. If this was the visa section, it was not impressive.

'Can I help you?' asked the woman. She didn't appear to be expecting them.

'I'd like to arrange for visas to the United States for my two friends here,' said Cooper, indicating his companions.

The woman asked them to sit down at an adjoining desk, then gave them some visa application forms to fill in. Whilst they were completing the forms to the best of their ability, Cooper chatted to her.

'My friend, Mr Kray, wants to visit a sick relation in the States,' he remarked. 'I'm afraid she's dying.' The woman glanced at Ron Kray, looking genuinely concerned. Cooper had a look at the forms before he handed them back to her.

'My friends aren't used to filling in applications like this,' he explained with a confident smile.

'You understand,' the woman said to Ron Kray, 'that I can only give you a visa for a seven-day period so that you can visit your relation. If you need to stay longer, you will have to apply in the United States.' It was good enough for them, and before long the three men left the office with seven-day US visas for Ron and Dicky Morgan.

'They can't check on any UK crime record here in France,' remarked Cooper in an off-hand way as they made their way back through the maze of corridors. 'As long as you know what you're doing there's no problem.'

This was Cooper's territory, said Ron to himself, remembering the authoritative way Cooper had taken care of their visa applications, but could it really be so easy? He thought back to Reg's arguments against coming here, but then he dismissed them. He had wanted a visa and now he had got one — he didn't really care how it had been obtained. Later on, he would be telephoning Reg from the hotel — he was looking forward to hearing Reg's reaction when he discovered that his brother would soon be on his way to visit his Mafia allies in New York.

'Would you like a cup of coffee, sir?'

Ron Kray thanked the smiling air hostess and sat back in his comfortable first-class seat to analyse events so far. On the telephone the night before, Reg had repeated his doubts about Cooper, but had wished his brother well with his mission. There was no hint of animosity between the brothers — Reg knew that so far, Ron was ahead of the game.

Now Ron, Cooper and Dickie Morgan were on their way to New York, where Cooper had arranged for an old friend to meet them at JFK Airport. This was Joe Kaufman, who had been over to London many times on behalf of the Mafia, delivering stolen bearer bonds and representing his bosses in other dealings. He knew the Krays well, and he and his wife, Marie, had even been on holiday to Spain with Charlie Kray and his family.

Ron was pleased to be meeting him again and was sure that Little Joey, as he was sometimes called, would have fixed him up a few meetings in New York. He was especially looking forward to meeting the legendary Meyer Lansky.

Only a few months earlier, Ron had met Tony 'Ducks' Corallo, a lieutenant in the Lucchese family of Brooklyn, one of the five Mafia families of New York. Corallo had been over to London on a scouting expedition, investigating gambling potential in the UK, and the Kray twins had met him at an apartment in Knightsbridge. Corallo and his two powerfully built bodyguards had impressed the Krays, and they had discussed possible business ventures for two hours in a very congenial atmosphere. Tony 'Ducks' Corallo was certainly another possibility in New York.

Then, of course, there was Ron's old friend, Angelo Bruno of Philadelphia. Maybe they could make a trip down to see him too, but time would tell. Anyway, Kaufman would take care of things — he knew everyone worth knowing in New York and it would be up to him to present Ron's credentials to the Mafia families and arrange the necessary appointments. Ron was hoping he would have a busy schedule lined up.

As Ron sat there thinking, he began to picture his successful trip to New York with maybe, just maybe, a boy or two to while away the early morning hours. His eyes began to close and he slept, a smile on his face, while his plane headed out across the Atlantic.

While Ron Kray was heading for New York, Nipper Read was searching the whole of London for evidence against the twins. He knew where Reg Kray was staying but Ron hadn't been sighted for a few days and that worried him a little. What were the Krays planning now?

Back in September 1967, Read had left Scotland Yard and set up his office in Tintagel House, taking a team of twelve officers with him. John du Rose, head of the Murder Squad at Scotland Yard, had arranged for Read and his team to transfer to the towering block of government offices on the south bank of the River Thames. He was worried that the Krays might have someone inside Scotland Yard itself. The twins had always said they had an informer in the Yard, and though Du Rose claimed he did not believe the rumours, he was not taking any chances. He wanted the Krays — badly.

'We're coming into JFK, Ron,' said Cooper.

'Good.' Whatever was going to happen in the USA, Ron was looking forward to it.

Ron nudged Dickie Morgan awake. Having been a friend of Ron's since their schooldays, the tall, dark-haired Morgan was one of the few members of the firm who knew him well, even though he was only on the fringes of the gang. He was not the type to get involved in any violent activity and violence was an ever present aspect of gang life in London. Instead, he had been involved with Charlie Mitchell in some of the long firms set up by Leslie Payne. But he was always good company and Ron liked having him around.

The Air France flight to New York touched down right on schedule, and the passengers were soon making their way to the immigration hall.

'Now don't go volunteering information,' said Cooper. There was no answer from his companions — the warning wasn't necessary.

The immigration officer flipped through Ron Kray's passport. 'Where will you be staying in the United States?'

'New York.'

'How will you be supporting yourself?'

'With money.' Ron pulled out his wallet to show a large wad of dollar bills.

'Enjoy yourself,' said the man, obviously satisfied.

Ron walked casually on, followed by Dickie Morgan, who had no problems either.

'That was easy,' said Dickie as they waited for their luggage.

'It was arranged,' said Cooper. 'I told you everything had been taken care of.'

Out in the arrivals hall, thronged with people of every race and nationality, the three men looked around for Joe Kaufman. Soon they saw his slight figure approaching through the crowds. He was clearly pleased to see them.

'Welcome to New York.' The little Jewish–Sicilian shook hands with Ron Kray first. 'I'm glad you could make it.'

'So am I,' said Ron, with feeling. The second round had been won. He was safely in New York whilst Scotland Yard were no doubt chasing around London at this very minute trying to find him. It was all very satisfying.

'I've booked you in at the Warwick Hotel,' said Joey Kaufman as he ushered them outside to his large American car. 'It's just off Broadway.'

As they drove towards Manhattan, AB Cooper was feeling quietly pleased. He had proved to the Krays that he was as good as his word — he did have exceptional contacts in high places. Now they would certainly be more willing to listen to him in future.

The Warwick, on West 54th Street in mid-town Manhattan, is a first-class hotel in a prime position. It is located just south of Central Park, squeezed in between Fifth Avenue and Broadway. During the next seven days there, presuming discussions to be fruitful, Ron Kray would be creating a new liaison with the Mob families of New York. If any of the five Mafia factions wanted to do business in England in future, he would make sure that the first name that came to mind had to be — Kray.

Ron Kray shut the door of his elegant room and pulled a beer from the fridge. The Budweiser tasted good — not like English beer, but fine. He liked the look of New York from what he had seen so far. He liked its brashness, its pace, its variety and its rude vitality. In a place like this, he thought, a man could accomplish much in seven days.

Before long, AB Cooper tapped on the door. He had disappointing news for the English gangland leader.

'I'm afraid I can't get through to any of my special contacts here at the moment,' he said, looking downcast. 'I'll have to try again later.'

Joe Kaufman, on the other hand, had been more fortunate. He had managed to speak to Angelo Bruno in Philadelphia, just to let him know that Ron was in town — it was the courteous thing to do. Bruno was pleased to hear from Kaufman and sent his regards to Ron Kray, but unfortunately he could not get to New York. He told Kaufman that they were all very welcome to come and see him in Philadelphia — a two-hour drive away — if they had time for a brief visit.

That was fine, thought Ron Kray, but Bruno could be kept in reserve. He already knew the Philadelphia Godfather well and had built up a good working relationship with the man some years earlier.

Kaufman also confirmed that he had tried to contact a good friend of his in one of the Brooklyn families. He had been unable to get hold of the man, a well-known Mob member called Crazy Joe Gallo, but he was sure he would be able to reach him within 24 hours.

Gallo was one of three brothers belonging to the Colombo family of Brooklyn. The others were Larry and Al. Joe Gallo had always had the reputation of being a hard man to do business with, and a recent seven-year period in the state penitentiary hadn't improved his manners. He used to be involved in the jukebox and vending-machine rackets in and around New York, but he was not highly successful, mainly because of his outrageous strong-arm tactics. In 1961 he had been sentenced to serve from seven to fourteen years for attempted extortion.

It was his business methods that earned him the nickname of Crazy Joe, and he certainly was not a person to disregard. His own family boss, Joseph Profacci, learned this when Joe Gallo led a bloody insurrection against him. The new ruler of the family was now Joseph Colombo, who counted the Gallo brothers amongst his staunchest supporters.

Reg Kray tells a story concerning Crazy Joe Gallo and the singer Billy Daniels which illustrates Gallo's way of operating. Billy Daniels, a friend of the Krays, once asked a lovely air hostess to go out with him. She

245

declined. He had almost forgotten the incident when he was asked to go and see Crazy Joe Gallo at a house in Brooklyn. Daniels didn't know why Crazy Joe wanted to see him, but since the Gallos were honourable men he decided he had better keep the appointment. When he arrived, he was immediately taken down to the basement of the house, where Crazy Joe kept a fully grown lion in a cage. No one knew why Crazy Joe kept the lion, because no one ever dared ask.

When Billy Daniels reached the basement, he was a very worried man. He was seriously wondering if he would get out alive. He asked Joe Gallo not to do anything that he might regret later. Gallo said that wouldn't be a problem as long as Daniels stayed away from a certain young lady friend the air hostess who had rejected the singer some while back.

A terrified Billy Daniels assured Crazy Joe, at length, that he would never, ever, in any circumstances, go near the young lady again. At last Crazy Joe let him go, and the singer got out of that basement as fast as his legs would carry him. Needless to say, Daniels kept his promise — he knew how very near he was to being put into that cage with the lion if Gallo had decided not to believe him.

This was the kind of person that Ron Kray could look forward to meeting if Joe Kaufman managed to set up a rendezvous. Ron hoped that he would succeed — he relished the idea of a get-together with Crazy Joe Gallo, who was a man of action like himself.

On their first evening in New York, Ron and his companions were invited out to dinner by Joe Kaufman and his wife, Marie. Marie was a pretty woman and good company. She had been a movie actress and once, early

in her career, had been in a film with William Holden.
She was proud of her acting achievements, and rightly so.

The evening was a pleasant one, but going out to
dinner at a local restaurant was not what Ron had come
to New York for. Both AB Cooper and Joe Kaufman
assured him that things would start happening the
following day. Meanwhile, it was best to relax and try
and get over his jet lag.

'Don't forget Meyer Lansky,' Ron urged as they
parted for the night.

'Don't worry, Ron,' said Joe Kaufman. 'He has
top priority.'

Two days later, Ron Kray sat waiting in the lobby of the
Warwick. He was alone, but he was a happy man. Any
time now, Joe Kaufman would be arriving to take him
to see a top lieutenant in the Colombo family. His
name was Frank Ileano. This meeting, Ron had
decided, would be attended only by himself and
Kaufman. He had managed to get rid of Dickie
Morgan, who was off shopping in Bloomingdales, and
AB Cooper, who was out trying to raise his so-called
good contacts in New York.

Not that Ron saw Morgan as any sort of threat. He
certainly was not a key player in the game, but even so it
would be better if he didn't know too much about Ron
Kray's business dealings with one of the most powerful
Mafia families in the whole of the USA.

AB Cooper, on the other hand, was a more doubtful
quantity. Ron knew that he could be a danger to the
Krays if he knew too much, so he had decided not to
involve him in any coming discussions. Indeed, he had
told Joe Kaufman that he was not even to mention

Ileano's name to the banker, but refer only to a possible meeting with Crazy Joe Gallo.

Ron Kray looked around at the smartly dressed people in the lobby. He was a smart man himself, but they dressed differently here. Still, he was proud of being English, in fact he liked to think of himself as an ambassador for his country. He hadn't let the side down in Nigeria and he would not do so here. He didn't want to look like an American — secretly, he felt that his nationality gave him that little extra touch of class.

Status and respect had always been important to Ron Kray, and he was sure the Mafia understood the need for them as well as he did. After all, they were honourable men.

Soon, Joe Kaufman arrived to meet him. The two men made their way out to his car, the usual big black limousine. Nothing too pretentious — Joe Kaufman didn't want them to be conspicuous.

'Where's the meeting, Joe?' asked Ron as the engine began to growl.

'It's over in Brooklyn, at a place near Prospect Park.'

This didn't mean anything to Ron. He had heard of the famous Brooklyn Bridge, but that was all.

'Shall we take the scenic route,' Joe continued. 'We can drive down Broadway, through Times Square, past Macy's, into Little Italy and Chinatown, then across the bridge. How does that sound?'

'It sounds like a long way,' Ron looked Out through the tinted windows, 'but as long as we're on time that's fine by me.' He was truly fascinated by New York.

However, it was not too long before they reached Brooklyn Bridge and headed across the East River. They drove towards downtown Brooklyn, past the Civic

Centre, and soon they were on another Fifth Avenue. This one, though, was very different from its Manhattan counterpart. There were no high-rise towers here and the whole atmosphere was completely different. It was all very suburban, all somewhat run down and dishevelled. Brooklyn had obviously seen better days.

'We're almost there, Ron,' said Joe. 'The house is on President Street. It's owned by the Gallo brothers.'

Ron Kray's thoughts went back to the story about his old friend Billy Daniels. Would he really be stepping into the proverbial lion's den? They turned off Fifth Avenue on to President Street. It was peculiarly peaceful. Surely, he thought, they wouldn't keep lions here.

There was a moment of silence as they stopped outside a nondescript Brooklyn house and Joe switched off the engine. It was now or never. Ron knew that he had to impress these people straight away. 'Let's go,' he said. 'It's time to do the business.'

Little Joe Kaufman knew Crazy Joe and his brothers Larry and Al very well. He had already told them a lot about the career of Ron Kray, the lad from the East End of London who was now the most wanted man in the United Kingdom. But the Mafia are always suspicious when a newcomer enters their ranks, and the Gallos certainly weren't about to welcome the Englishman with open arms. Ron realized from the outset of the meeting that, however good his credentials, he was in for a hard time.

Joe Kaufman did his best with the introductions, but as they waited for Frank Ileano to appear, conversation was sticky to say the least. Ron was asked to sit down, but the fact that a man stood behind his chair didn't make him feel any more comfortable. There wasn't even the offer of a drink, something which Ron would have found very welcome.

Ron tried to stay cool. He knew there was no point in losing his temper even though the longer they waited the more trying he found the situation. No one could call him a nervous man, but he was reminded of how he used to feel in the last minutes before a big fight. If anything, this was worse. As the minutes ticked by he began to question his sanity in coming to New York at all.

At last, Frank Ileano appeared. He was a big man with a powerful personality and he took control of the meeting immediately. Joe Kaufman, making the introductions again, knew there was no point in overselling Ron to him. One thing he did say was, 'He's already got his button' — Mafia slang meaning that Ron had already killed a man. He also told Ileano that Angelo Bruno knew Ron well, and they they had worked together in London for some years, with good results. 'Maybe you'd like to check out Ron with Angelo Bruno,' he suggested.

This was a smart move because Bruno was on the *commissione*, the Mafia's governing body. This made him a very senior figure in the US Mafia, and someone whose recommendation it would be bad policy for the Colombo lieutenant to ignore.

'I'll do just that.' Frank Ileano left the room to make the call. The Gallo brothers, who had been staring suspiciously at Ron throughout this conversation, watched him even more closely once their boss had left. So did the evil-looking little guy standing behind his chair. Ron and Joe just sat and sweated.

A few minutes later, Ileano returned. To Ron's

enormous relief, he was smiling. 'I'm sorry to have kept you waiting, gentlemen.' He looked at Ron. 'I've checked you out with Angelo Bruno, and he says you're OK. Now let's get down to business.'

The tension in the room drained away — all at once it seemed quite a comfortable, homely place. 'How about a coffee?' asked Crazy Joe. The Gallo brothers looked a lot less menacing when they smiled and even the little thug behind Ron looked marginally more pleasant.

'But before we begin, there's just one thing I think you should know, Ron.' Frank Ileano's voice was serious again. 'You're being followed by the FBI.'

So Joe Kaufman had been right, thought Ron. Earlier in the day they had lunched in Greenwich Village with Rocky Graziano and Tony Zale, two of Ron's favourite boxers. They'd had a good time, but Dickie Morgan had thought he noticed two men following them. Joe Kaufman had later checked with one of his contacts, who told him that there was an unusual amount of FBI activity, and that the Feds seemed to be keeping tabs on Ron Kray.

Joe was surprised. He had supposed that he himself would be the subject of the FBI's interest. Ron Kray hadn't been in the country long enough to have committed any crime, and for the FBI to be tailing him already they must have had advance warning of his visit to New York. This seemed improbable, given that Ron had obtained his visa so recently. How did the FBI know about Ron, and what were they after?

Frank Ileano reassured Ron that their meeting today had been arranged in such a way that the FBI could have no knowledge of it. The Gallos were very experienced at this sort of thing. Joe Kaufman also confirmed that, without wishing to disturb his English guest, he too had taken precautions. The 'scenic' route they had taken to Brooklyn was designed to enable him to throw off any tail.

Ron appreciated the trouble that had been taken on his behalf, but the whole situation raised some unpleasant questions, and increased his nagging doubts about AB Cooper, whom neither he nor Dickie Morgan had set eyes on all day. Cooper was supposed to be trying to arrange meetings for Ron, but with nothing to show for his efforts, Reg's warnings about watching out for the Yank kept repeating themselves in his brother's mind.

Even so, Ron was determined to take advantage of his introduction to the Colombo family. He spent the next three days discussing business with Frank Ileano, and the two men began to build up a good relationship.

Joe Kaufman was still trying to arrange a meeting with Meyer Lansky, but this was looking increasingly unlikely, given the FBI's level of activity. Tony 'Ducks' Corallo of the Lucchese family was having similar problems. Both men passed on their best regards to Ron through Kaufman, but it seemed as if that would be the extent of their contact.

Ron was not too worried. This new connection with the Colombo family was looking more and more promising, and Frank Ileano had some very positive propositions for him. The main subjects of their discussions were gambling and drugs. Gambling, of course, interested Ron a lot, but drugs were something the Krays had always preferred to stay away from. On the other hand, Ron knew that if he turned down the opportunity to get involved in the lucrative drugs trade, the Mafia would almost certainly contact other gangs in the UK — gangs who, if the price was right, would have far fewer scruples than the Krays about how they disposed of the merchandise. It was a delicate issue and he didn't want to make a final decision right now — this was one he and Reg would have to talk over carefully.

As well as business discussions, Ron's stay in New York was a never ending round of parties and dinners at which he was guest of honour. He loved all the attention. Public relations had always been his big thing, and he was making a lot of important friends in New York — friends whom he hoped would help him to new heights of achievement and fortune. The fortune would be made through crime, of course. Ron had never been able to envisage making serious money by any legitimate means.

As well as drugs and gambling, there was another topic discussed in negotiations with Frank Ileano which Ron found very interesting indeed. This was the possibility of setting up a Mafia-style operation in Great Britain run by the Krays themselves.

Ileano talked at length about the internal structure of a Mafia family and of the various techniques used to dissociate the family boss, or *capo*, from the actions of the soldiers, or *soldati*, who carried out the *capo*'s orders. For example, if someone had to be dealt with, either temporarily or permanently, then the boss of a family would bring someone in from out of town to do it. This was especially important when someone had to be killed. It was always better to use a so-called button man, from outside the immediate family.

This system is called by the Mafia the buffer or *cuscinetto*. The boss gives his orders to a go-between, one of his lieutenants. The go-between then passes the instructions on to those who will carry them out. The theory is that the more people there are between the top man and those who actually carry out his orders, the safer he is.

Ron thought the Krays could learn an important lesson from the Mafia way of operating. They didn't have to do everything for themselves, in fact it would be far safer if they did not. Especially now when, back in England, Nipper Read was getting far too close to them for comfort. Ron had always said that if anyone was going to catch them, then it would be that persistent little Scotland Yard Inspector.

Ron remembered a piece of good advice once given to him by Angelo Bruno. 'When the shit hits the fan,' Bruno told him, 'stay away from the shit.' It seemed to make a lot of sense. Ron decided that he would definitely suggest to Reg the idea of setting up a Mafia 'franchise' in Britain, as soon as he got home.

A few days into his trip, Ron phoned England to tell Reg how he was getting on. Reg was delighted with Ron's progress and said that he was looking forward to hearing all about it when his brother got back. 'By the way,' he told Ron, 'Nipper's furious. He can't find you anywhere.' Both men thought that was very funny.

While Ron was having his meetings with the Colombo family, AB Cooper was still running round trying to set something up through his own contacts. Somehow, he seemed to find it impossible to do. There was always some last-minute hitch. Ron had never seen anyone try so hard with so little success. He found it difficult to understand how the man who had succeeded in getting him a visa in Paris could be so ineffective right here in his home territory.

Dickie Morgan commented that Cooper seemed to be stuttering more each day. He wondered if it was a sign of nerves, but if so, what did Cooper have to be nervous about? Apart from letting Ron down.

Cooper couldn't have been more apologetic about his failure. As they got closer to the seven-day time limit of their stay, he suggested they take a quick trip to Las Vegas — he was sure he would have more luck there. Or perhaps they should head for Los Angeles, to see Ron's old friend George Raft. Or make that visit to Angelo Bruno in Philadelphia.

But Ron had stopped worrying about what Cooper was up to. His trip to New York was living up to expectations as far as he was concerned. He had got a long way in his negotiations with Frank Ileano — the New York Mafia would no longer have any excuse for wondering about Ron Kray's credentials. He'd had a good time into the bargain. He'd been wined and dined all over town by the Colombo family and he'd seen all the sights -the Empire State Building and the Statue of Liberty, Carnegie Hall, the Rockefeller Center, the Museum of Modern Art and Radio City Music Hall. He'd even been across the Brooklyn Bridge.

Ron wasn't interested in going anywhere else in the USA. He was enjoying himself too much in New York. He was so happy that he had even turned down Joe Kaufman's suggestion of getting in touch with some of his showbiz friends such as Barbra Streisand and Tony Bennett. He didn't even want to see Judy Garland.

Ron had one last task for Joe Kaufman before he left the country — to confirm that a fresh batch of negotiable bearer bonds would soon be on their way to England. Then there was just time for one final fling in

New York — an outrageous evening of drink, drink and more drink. It was the kind of night out Ron had often enjoyed back in the East End, and Joe Kaufman made sure there were plenty of pals around to drink to his health and wish him bon voyage. Ron Kray had beaten the odds. He was treated like the 'King' of New York. This was to be the beginning of a new era — and Ron just couldn't wait to get back to London, so he could make arrangements for the 'Mafia Franchise', as described in full by the Colombos. In future he would organise the London underworld along Mafia lines, together with the only partner in crime that he ever felt comfortable with — his own twin brother Reg.

14
NEMESIS

When Ron Kray and his companions arrived back at Heathrow, Ron and Dickie Morgan took a cab to the East End, and AB Cooper took the next flight to Paris. Banking business, he said.

Ron returned home to a hero's welcome. He had presents from New York for everyone, just in case he needed to prove where he'd been, but no one doubted his story. The trouble was that Nipper Read soon knew all about his New York trip too, and he was livid. So was his boss, John Du Rose. They had been trying to put the Krays away for a long time — now the problem was more urgent than ever.

Unfortunately for them, although they believed, quite

rightly, that both Cornell and McVitie had been murdered by the Krays, they had absolutely no proof of it. All they knew was that both men were dead, although McVitie's body couldn't be found. They had to find someone who would talk, but while the Krays were walking free round London that was a very difficult thing to do.

Meanwhile, both Ron and Reg were making plans for the future. Ron decided to move out to his country home, The Brooks, as soon as possible. He loved the Suffolk countryside, and anyway he felt that spending some time out of London would be no bad idea at this moment. Reg, too, was thinking of leading a more settled life. He was even considering getting married again.

As the twins saw it, they now had two options available. They could revolutionize organized crime in the UK by setting up the Mafia franchise, as suggested by the Colombo family. Or they could leave crime behind, invest their gains in legitimate business ventures, and enjoy their new status as country squires. Reg favoured going legitimate. Ron favoured the Mafia franchise.

Charlie, who had never been happy with many of his brothers' activities, urged the twins to invest in some bona fide businesses. Amongst other things, he suggested clubs, betting shops, car sales and property development. Anything, he told them, was better than carrying on the way they had been doing. If they did not give up their life of crime, he was convinced they would soon be caught. Ron and Reg listened to what Charlie had to say — but their elder brother had never been very good at persuading the twins to do anything.

Shortly afterwards, AB Cooper returned, still

stuttering, from Paris. He had a new piece of business for Ron and Reg — to arrange for the killing of a man named George Caruana. Caruana was a London nightclub owner. Though he lived in Britain, he held a Maltese passport. Cooper told the twins that he had been in contact with members of the New York Mafia, whom he said would appreciate the Krays getting rid of George Caruana for them.

The hit man for the job was hired by Cooper himself. But the murder attempt was as ineffective as so many other set-ups involving the New York banker had been. It did, however, cause Nipper Read to take Cooper into Tintagel House for questioning.

This was a mistake on Read's part, because Cooper had, all along, been spying on the Krays on behalf of Read's boss, John Du Rose. He also claimed to be an FBI agent who had worked for two years at the FBI's European headquarters in Paris.

Nipper Read probably knew that Cooper was passing information to Du Rose, though he has always claimed that he was not aware of any deal between the two. He certainly did not know about the FBI connection, but when he checked Cooper's story he found that it was true. Cooper had been acting as an agent provocateur on behalf of the FBI. That was why all his murder attempts had mysteriously failed, why Ron Kray had been able to get his visa in Paris, and why Cooper had flown to the French capital immediately after returning from New York.

Cooper himself was amazed at being arrested. If Read did know of his status as an informer, the Scotland Yard detective was making a ridiculous mistake. The attempted Caruana killing was a complete set-up, organized by

Cooper to frame the twins. Cooper told Du Rose that he had been very near to getting damning information on the Krays that would put them behind bars for many years. But Read's arrest of him had put paid to any chance of incriminating them.

The next attempt to fabricate evidence against the Krays was a joint effort by Read and Cooper, who by now had made his position clear to Scotland Yard. It involved Little Joe Kaufman, the Krays' New York friend, who was in London again on Mafia business.

Cooper let it be known that he was unwell and had been admitted to a London clinic. The illnesss was a fake — but it gave Read and his team the opportunity to wire Cooper's room in the clinic for sound and record all his conversations there. At first the plan seemed to have failed — though Cooper repeatedly asked the Krays to visit him, they sensed that something was wrong and stayed well clear.

Joe Kaufman was less wary. He strode into Cooper's room with a bunch of flowers and a big smile on his face. Cooper immediately asked him what the latest was on the bearer bonds. Good news, said Kaufman. More bonds would soon be arriving by mail, direct from the USA, and would be delivered to his room at the Mayfair Hotel.

It was all taped by the police. At last, Read had something on the Krays. It was not the firm evidence he needed, but the link to the stolen bearer bonds via Joe Kaufman was better than nothing. He also had a 200-page statement taken from Leslie Payne at the end of 1967 about his association with the Krays, but that again was not good enough — Payne had had nothing to do with the murders.

Nipper Read and John Du Rose wanted the Krays behind bars right away. They knew that if they didn't move fast, Ron Kray would have time to reorganise his firm along Mafia lines. They decided to put their jobs on the line and take a huge risk — arrest the Krays now, lock them away in a secure jail, and pray that someone would start talking.

On 9 May 1968, in the early hours of the morning, Ron, Reg and Charlie Kray were all arrested. Ron and Reg had only just gone to bed. The following day, Charlie Kray's old friend Gordon Andersen was arrested. So too were most of the Kray firm, including Charlie Mitchell, Dickie Morgan, Connie Whitehead and John Dickson. Soon others joined them in jail — the Lambrianou brothers, Freddie Foreman, Ronnie Hart, Ian Barrie and Ron Bender. Joe Kaufman was also arrested, with almost $20,000 worth of bearer bonds in his possession.

Fortunately for Read and Du Rose, their gamble paid off. People began to talk, since the twins were locked away and there could be no retribution, no silencing of unwilling witnesses. Kaufman made a complete statement to Scotland Yard about his involvement in the bearer bond deals and Frank Mitchell's girlfriend, Lisa, revealed the truth about the killing of the 'Mad Axeman'. Although it was already too late to add the Mitchell killing to the prosecution's case against the Krays, since they had already been tried and acquitted for his murder, the evidence was beginning to mount and Scotland Yard knew they were right in stopping the Krays when they did. But Read soon had the names of a whole list of customers who were in The Blind Beggar when Ron Kray strolled in and shot George Cornell and members of the firm itself began talking openly to Read about the knifing of Jack 'The Hat' McVitie.

The May 9th grab of the Krays and their firm was a great risk on the part of Read especially, who had everything to lose. But his slow, methodical probing resulted in statements and confessions — enough to secure victory on March 8th 1969. The only point of interest, as far as Read was concerned, were the killings; he wanted the Krays to go down for murder and nothing else would do. The Mafia deals, the protection rackets, the long firm frauds, the extortion and all other possible offences against the state were shelved, in favour of the murders of two sordid gangsters, George Cornell and Jack 'The Hat' McVitie.

The Cornell killing had taken place nearly two years earlier. George Cornell was a member of the powerful Richardson gang, a south London firm who were becoming rivals of the Krays. One day, Cornell called Ron a 'fat poof', in public. Ronnie couldn't put up with an insult like that — it was a direct challenge. On 8 March 1966, Ron was told that Cornell was at the Blind Beggar pub in Whitechapel. The night before, the rest of the Richardson firm had been arrested after a shoot-out at Mr Smith's club in Catford. Cornell was the only gang member still at large, but Ron decided that he was not going to be let off the hook so easily.

He asked John 'Scotch Jack' Dickson to drive him and his minder, Ian Barrie, to the Blind Beggar. First they paid a visit to 178 Vallance Road to collect a gun or two. When the three reached the pub, Dickson was told to wait outside. Ron handed Barrie a gun and told him to follow him into the pub. The Blind Beggar was not one of the Krays' regular haunts, but for Ron Kray it was confrontation time — he had to show everyone who ruled London.

When they entered the saloon bar, Ian Barrie fired a few shots in the air. Everyone dived for cover. Except George Cornell, who was drinking a light ale at the bar with a couple of friends. The friends suddenly vanished, but Cornell stood his ground. 'Well, look who's here,' he said, as he raised his glass. He probably thought he had nothing to fear from Ron Kray in a crowded bar. But he didn't know Ron.

Ron stood perfectly still for a moment. Then he slowly pulled a Mauser 9mm automatic from his coat pocket, and shot George Cornell in the head. The pub jukebox was playing 'The Sun Ain't Gonna Shine Anymore' by the Walker brothers. Those words came true for George Cornell.

Unhurriedly, Ron and Ian Barrie left the pub. They got into the car and Scotch Jack Dickson drove them back down the Mile End Road, towards home territory. As they crossed the River Lea, Ron Kray wound down one of the windows in the rear of the car and threw the Mauser 9mm automatic into the water. Here it was to rest for the next 20 years or so, until it was discovered in a dredging operation. After forensic tests it was placed proudly in Scotland Yard's Black Museum. Dickson himself still had no idea what had happened inside, but the pub had been crowded with early evening drinkers so soon most of London would hear about the killing. No one would talk to the police about it, though.

Ron himself felt good. He had dealt with an insult to his honour, and he had realized one of his life's ambitions — to kill a man.

The McVitie killing was a less cold-blooded murder. Jack 'The Hat' McVitie was a hard man who sometimes did jobs for the Krays. He started making mistakes — getting drunk and causing trouble. On more than one occasion he took money from the twins to do a job, then failed to go through with it, but kept the money. One thing he failed to do was kill Leslie Payne, the Krays' former business manager.

The twins decided McVitie had to be taught a lesson. On 28 October 1967, McVitie drove to what he had been told was a party at a basement flat in Stoke Newington. The flat belonged to a girl called Carol Thompson and Carol Skinner, also known as Blonde Carol, but she was told she wasn't wanted and had to clear off for the night, together with her two young children. With McVitie were the Lambrianou brothers, Chris and Tony, and a couple of friends from out of town. They had all been drinking at the Regency Club for most of the evening and McVitie was well away. He should never have been driving his big Ford Zodiac — and certainly not to that basement flat.

When they arrived at the flat, Ron Kray greeted McVitie by thrusting a glass into his face. 'Now fuck off!' he told him. Everyone was amazed when Reg, who had also been drinking heavily all evening, then pulled out a gun and tried to shoot McVitie in the head. For some reason the gun didn't go off, but Reg kept trying again and again to fire it.

Ronnie Hart and two boys who had come with Ron Kray grabbed McVitie and urged Reg to deal with him. While Ronnie Hart was still holding McVitie, Reg grabbed a knife from the kitchen and stabbed him in the face. He stabbed again and again, in a furious drunken rage, not really knowing what he was doing or why. Blood poured from the facial and neck wounds, soon there was blood everywhere. Carol's pretty little flat soon looked more like a slaughterhouse than a trendy gangster moll's hideaway. Jack 'The Hat' McVitie sank to the ground in a pool of blood. He was very dead.

Ronnie Bender, who came into the room from the kitchen just after McVitie had drawn his last breath, couldn't believe his eyes. This was not like Reg Kray at all. The firm expected this sort of behaviour from Ron, although killing someone was normally regarded as overdoing it, but not from Reg.

Reg, Ron and Ronnie Hart drove off. They left Tony Lambrianou, Ronnie Bender and a startled Connie Whitehead, who had just arrived for the party, to deal with McVitie's bloodied and battered remains. Eventually Jack 'The Hat' McVitie was fed to the crabs, somewhere off the north coast of Kent.

In the end, there were too many witnesses for Reg to get away with the killing. Tony Lambrianou was one of the few people in the room who didn't give evidence against him at the trial. He served fifteen years, though he took no part in the actual killing. Ron Kray's 'boys' didn't give evidence either –they were away as fast as their feet could carry them, shocked by the bloody events they had seen.

So after almost a year of investigation Scotland Yard knew the details of the McVitie killing, but there was no body and no real evidence — apart from the statements given by members of the firm itself. Most of these people could not be trusted and would say anything to get out of a jail sentence, so Read was still looking for hard facts. He found them when police forensic units later visited the basement flat and found dried blood, still lying between the cracks in the floorboards of the room where Reg Kray had killed Jack 'The Hat'. The blood group matched and at last Nipper Read had real tangible proof of a crime.

It was all over bar the shouting, and there was plenty of shouting in court as a procession of former members of the Kray firm gave their evidence against the twins. Ron and Reg were sentenced to 30 years apiece. Their brother Charlie was given seven to ten years for being an accessory to the murder of McVitie. This was in spite of the fact that Charlie Kray was not present at the time and did not help to dispose of the body, as claimed by the prosecution. But he was a Kray, so he had to go down with the others.

Ron and Reg did in fact try to do a deal with Nipper Read over Charlie. They said they would plead guilty if Read would let their brother go free. Nipper Read refused — he was determined to have all three of them. So Charlie spent seven years in prison for something he didn't do.

Whether or not Ron and Reg Kray would have recreated their gang along the Mafia lines suggested by Frank Ileano in New York, no one will ever know — their arrest came too soon. But they are still the most powerful underworld figures Britain has known, and their fame lives on in an extraordinary way.

Of the other players in their story, Joe Kaufman was released within a year for lack of evidence. He returned to the USA as fast as he could. Although not before Reg Kray had the pleasure of knocking some of his teeth out while they were in Brixton jail together. Gordon Andersen was also released. He went to live in Italy.

The members of the Kray firm who had given evidence against the twins were set free into the society of London's East End. Some went abroad, but most simply resumed their activities under a new umbrella.

In the USA, Crazy Joe Gallo was shot and killed in 1976. His boss, Joseph Colombo, was also killed. New faces took over the Colombo family and its internal struggle continued. Tony 'Ducks' Corallo, the all-powerful boss of the Lucchese family, was finally sent to the state penitentiary in 1986. His sentence was 100 years.

And what of Alan B Cooper, the banker and FBI agent? What was he really up to? After the Kray trial, he eventually turned up in the USA again, where he was arrested by the police. He spent five years in jail in his home country, but as the US Mafia had been after him at the time of his arrest, he was not too worried. At least he was safe inside.

Though it seems clear that Cooper did work for the FBI at some time, he also appeared to be playing them off against Scotland Yard. He was also playing off his dealings with the Krays against dealings for his own profit. For example, it emerged after Joe Kaufman's arrest that Cooper had never told the Krays about Little Joe's final trip to London with more bearer bonds. It appeared that he intended to take the bonds himself and sell them for his own profit without the Krays knowing. Which, if the twins hadn't been arrested, would have been an extremely stupid thing to do.

At the Kray's trial a certain amount came out about Cooper's activities, but the full story will probably never be told. One fact that did emerge, however, was that the 'visa office' Ron had visited at the US Embassy in Paris was really the European head office of the FBI. No wonder there was no sign on the door.

It was at the time the most expensive and extensive case in the history of crime within these shores. The sentences were impressive and the tough stance taken by the judiciary was designed to help deter and prevent the re-emergence of gangland London and dominance by one fraction of the underworld. In this they succeeded, but the result has been a fragmentation of crime where boundaries are limitless. The criminal fraternity has spread its wings — even to the City of London itself. Crime is everywhere.

An era came to an end with the conviction and imprisonment of the Krays. The status quo between criminal and police has gone for ever. No more the friendly rivalry — one trying to catch, the other trying not to get caught. The gloves have now come off and there are no holds barred. Crime today is a very different animal and I would be very much surprised if the Krays themselves — the greatest gangsters this country has ever known — would even recognise it today, as we near the start of a new millennium.

The kings of crime are gone for ever — but they will never be forgotten.

EPILOGUE

I FIRST MET CHARLIE KRAY in a London pub in the mid '80s when I was on a visit to see some of my record business colleagues. The trip had gone well and I was soon to return to Copenhagen where I had lived for some 17 years, but a friend had asked me out to experience some of London's nightlife and that included a bit of a pub crawl.

He was introduced simply as Charlie Kray, a man with connections in the music world. During the evening, one of my acquaintances told me that Charlie had two brothers and that they were twins. Being a twin myself, I asked politely what line they were in.

There was a slight look of embarrassment on his face as he told me that they were in jail. 'They are both in prison,' he told me straight. 'But they are great guys and should be out soon.' He was obviously used to talking about his brothers.

A friend took me to one side and told me that his brothers were the notorious Kray twins, men of steel.

'Who?' I asked, not remembering them at all from my days in England.

'Ron and Reg Kray,' he told me. 'They were the bosses of organised crime and have been in jail for 18 years.'

This was indeed a revelation, since my own early memories of London were confined to parties at the colleges and to the Oxford–Cambridge Varsity rugby game at Twickenham. Gangsters never interested me, likewise boat races.

'I am a twin, too,' I told Charlie, as a way of getting back into conversation. A sip of beer later and I was getting curious. 'So your brothers are gangsters,' I said quietly. I was never one to beat about the bush.

'That's right — haven't you heard of them?' he asked me.

A shake of the head told him that it was all new to me and my body language told him that I was not one of those with preconceived ideas about the Krays — I was neither cop nor crook, I was no-one to fear. Suddenly he was talking openly and apparently honestly about his brothers — it was as though he was genuinely relieved to talk to a stranger.

When we parted that evening, he gave me his telephone number and told me that he could possibly get what I was looking for at the right price.

'Get in touch when you're coming over next time and I'll see what I can do,' he told me cheerfully with a warm handshake. It was as though that handshake was important but I didn't realise it at the time — I shook everyone's hand, so one more made little difference to me.

That was my first meeting with the man who became known to me as 'Champagne Charlie' Kray, a man with twin brothers who were once the most feared men in London and a man who could supply almost anything at a price.

'I'll meet you there at lunchtime,' he told me as he hung up the phone. Charlie Kray was in a good mood, possibly because he could smell a nice little earner. He had just arranged for me to meet some of his friends who had music product for sale at very keen prices — how keen I was soon to find out. It was my first visit to the UK since the summer of '85 and now with the leaves falling and the cool nights closing in, everyone was beginning to look forward to Christmas. And you know what Christmas means to people in the music business — money!

I arrived at Wickham House, just off the Mile End Road, at around 12.30pm and headed straight for the canteen. I soon found Charlie and some of his pals at their usual table and I was introduced as a business friend from Denmark. I can remember that Barry Bethel was there, so too was Laurie O'Leary, an old friend of Charlie's and a good pal of the twins.

'Cup of tea?' asked Charlie as I sat down to join them in idle chat.

'Thanks,' I replied as I pulled up a chair next to

Charlie. I waited while one of my new friends went to get the tea and slowly I joined in the conversation.

'This is my son, Gary' said Charlie as he introduced me around the table. He was his usual suntanned self and he was in total control. No one asked me to pay for the tea.

The talk drifted over to the bodyguard business, something that Charlie knew a lot about.

'We have an office in Copenhagen, you know,' he told me.

No, I didn't know.

'And Pauley here is my own personal bodyguard.'

He nodded over towards one of the men seated around the table, a big man with dark hair and huge fists. He looked a good choice — I couldn't see anyone deliberately wanting to pick a fight with him!

The tea and gossip over, it was time to meet Charlie's business connections at a pub, south of the river, as they all called the River Thames. I was getting used to hearing the cockney slang and general jargon of the East End of London, a culture that I freely admit I had never experienced before. I always thought that London ended at the City, coming as I did from West London. But I never got used to the slang for money. What is half a monkey? And how about a drink?

Pauley led the way out to Charlie's car and we were soon on our way. Apart from Charlie and Pauley there was another man with us, introduced to me as Wilf, an old friend and a trusted associate. I can't remember much about the drive across the river, but I do remember thinking that the car was a little old and decrepit for a man of Charlie's apparent social standing. He had obviously noticed my disapproval when he said, 'I only use this car in town. No one would think of looking in here. There are a lot of thieves around, you know.'

I had the distinct impression that he was right. This was, after all, his world and not mine. For the moment, then, my curiosity was satisfied.

'We're here,' said Charlie as Pauley pulled up outside a dismal-looking pub. We all disembarked eager for a quick pint before the business could be discussed in earnest. This was the way with this crowd — drinks first and business afterwards. Soon we were standing at the bar with more handshaking going on. Drinks materialised as if from nowhere and no money changed hands.

Another aspect of dealing in this way, I was to find out, was the incessant waiting and this day was to be typical of many, spent in dubious banter about everything and anything of absolutely no importance at all. I was never very good at this and I am pleased to report that I have not changed in that respect. But this day proved to be long indeed, since Charlie's contacts refused to show.

'Pauley has just got out of the mental home,' Wilf told me, trying to put me at ease when the waiting started to become stressful. It didn't help. In fact nothing I was hearing helped, since it was becoming blatantly obvious to me that the records we were all talking so nonchalantly about were in fact being stolen to order. Someone had thought it a good idea to get the goods abroad, where they could be sold quietly on the open market, thus creating a good profit for everyone concerned. I was slowly but surely getting very cold feet. It wasn't, after all, high on my agenda to get involved with stolen records in this way. But fortunately for me, the deal never happened since the men never showed at the pub. We spent the whole afternoon behind closed doors drinking everything and anything that the landlord provided, with Charlie telling more and more stories about the old days. And still no money changed hands!

What I did learn, however, was that Charlie was a very interesting person to know and he even promised to introduce me to his brothers, if I was interested. The stories or 'exploits' he recounted were full of East End promise and charm and it is probably at this time that I really started to take serious notice of the potential of these tales. But it was only when I met Ron and Reg Kray that I realised I could be of help in writing a storyline for a possible new film. It was this work that ultimately paved the way for *Doing the Business*.

The film idea built around 'The Mafia Franchise' hasn't yet materialised, but my film treatment was translated into a book with the able assistance of Champagne Charlie himself and Blake Publishing have now authorised a new revised version, due to the untimely death of Charlie Kray at the age of 73. Much has changed since the book was first published in 1993. Ron Kray has died in Broadmoor, killed by the cigarettes that he loved so much; Charlie Kray is now dead, having suffered a heart-attack in prison after being found guilty of cocaine trafficking in 1997; and Reg Kray finally lost his fight against cancer as he struggled to survive, constantly shuffled from prison to prison in search of the route away from custody and into the outside world. Even their old pal Frank Sinatra couldn't beat death.

It would be only fitting, therefore, to add a new chapter to *Doing the Business*, a true epilogue, one that brings the whole story of Charlie Kray and his brothers completely up to date and comprising some reflection on the achievements and importance of the Krays in the history of the UK and in the history of crime itself.

But the strange initial conclusion of any analysis of events past and present is that the Krays, over the last seven years since publication, have become more popular than ever, even now at the start of the new millennium. When Rodney Trotter (alias Nicholas Lyndhurst) mentioned Ronnie and Reggie to his brother Derek (alias David Jason) in the Christmas edition of *Only Fools & Horses* (BBC 1996, repeated in 1997/8) it was obvious to everyone watching the show that he was talking about the Krays. They are now a symbol of their age and of their chosen profession — some would even say that they are now part of the Establishment.

It is undoubtedly certain that Ron and Reg Kray are now dead — but will they ever be forgotten? The media have now adopted the name of Kray as an image of the bad guy, a name that tells it all without the need for going into trivial details of actual events. They are indelibly part of the myth of society and the legend will almost certainly stay with us for a long time to come — maybe for ever!

*   *   *

The story of the Krays is constantly in the press, always on our minds. But these brothers were all special, all different, all worthy of note in their own right. So what was it that made them stand out in a crowd — and why should we remember them at all?

'Oh God, Mother — help me!'

These famous last words marked the demise of Ron Kray, who died in the spring of 1995, when smoking finally got the better of him at Broadmoor Hospital. He had been frail for some time and there had been a number of minor heart-attacks and other complaints. But through it all he kept his humour and his dignity, something that may be somewhat difficult for many readers to understand and accept.

Personally, I well remember how alive he looked when he was telling of past glories; of how he escaped from Long Grove Asylum and of how great he felt when he shot and killed George Cornell. He loved to talk of all the places he would like to see, of the people he would like to meet, of the things he would like to do. He knew that his dreams would never come true, but that didn't stop him hoping. After all those years in Broadmoor, hope was all he had.

My visits to Broadmoor were a magical mystery tour of sorts — I never knew what was going to happen. On my first visit I told him that I, too, was a twin — I had an identical twin brother. That did the trick — from then on, we were life-long friends.

'I knew it when I saw you,' he told me. 'What do you want to know?' he asked as he began to talk about he old days.

Once there was a journalist doing an interview for a major newspaper, but Ron didn't like his stutter so he kept telling him to, 'Fuck off!' This was a secure, controlled environment, but I am sure the poor young man was shaking in his boots — and the more Ron kept at him, the more he stuttered. Then there were the visits by Kate, Ron's wife. She was always chatty and cheerful, but sometimes she said just a little too much and Ron would get angry. But he was careful not to say anything when others were present — a look was enough. And if you have ever been stared at by Ron Kray then you know exactly what I mean. His stare was known throughout the East and West Ends alike — it was sign, a signal, and it said 'be careful'.

On one occasion, Ron was close to tears as he talked about his old pal Frank Mitchell. 'I like to think of him wandering the outback in Australia,' he told me. But his eyes told me that he was the one who had given the orders — orders to kill and silence the 'Mad Axeman' once and for all.

The Krays had helped Frank Mitchell escape from Dartmoor Prison, and they drove him to a safe house in London. But he was getting troublesome and even a happy hooker, Lisa Prestcott, couldn't quiet him down. So Ron, Reg and Charlie all had a meeting with a fellow gangster from south of the river, a man by the name of Freddie Foreman. Along with Gerry Callaghan and Alfie Gerrad, Ron agreed to get rid of Frank Mitchell by filling him full of holes and then burying him at sea.

The East End of London, however, gave Ron a hero's funeral — with the media there in force to cover each and every sordid detail. They sang songs in his honour. They threw flowers in the path of the hearse as it was pulled by huge black horses, plumes and all. They praised all the good things he had done. Somehow, everyone forgot all the bad and the evil that the Krays stood for, all their lives.

It was always Ron Kray's ambition to become the Al Capone of British criminal history. He has now won that battle. He has also escaped the degradation and humiliation of Broadmoor, so he is free to enjoy his life hereafter as only the ghosts can.

Last of the Krays — first there were three, then two, then one — and there are none!

When his brother died, Reg Kray was heartbroken. His twin was no more. He was alone. Through the years he had visited Ron each and every six months, but for some reason his latest visit had been delayed and he never got to see his twin brother in hospital, to pay his final respects and to remember the good times that they had undoubtedly had together. It was a bond that was only broken by death.

Reg Kray is still in the news, with the latest reports talking of psychological tests that he has just undergone, so the parole board can evaluate his mental condition. But I find it very hard to believe that a man who has been in prison for 32 years, and 17 years of that in Parkhurst on the Isle of Wight in a major risk category, can be 'normal' psychologically. Normality is something that doesn't appear to come readily to mind when thinking of the Kray twins.

In the spring of the new millennium Reg Kray was still in the news, with the latest reports talking of psychological tests that he had just undergone, so the parole board could evaluate his mental condition. But I found it very hard indeed to believe that a man who had been in prison for 32 years, and 17 years of that in Parkhurst on the Isle of Wight in a major risk category, could be 'normal' psychologically. Normality is something that doesn't appear to come readily to mind when thinking of the Kray twins.

But his 30 years were up and he should have been free — in fact he was then into his 33rd year. The country had had its retribution and he had paid the price in full. Even after two attempted suicides, he was still alive and apparently reasonably well — and in his mid-60s he could no longer be seen as a threat to society. And he was no longer alone to dream in silence, since he had married again, this time in Maidstone Jail. His wife, Roberta, moved with him as he was transferred from prison to prison, waiting for his eventual day of release. He knew it wouldn't be long, but the authorities were playing a waiting game, teasing him every minute of the way. In April he was told that he must spend at least two more years in an open prison prior to release, but at least his psychological evaluation had gone in his favour — this surely showed character. But strange things have happened before, especially when the Krays have been concerned, so he waited — and he waited — and he waited.

So with Ron dead, elder brother Charlie dead and Reg now recently deceased, there isn't any chance of the brothers getting back together again — at least not in this life. It looks as though it's all over for the Krays. It was most unfortunate for Reg that cancer intervened as it did: he had a new life to look forward to and a new wife to enjoy it with him. There would undoubtedly have been many fraught years ahead, with numerous difficulties and some overwhelming decisions to be made, but they deserved a chance. That chance has now been denied them.

Reg passed go many years ago and he collected many a prize, a fee, a payment along the way. His last deal was to collect his final pay-check, in the form of a lucrative publishing deal for his book *A Way of Life*, to be published in November of the year 2000. And the newspapers made sure he was a wealthy man on release, as they all lined up for his autograph. So the country had nothing to fear from Reg Kray — he had become a part of the establishment. The future would have compounded that position, had he not lost his last and greatest fight with cancer. Through the years he had managed to keep himself fit, like the boxer he used to be. But this was not enough, he was never able to enjoy the best years of his life.

The only way Ron, Reg and Charlie Kray will ever get together again is in whatever life they may achieve after death. They are, however, indelibly imprinted in the history books as being the Godfathers of Crime, and in that respect they will always be with us — be it heaven or hell.

★   ★   ★

'*Not guilty!*' — but Charlie Kray was never innocent, always connected.

When *Doing the Business* was completed and finally edited for publication, Charlie Kray expressed a wish to include a Postscript, including a personal message. This, unfortunately, never came about. But his proposed statement now shows, in retrospect, a poignant irony.

He asked me to include the following:

> '*I've heard all the stories about my brothers, but I hope this book shows a different side of the twins.*
>
> *They have done so many good things in their lives and they are still doing them.*
>
> *My brothers are the strongest characters that I have ever known — they are real men.*
>
> *Yes, they did the crime, but now they've done the time.*
>
> *My greatest ambition in life now is to stand beside them once more outside prison — all three brothers once again FREE MEN!*'
>
> Charlie Kray, 1993

EPILOGUE

But the irony of the Kray saga took a sharp and wicked turn in 1997 with the imprisonment of Charlie Kray for his apparent involvement in cocaine dealing. He was caught red-handed, selling drugs to an undercover officer. It was a sting, set up by Scotland Yard to capture the last remaining Kray. It worked. Charlie Kray was given a 12-year sentence — he knew he would die in jail. For Charlie it was a deal too far. He just couldn't resist the lure of ready cash. He knew it was probably his last chance of making the big time. On a personal note, I feel that Charlie was just after the money and that he was forced into going through with the deal by the pressure exerted by the police. Was this police action morally justifiable? But he did the deal, make no mistake about that — but at the age of 70, did he really deserve 12 years at Her Majesty's pleasure?

Down on his luck, Charlie Kray tried his hand at many things over the last ten or more years. In business he had not been successful. The deal with the Mob in New York to set up a music company to launder Mafia loot had not come off — they didn't trust him. And the deal importing fruit and veg from Nigeria had gone rotten — nobody could see Charlie Kray selling bananas. But the pièce de résistance came when he tried to set up a company with the aim of 'cleaning up the oil fields of Kuwait'. None of these ventures got off the ground — they all ended up buried in the sand, another good little earner gone sour.

His long-lasting relationship with Diana Ward broke up a few years ago as he drifted from woman to woman. She had had enough of his meanderings, but Charlie couldn't keep his hands off the women, who were always there to tempt him. At the time of his arrest, his lover, Judy Stanley, maintained that she would stand by her man, at least for the time being, but she soon realised that she would have a long time to wait. At 70 years old, Charlie Kray had a long way to go before he could gain parole — he never made it. Time waits for no man!

His 'Del-boy' lifestyle was all he had. He loved the glamour, the money and what it could buy — but he never had it himself. He was always poor, always a fake — but always 'Champagne Charlie Kray'.

One incident that sheds light on the true nature of Charlie Kray — ex-gangster, ex-hot shot, ex-celebrity — was the time when he came down to Salisbury to open a public house. It is the story of a man who was eager to please, charming and cheerful with the ladies, and always on the look out for a nice little earner.

The time was mid-summer, the year 1986, and my twin brother had recently purchased a pub called The Fisherton Arms. It had been run down for many years and there was much redecorating and refurbishing to do, but there was potential, my brother having bought it when he retired from the Fire Service, after many years as Station Officer.

My first visit to the place was an eye-opener. It was dirty, dusty and completely dilapidated but my brother Rod had managed to get some willing helpers — members of a biker gang or, as they are more commonly known, the local division of Hell's Angels. There they were all dressed up in their obligatory leather gear while painting, decorating and sweeping out. My brother had done a deal with them — they could use the pub for their get-togethers and they could park their bikes in the huge car park out back, if they helped to sort things out and got things operational again. The response was instant, and they did a great job.

When it came to opening the pub for the first time under the new management, Rod wanted to get a 'celebrity' to open the place, and he wanted my advice. With all the bikers listening attentively to our conversation, I promised to ask Charlie Kray to come down and do the honours. I was very surprised when he agreed, as a personal favour. At the time we shared an office just off the Mile End Road in the East End, so we were in contact regularly, but to get Charlie away from London was something new for me, and different for him. It was all set.

On the day, Charlie came down in a white Rolls Royce, all dolled up with his gold imitation Rolex, his fake heavy gold chains and his famous smile. He was the epitome of the gangster as he entered the pub, along with a few pals who just happened to be coming down our way, just for the ride. The Roller was parked out the back and Rod welcomed Charlie to Salisbury. They entered the pub by the back door — there was no fuss, no crowds, no reporters.

Charlie had arrived early as planned. He had borrowed the Rolls for the day — the owner, too. It was all part of the show — people would be coming to see Charlie Kray and Charlie wanted all the razzmatazz that went along with being the elder brother of the Kray twins. As the time for opening approached, the queues began to form outside on the street, and quite a long way down it. There they were, all the members of the Hell's Angels, all quiet and respectful, all expectant and hopeful — would they get to meet Charlie Kray, would they shake him by the hand, would he make their day?

283

They did and he would. It took a long time for Charlie to shake all their hands and to kiss all the girls, but he did. He was their hero and he wouldn't disappoint them. The bikers were so polite, so welcoming — we all had a great day. My brother laid on the drinks, so Charlie didn't have to reach into his pocket. He was, after all, the guest of honour, and he was Charlie Kray.

The evening went well, very well. Everyone was so well behaved. At the merest hint of trouble, the gang leader took charge and made the intruder leave, sternly and without question. There were no disturbances, no hassle — just good cheer for everyone there. Charlie was a hit with them all, even my mother and father were there to greet him and to drink his good health. Charlie smiled his way into their hearts, one and all. On a particularly warm part of the evening, I took a step outside into the car park, and I was immediately struck by the hilarious sight of one solitary white Roller among a mass of high-powered motorbikes.

That night, Charlie stayed over at one of the local hotels — a double room, booked for one but suitable for two. I was told that the ladies were queuing up outside his room, just as they had done earlier in the day on the streets of Salisbury. Just how many managed to get inside is anyone's guess. But the following morning Charlie was his normal cheerful self — and there was a definite glint in his eye. He had had a great time in Salisbury but it was now time to leave — back to his beloved East End of London. Rod gave him a wad of cash, a token of respect for his professional services, and Charlie pocketed the dosh without even a glance. He knew he would be taken care of and we all knew he would do the business!

Rod had the pub for some years and he was never

bothered by trouble-makers — and he was never bothered by the police. The day before Charlie came down to Salisbury he thought he should notify the police of Charlie's arrival, just in case of trouble. They were sympathetic and thanked him for his courtesy. 'Have a nice day,' they told him. The Fisherton Arms was never raided by police, there was never any real trouble at all, even though the local Bernie Inn, just across the road, was raided on three separate occasions when the police were looking for drugs.

The day after the event, the local newspaper contacted my brother for a story — they had heard that Charlie Kray was visiting and wanted some up-to-date news.

'It was a charity event,' Rod told them, but he didn't tell them that it was Charlie's charity. A small piece appeared in the newspaper the following week — again, no fuss, no bother, no problems at all.

My twin brother has a momento of that day — a photograph of Charlie standing behind the bar of The Fisherton Arms. On either side stand Rod and myself, drinks in our hands and smiles on our faces. He has the photo framed and now it stands behind the bar in his home in France, for every visitor and welcomed guest to see. There is a caption underneath — it says simply 'Charlie Kray — and the twins'.

This was the life of Charlie Kray and this was his true nature. But sometimes he would stray along a dangerous path — a divide between right and wrong. When times were good, he had no need to get involved in crime, but when times were bad he would listen and sometimes be persuaded to join in — to be the crook he used to be.

When I met Charlie at Waterloo Station once, back in the late '80s, he pulled me over to the other side of the street away from Buster Edwards, the ex-Great Train Robber, and his flower stall. When I asked why, he gave me the somewhat ironic reply, 'It's that Buster, he's always trying to get me into trouble!'

POSTSCRIPT

BY HOOK OR BY CROOK

THE KRAYS ARE NO MORE. On the very first day of October, in the first year of the new millennium, Reg Kray died of the cancer that had invaded his body during those last years of anguished and tormented imprisonment. He never made his sixty-seventh birthday. But how did it happen so quickly? A natural-born fighter, he didn't give up easily. But one day he is apparently well, the next gravely ill, the next again he shows some improvement — and then he is dead!

Reg had already lost a lot of weight, even prior to brother Charlie's funeral earlier in the year — but afterwards he lost hope, he became frail and fragile, and he lost another stone in weight. The authorities were concerned about him. Previously a boxer, he had been a a fitness fanatic and in robust shape — a superman among the hard men of long-term prison life. But now he was beginning to let go, his reason for living was slowly but surely fading away.

However, Reg was still a Kray after all these years and still super-active behind bars doing what he did best — making lots of money. The books, the films, the merchandise — they had all added to the coffers and helped to make Reg Kray a wealthy man. Unlike his twin brother Ron, who gave everything away, Reg Kray had been piling up the dosh waiting for the day when he could enjoy the rewards of his industry and openly display his wealth. And now, just after the start of the new millennium, he was the sole survivor, keeping the Kray name alive and keeping all the money to himself. Not that Reg was uncharitable — far from it — but he was saving for a rainy day. He had plans and that was all that kept him going, and focused on the future.

But he had been forced to lash out in recent years. First there was Ron's funeral, then Charlie's. It had all cost an awful lot of readies, and Reg was the only one who could meet the bill. He even paid for Gary's funeral, Charlie's son who died of cancer a few years ago, when Charlie was absolutely destitute. So how had Reg Kray been able to cover all these costs, all this grandiose expenditure, this show of wealth that both bewitched and beguiled?

The money had been good — first the books, from which the twins received a staggering £100,000 advance from Sidgwick & Jackson for the Fred Dineage book *Our Story*. Then came the film *The Krays* from which the brothers shared £300,000 for the use of their name and the use of their reputation. The film company involved didn't really have to pay them anything — the Kray story was all in the public domain — but I think they cherished their knee-caps. And in the spring it had been widely reported that Guinness were prepared to offer Reg Kray £50,000 for the use of a David Bailey photo, advertising their particular brand of liquid refreshment. And the money kept rolling in.

Whether or not current Bills going through Parliament would have changed all that is a great unknown. But it appears that both the Government and the police are keen on getting their hands on the assets of crooks and criminals throughout the country — and Reg Kray's ill-gotten gains may well have come into that category. Can it be morally justified to pay a convicted killer for advertising the fact that he is a convicted killer, serving life behind bars?

When Charlie Kray was in court defending himself on the cocaine smuggling charges, it was rumoured that he had put out contracts on the policemen who had taken him into custody. But everybody knew that Charlie had no money — so where was the supposed £100,000 coming from?

When Reg had a falling out with his so-called adopted son, Pete Gillett, it was also rumoured that he had put out a contract on his life, so, again, many observers were asking the same question — where is the money for such payments? I can only hope that Reg Kray had a good accountant and that the source of his wealth is traceable. If not, then maybe the Government, even after his death, will get their hands on his assets — money and all.

So just how many years did Reg Kray think he had to serve behind bars — even the rubber bars of Wayland

Prison, where he had the key to his cell hanging around his neck '... so I can lock my doors at night — there are a lot of thieves around here'?

His sentence was for at least 30 years. Always a political decision, he was now in his thirty-third year. When he was sentenced, the files on the Krays, held by Scotland Yard, were put into storage and locked away from prying eyes for 30 years. But when this writer asked for permission to see these files, just prior to the expiration of the 30 years, he was told that they would be kept in secret for 75 years — a rule only normally reserved for state secrets. So was Reg Kray likewise facing a similar situation?

Certainly there was no rush to free him and surely if the files are important and warrant 75 years' secrecy, then what about the man himself — did he, too, warrant 75 years behind bars? What did he know — and would he tell?

Only the chiefs at Scotland Yard and the Home Office under Jack Straw know the truth about the Krays, but they are not talking. Today, the whole affair is as secret as the day of their trial, back in 1969. So who is hiding what — and from whom?

Instigating the use of the 75-year rule in the case of the Krays poses many questions — more questions than answers. But without freedom of information we are not empowered to ask — and to find out. So were the authorities simply answering these difficult questions by keeping Reg Kray locked up, quietly waiting and hoping for him to die in jail, like his brothers?

It appears that 'Watch this space!' is always the caption when considering the Krays. Whatever happens from here on in, Reg Kray has already confirmed his place in our history, in our society. He has become an indelible part of the establishment, the same one he tried to overthrow some 30 years ago and more.

. Reg Kray was 66 years old, a pensioner and of no danger to anyone. His health had been poor, due to a rigid prison diet for all those years — and his hearing was failing. Reg Kray could simply not have handled himself in the outside criminal world, where he was once the undisputed 'King'.

The Krays terrorised London in the '50s and '60s, ultimately killing their way to the top of the criminal food chain. But they were not just killers — they had their fingers in every crooked pie, from gambling joints to nightclubs, from protection rackets to extortion and fraud, from fencing stolen goods to money-laundering for the US Mafia.

But they were only convicted of one killing each; none of their rackets and gangland ways were of consequence to the police at the time, so why should we consider these misdemeanors now? The answer, of course, is that Scotland Yard didn't feel that they had material strong enough for conviction — so why bother then and why bother now?

Ron Kray always used to say, 'If you can't do the time, then don't do the crime!' Reg had been incarcerated since 9 May 1968 and many throughout the land were saying enough is enough. Even the man who captured the Krays, Leonard 'Nipper' Read, said that the time was now right to free Reg Kray — 30 years was enough.

There is no doubting the fact that Reg Kray killed Jack 'The Hat' McVitie, but he had served his time honourably and with respect to the law of the land.

When attending the funerals of his brothers, he never once tried to escape, never once made it difficult for the officers around him protecting the public from the old enemy — Public Enemy Number One. It would have been harsh indeed if all three Kray brothers were to die in jail. This, as we now know, was not to happen — but it was close.

So what brought about the deterioration in Reg's health, this apparent loss of hope for the future — any future?

Soon after Charlie's funeral, old pal Freddie Foreman was again in the news. This time he had admitted on prime-time television that Ron and Reg Kray had given him money to kill Frank Mitchell, the 'Mad Axeman'.

On 25 May Freddie Foreman, 68 years old and a fellow pensioner, was arrested; the charge, 'suspicion of perjury and perverting the course of justice'. He had openly admitted taking money from the Krays and killing 'Mad Axeman' Frank Mitchell. He had also admitted to killing Tommy 'Ginger' Marks. These confessions had previously appeared in a book, written by Foreman back in 1996, but his recent appearance in a television documentary about the London underworld, where he again confessed to the killings, sparked immediate action at Scotland Yard. Foreman could not be charged for the murders, since he had been cleared of both back in the '60s, where he stood trial at the Old Bailey, but he was now a wanted man, all over again.

Back in 1969, he received a ten-year jail sentence for his part in Kray activities — and later, in 1989, a six-year sentence for his part in the 1983 £7 million Security Express robbery, in which Ronnie Knight was also involved and imprisoned.

POSTSCRIPT

This was not the news that Reg wanted to hear. The public could read the book and now they could see the television documentary — the Krays did it after all, they had Frank Mitchell killed. According to Freddie Foreman, even Charlie had been involved, since he was present when the order was given and the money changed hands. Reg waited, and waited. Surely it couldn't get any worse.

In June, Kate Kray made the news with a new book all about the hard men of the underworld. As the ex-wife of Ron Kray, Reggie's twin brother, she knows a thing or two about hard men. The Kray name was again front page news.

At the beginning of July, the first signs of serious trouble for Reg Kray made the headlines. Doubling up in agony in his cell was a new experience for the 'Godfather' of crime — and he was rushed to the medical wing of Wayland Prison, where he was immediately given antibiotics to stave off infection. His liver was inflamed and things were not looking good. A prison source said, 'There is no doubt about it — he's caused some serious damage with his drinking.' This is a strange admission for anyone to make, since alcoholic drink has never been allowed in the jails of this country — so where was he getting this illicit liquor?

I now feel forced to tell the story of how I first met Reg Kray and about his most secret of hobbies — drinking. It all happened in 1992 when I went to see him in Nottingham jail. We were talking about the old film, *The Krays*, and about a possible new venture about their dealings with the US Mafia, when suddenly I noticed that Reg was getting slowly but surely drunk. But where was the source of his alcoholic haze? A quick glance at the family at the next table showed me the reason for the smile on his face — the vodka had been hidden in a baby bottle and topped up with a little orange juice, for camouflage. Now and again, Reg would reach for the bottle, under the enquiring gaze of the child — and top up his glass. The child's eyes kept saying 'Who's that man, Mum?' and 'Why's he taking my bottle, Dad?' None of the other people at that table were asked if they would like to indulge. This was Reggie's little treat — his and his alone.

By mid-July, Reg Kray could read the news all about his goddaughter, Patsy Kensit, and her troubled relationship with Oasis singer Liam Gallagher. All the stories told of her father, a well-known London pick-pocket called Jimmy the Dip. And everyone could read about her connection with the Krays. But it was old news, rehashed for the public of today — again, nothing new here, no revelations, nothing that could do his hopes for parole any harm.

Reg Kray filled in time by writing pages on his website. He thanked Mike Tyson and old pal Don King for saying kind things about him on television after Tyson's fight in Scotland, and he thanked everyone for their interest in his health. When Reg couldn't write any more, Roberta took over, telling of how wonderful everyone had been, so helpful and considerate, so pleasant and cheerful — all, that is, except the Home Office.

Later in the month, Patsy Kensit again made the front page of many a tabloid, where she openly admitted to having an affair with Jamie Foreman, son of Kray cohort Freddie Foreman, the man who had recently admitted murder on television. Things went from bad to worse as Jamie Foreman was being sought by the police for possession of cocaine — a warrant for his arrest had been issued and he, like his father, became a wanted man.

Brother Charlie had been jailed for cocaine; so had Pete Gillett and Joe Pyle, one of the fierce henchmen who ran the old 'Firm' with fists of iron. Drugs and the Krays was not what he wanted to see. Reg could only wait and see, listen and pray — and hope for the best.

Soon the Krays were again featured in the newspapers — this time the *Sun* of Friday, 14 July where 'The Kray Connection' was the title for an article on the *EastEnders* cast and their connections with the Krays and their pals. All the usual suspects were there — Freddie Foreman and son Jamie, Barbara Windsor and her 'ex' Ronnie Knight, Mad Frankie Fraser and his pals Dave Courtney and Lenny McLean, Martin Kemp and fellow actor Craig Fairbrass, along with another photo of Patsy and a silhouette of her dad, James Kensit, or Jimmy the Dip. The myth was alive and well, and perpetuated by the media. It was all gossip and showbusiness gas and it helped to maintain Reggie's celebrity status, something that he saw as his path to riches. But, strangely, brother Charlie was nowhere to be seen.

Events were now occurring at a rapid pace and things were soon to go downhill — big time. By the end of July, Reg Kray was again taken ill in his cell. 'I feel like I'm dying,' he told friends as he was treated at the medical unit of Norwich Prison, some 20 miles away.

A prison spokesman said, 'Reggie was found in pain, clutching his stomach. He is very ill, and he's also lost the will to live. No one knows what will happen.'

Reg Kray was still losing weight — he was not well at all. He was being kept alive on liquid food and painkillers. Was this to be the end of the last surviving Kray?

Reg was rushed to The Norwich and Norfolk Hospital on 3 August to undergo surgery for a suspected tumour. By the end of his first week, surgeons had removed a malignant tumour from his small intestine during a four-hour operation. Roberta, Reggie's wife of only three years, told journalists, 'The obstruction is a secondary growth and we are awaiting further scans to determine the source.' Roberta also confirmed that they were asking for Reggie's release on compassionate grounds. A Home Office spokesman said simply, 'Compassionate parole is only given in exceptional circumstances.'

Within days, Reg underwent another operation to remove another tumour. The Home Office admitted on 19 August that Reg Kray was gravely ill. A spokesman said, 'Reg has terminal cancer and there is nothing anyone can do for him. Doctors have still not found the source of the cancer so there is more out there — it is terminal.'

A scheduled parole review had to be postponed because of his illness, but lawyers were now in deep discussions with the Home Office — and Jack Straw.

Voices were beginning to be heard from far and wide. Soap stars such as Barbara Windsor, Mike Reid, Billy Murray and Johnny Briggs were urging his release. Pictures made public by Roberta showed Reg in bed in The Norwich and Norfolk Hospital wearing an oxygen mask, gasping for breath. Was this to be his 'death bed'? And still the Home Office said he would only be released when he was no longer considered to be a threat.

The Sunday People, of 13 August, carried the exclusive pictures of Reg, taken just after his first operation. Gone was the glint in his eye and the staring menace of a villain. His sunken eyes now showed that he was dying, he was just a frail old man dying of cancer.

'There is no greater punishment this Governmant can inflict upon him now other than denying him his last, small taste of freedom,' said Roberta. 'We've written to Jack Straw on numerous occasions but never once had a reply from him, not directly,' she told the press.

Trevor Linn, Reggie's solicitor, decided now to apply directly to the Home Secretary. Surely there were suitable grounds for compassionate release? He told the press, 'I believe that the authorities are delaying hearing the release application ... hoping that nature takes care of the problem for them.' He then added, 'Jack Straw doesn't want to be the man who frees a Kray, even though our petition will show Reggie meets the strict criteria laid down in the Prison Service operating standards and Section 36 of the Criminal Justice Act 1991.' At last, the lawyers were getting their act together.

On 21 August, the *Times* spelled it out. The medical report had first to be seen and confirmed by the Governor of Wayland Prison who would then, if found to be suitable, send a recommendation to the parole board. Then the Home Office would enter the proceedings, where it would undoubtedly find its way to the desk of the Home Secretary. The petition could then be sent to another parole board and so on — a long way to any final decision.

Again, Roberta Kray had to wait — just like her husband Reggie. She was getting used to it, but she didn't like it. There was, however, a good side. 'I'm virtually living at the hospital and stay in a room overnight,' she told reporters. 'It's been hellish, but the one good thing is we've been able to spend time together since he's been here.'

The bad news was that Reg Kray's name had been included on a list of some 25 prisoners throughout the UK who should never be released, no matter what! This was indeed a testing time.

Trevor Linn, acting for Reg and Roberta Kray, made the details of his letter to Jack Straw public. 'I have now been informed by Mr Kray's treating consultant that Mr Kray has cancer of the bladder, with other secondary tumours,' he told the press. 'His condition is terminal. The cancer is not operable and will not respond to chemotherapy.' He added, 'In the circumstances, I request that you order Mr Kray's immediate release.'

'I have always said it is time to let Reggie out. In light of this latest sad news about his cancer it's only right to let him come home with Roberta,' said Barbara Windsor.

Johnny Briggs, of *Coronation Street* fame, said, 'Reggie has been in prison a long time and has paid his debt to society. It's time to let him go home.'

Even tough-guy actor Billy Murray showed compassion. 'Reggie has more than done his time,' he told the press. 'It would be only humane to let him go home. Reggie needs to be with his family.'

London's Burning star Glen Murphy put it simply: 'Reggie should be allowed home. He can't harm anyone now. He should be freed to spend this time with his family.'

In a poll run by *The Sunday People*, over 93 per cent of those who responded agreed. By a large majority, they all shouted 'Free Reg Kray'.

On Saturday, 26 August 2000, Reg Kray was officially

freed from jail by Home Secretary Jack Straw. The reason — compassionate grounds.

All the old news was featured and all major newspapers, radio and TV channels ran with it. 'In the early part of August, Reg had been rushed to The Norfolk and Norwich Hospital from Wayland Prison, complaining of severe stomach pains,' they said. 'The trouble that had started back in the summer of '96 had once again reared its ugly head — he had stomach cancer.' A spokesman put it bluntly: 'The operation to remove the tumor went well, but the cancer had spread — most of his internal organs were now infected, especially damaged were the bladder and bowel regions. It is clear to everyone concerned that Reg Kray doesn't have long to live.'

When the news of his imminent release reached his hospital bed, his wife Roberta was there to console him, to congratulate him, to laugh and cry with him. Tears were definitely the order of the day. The handcuffs were removed and the police guards slowly but surely detached themselves from the scene. Reg and Roberta were alone — not a hostile face in sight. They were alone all right, but how long had they got? A free man at long last, the hospital refused to allow him home. And anyway, where exactly was home?

Reg Kray had seen most of the country over the last 33 years, mainly from the inside of a prison van as he was escorted from jail to jail, from prison cell to prison cell. His home went with him, along with his few prized possessions — the photos of his mum Violet; the books; the letters from his brothers Ron and Charlie. Reg Kray had not seen his new home, set up for him by his wife Roberta and a few close friends —

it wasn't far away, but a place kept secret from the prying eyes of the press.

But Reg Kray had these same media folk to thank for his release. In the preceding months, many a newspaper had carried the banner 'Free Reg Kray'. And it was not a surprise when the vast majority of readers confirmed their thoughts and feelings about his outrageously lengthy prison sentence, especially now his cancer was front-page news. The compassion of the British people eventually moved Jack Straw to similar compassion — and to release Reg Kray.

The switchboard at The Norwich and Norfolk Hospital was jammed with well-wishers offering sympathy and a cheerful word. The hospital's own Bob Atkinson was forced to issue a statement asking for people to mail in their messages. 'Please write to him,' he said. 'The number of calls being received is causing a great strain on the switchboard staff and may also prevent urgent calls getting through.' The celebrity bandwagon was up and rolling.

'It's brilliant news. Now he can spend some time with his loving wife,' said Barbara Windsor, once upon a time Charlie Kray's closest companion. 'I sent flowers to the hospital a couple of weeks ago,' she told the press. 'Reg is an old man now — he is dying,' she added, close to tears.

Others were soon to add their congratulations. 'It's about time they released him,' said *EastEnder* Mike Reid. 'I'm over the moon for him and his family.' Fellow actor Billy Murray again endorsed the message. 'It's wonderful news, but it should have happened sooner. It's a shame it's so late because he is very ill, but hopefully he will get to spend some quality time now with Roberta.'

POSTSCRIPT

Later that same day, 26 August, the acting chief executive of The Norfolk and Norwich Hospital, Anne Osborn, confirmed that Reg Kray was then too ill to leave hospital. He was freed from the shackles he had worn for over three decades, but he was not free to go.

Roberta spoke to the media. 'I'm pleased that he has got his freedom,' she said tearfully. 'It is something that he has been waiting so long for. But he is seriously ill. He will not be leaving hospital in the immediate future. However we are hoping that he will be able to get out for a few days. He is conscious and able to speak, but it is a difficult time.' And what was Reggie's comment on his release? 'He was overjoyed!'

Reg Kray had been ill for some considerable time. He knew that his days were numbered back in the summer of '96 — only his great physical and mental strength kept him going. This now frail and feeble pensioner could do no one any harm — or could he?

When I saw him in the spring of 1992, in Nottingham jail, he showed me his secret masterpiece — a manuscript that he had been compiling ever since his first few days in prison. He couldn't show it to a publisher or to any newspaper people, he told me — this was his life story inside jail and it wasn't yet finished.

'There'll be a lot of aggro when this is published,' he said with a glint in his eyes, 'that's why it'll only be released when I'm dead!'

Even then he was planning to stick two fingers up at the prison service and the Home Office — even then his brain was in overdrive. By far the brightest of the Kray brothers, Reg had planned his way through 33 years of torment, of hatred, of bitter resentment.

Things were even beginning to hot up for me. Having

written two books on the Krays, I was again in demand. On 30 August, I did a radio interview with the BBC in Newcastle in which a caller made the remark that the East End of London was a safe place when the Krays were around. 'They were vigilantes,' he told the listeners, 'they kept the rapists and the muggers off the streets — and they only ever hurt other gangsters.'

This is often said of the '50s and '60s when the Krays ruled the London underworld. The streets may have been a safer place, but behind the scenes the villains were up to their dirty deeds — people were maimed, tortured and killed.

Ordinary people on the street didn't see their dealings with the US Mafia, through which they organised 'Murder Incorporated', intent on killing everyone and anyone to order. These same people didn't see the everyday violence meted out on shopkeepers, publicans and club owners if protection money wasn't paid in time and in full. And these same people didn't witness the stabbings, the shootings and the general persecution inflicted on ordinary people who just stood up for their rights, wanting a fair deal at a fair price.

Typical of these activities is the story of when a customer made a complaint about a car he had recently purchased from a dealer who paid protection money to the Krays. When the customer turned up at the dealership to complain in person, man to man with the dealer, Ron Kray pulled a gun and shot him. Afterwards, other members of the 'Firm' got him to hospital where he was given some ready cash and told to keep quiet — if he wanted to stay alive. It wasn't the money that kept his mouth shut — it was the fear!

Have people really forgotten all about the fire-bombs,

the shoot-outs, the razors slashed across the face of many an innocent bystander just because he said something that annoyed, or was in the wrong place at the wrong time? Selective memory has indeed helped to keep the Kray myth alive — or should that be mass hysteria? I for one carry no illusions regarding the Krays. The twins were vicious, ruthless in the extreme — they cut down anyone in their way. Charlie Kray was different — he was a 'prangster', a clown among crooks. His was a very different kettle of fish. He urged his brothers to invest in 'real' business, to make 'real' money. But Ron and Reg Kray wouldn't listen — the quickest way to the top was always with their fists, their knives and their guns.

But this is all history. With his brothers dead, Reg Kray should have been freed earlier to live what remained of his life in peace. With a doting new wife to keep him on the straight and narrow, there was nothing to fear from Reg Kray. He paid for his crimes, as did his brothers. He was, however, the only one to serve his sentence in full, and in this respect the only unanswered question is why?

During the latter part of August, I heard that his book was due to be published by Macmillan later in the year. A few days later, I heard that they were rushing it through for the end of September. Does this mean that Reg Kray, on his admission to hospital in the early part of August, had given up any hope of living? 'Only when I'm dead,' he'd said — maybe he knew he couldn't make November, or perhaps he just didn't care any more. Maybe then we'll know the real reason for the 30-year sentence.

When the news broke about his release, a Home Office spokesman said, 'We are satisfied that there is no risk of him committing further offences.' Well, they weren't taking any chances — at the time he couldn't even get out of bed! And why should he have wanted to get involved in crime? Crime was the reason why he had served 33 years behind bars, so why should he want to get involved in it when he could justifiably write about it and make a good living, given half the chance? And even then, after all those years, he was still counting the days.

But Reg Kray was still fighting. He was free, that was all true enough, and he was going home, wherever that might be. And he was about to have his first real hair cut for over 32 years. The hairdresser came to his bedside, to give him a trim, to cut off the grey and to restore some pride. Reg Kray was being cut — and he didn't mind at all.

Trevor Linn, his lawyer, was also at his bedside. 'I'm hoping Reggie will confound experts and leave hospital soon,' he said. 'He's a tough as old boots,' he added with a laugh — and didn't we know it.

On Monday, 28 August, the media was once again ahead of the game. On the front page of the *Mirror* was the photograph of Reg Kray in his hospital bed, alongside a photo of the house in which he and Roberta were due to set up home. So much for privacy. But no-one with the name of Kray can remain private for long. Could they really have kept the semi-detached home a secret?

But Reg was feeling better, breathing a little easier. It was now time to add his own voice to the proceedings — to tell it like it was, no holds barred. After all, it was official — he was a free man.

'I've been cooped up for 32 years. I want to be able to sit out and smell the fresh air, then I'll really feel free,' he told reporters. 'That will mean I can die happy. I might not have long left, but I intend to savour every moment of my freedom.'

The humour was there, the glint was returning to those sunken eyes, he even managed to crack a joke or two. 'All I'd like to do is sit down and have a nice gin and tonic by a swimming pool,' he said with glee. And I bet there were many around the country who'd have been willing to buy him that first drink.

Trevor Linn was full of information for the massed press pack. 'Pain is not the major problem for him, it's really the lack of bowel function,' he said. 'The surgeons have said weeks, rather than months or years. Having said that, if the next minor surgery is OK, he could live for up to three months.'

The news had also reached the press about a possible legal action to be brought against the Prison Service by Reggie's civil lawyer, Mark Goldstein, in which he said that the Prison Service should have been aware of the cancer problem much earlier. With stomach complaints going back to 1996 I would venture to say that he maybe, just maybe, has a point.

The following day, Reg was feeling better. Roberta even managed to wheel him around the hospital's garden, even though he was still not on solids and his condition was not good. But you can't keep a good crook down, he wanted his first taste of freedom — and he got it. Roberta, however, could not stay long. She had to leave Reg at the hospital, since an appointment had been made for her to see the Governor of Wayland Prison, to discuss the terms of his release. It was all true, Reg Kray had been freed from prison, and now she had it in writing.

The early part of September was a quiet one for Reg

Kray. He was ill — often too ill to talk — and he was dying. Two weeks after his release, he was still hospitalised, still occupying that same sick bed — still a prisoner. But he was free and it was time to get cracking, to take charge, to do the business. *A Way of Life* was now being publicised openly, it was to be his last great work. Reg even went on record saying that he would like to be remembered as an author, poet and philosopher. But Ron and Reg Kray will always be remembered for what they were — the 'Godfathers of Crime'.

Still, working was a way of forgetting the present. Even taking a shower was difficult with all those tubes connecting him to his life-support system, but he got through each and every day by concentrating on his work — and that, as usual, meant money. His new book was a nice little earner, then there were the newspapers all clambering for position. Even Macmillan, his publishers, were getting in on the act. They quickly set about publicising the book, and selling off the serialisation rights by way of auction.

Again, Reg would make a lot of dosh and he needed it all. He had already done his sums and a nice place in the country was a little more expensive now than at the time he was sent to prison. In fact, the only minus in the whole equation was the fact that he was dying. On every other count, he was sitting pretty — wads of cash and the promise of more to come.

This is Reggie's story, announced the publishers, already rubbing their hands in gleeful satisfaction and anticipation of rich rewards — a diary of his life, they told us, with reflections on the past and the role he found for himslef on the inside. It is a story of courage and remorse, revelation and friendship, they said.

POSTSCRIPT

Anyone with any inside knowledge of Reg Kray would not recognise the word courage. Did it really take courage to kill Jack 'The Hat' with a carving knife, with members of the 'Firm' holding him down? And no one would understand their apparent talk of remorse, since Reg has never, ever, expressed such feelings about the killing. Sure, he regretted being in prison, but that was it.

In fact, the book was a diary of prison life and events as seen by Reg Kray. But he was only telling us what he wanted us to hear and what he believed we wanted to hear — not necessarily the truth. There is no mention of his blatant homosexuality. This is a one-sided, single-faceted picture, told by an ageing and angry man who holds a grudge against society. But after 32 years in jail, who could blame him. And in any case, it was almost all over.

The hospital radio kept him informed about his newsworthiness. 'I heard I was being released on the radio news before they told me officially,' Reg told the press, now allowed to the bedside. 'Sure, I'm free,' he told them, sitting uncomfortably in a chair, 'but free to do what?' The reporters listened intently to what he had to say. After all, they had paid dearly for the privilege. He told them the usual things. 'I never wanted to be a criminal, but that's where the circumstances took us, Ron and me.' And with a wry smile, he added, 'I still can't get used to people bringing in my post — and it not being opened.'

'I was a loner in some ways,' he told the *News of the World*. 'But I always had my family to support me.' But Reg knew instinctively that he had said too much — he was in trouble, the wrong word had crept out of his mouth and into the press. 'Now, I don't want people to think that I'm talking about the Mafia family. I'm talking about close bonds with friends and family who have been loyal throughout the years.' But the slips kept coming. He'd mentioned 'the Mafia family' and 'bonds' — it all reminded me of the bearer bonds stolen in the USA by the Mafia and sold in Europe by the Krays all those years ago.

He had only kind thoughts and praise for Roberta. 'I suppose we knew we'd be together in some way from the first moment — Rob is the one for me,' he told everyone. 'No one sees what goes on behind the scenes. She's always mopping my brow and making sure that I'm comfortable,' he said, as she fetched a glass of water. But he had something else he wanted to say.

'I was very ill for a long time before anyone took notice and then it was too late. I was given Milk of Magnesia by the prison doctor and was told I'd get better.' he told the reporter from the *News of the World*. 'But the pain got considerably worse over a period of time.' Again, Roberta applied the water to his lips, as he rested back in his chair. Reg was thinking about his claim for damages, arguing that his cancer should have been spotted earlier. He smiled.

But Reg wasn't finished yet. Time was now precious, it was in short supply, but there was a message, something else to be said. 'And stay away from drugs,' was that message.

'I think drugs have been the most evil influence that I've seen in the prison system — just how badly people can be hooked.'

Strange, that brother Charlie should go down for drug dealing. Even stranger that Pete Gillett should also go down for drugs, in a deal organised by Reg Kray himself. I have even heard, from reliable sources, that Reg enjoyed a 'puff' or two, when available — to chill out between bouts of drinking. So all the talk about not doing drugs didn't include a joint or two in the joint. As they say, there is no smoke without fire!

The press were generally kind to Reg Kray. Even his parting remark had been carefully and cleverly contrived. 'I don't know what the future will be for us,' he told them, 'but obviously I'd like to go and walk by the seaside and have an ice cream and just hold my wife's hand — and wander around like normal people.'

Reg Kray could certainly have afforded the ice cream, no problem there, but 'wander around like normal people'? That was impossible — the last of the Krays was by no means 'ordinary' and anyway, in the end it was just a dream. He never had the jellied eels he longed for, he never had the gin and tonic by the pool, he never found freedom. His only treat was to have his ginger ale laced with alcohol — by this time even the nurses were turning a blind eye. Reg hadn't long to live, and he knew it. Even his book showed a certain poignancy.

On Sunday, 17 September, some six weeks after he had entered hospital, both the *News of the World* and *The Sunday People* spelt it out — Reg Kray had just two weeks to live. And Reg had even made plans for his own funeral.

The news, however, was all about the stories of old. There were the times he tried to commit suicide by slashing his wrists — three times in all. There were more photos of Reg in his hospital bed, all smartened up for the camera. And there were the usual sentiments about family, friendships and the future he was not allowed to see. The cancer had won the battle. Reg Kray was doomed to die a painful death.

DOING THE BUSINESS

A room was arranged for him at a local hotel, The Town House in Thorpe St Andrew, and he was quietly smuggled away through the back door of the hospital. He rode in a Rolls-Royce, like a celebrity, through the local Norfolk countryside but once installed in the honeymoon suite he was treated like any other guest. But Reg Kray could never be any other guest, the burly minders made sure of that. However, there were no public appearances — he stayed quietly in his room, waiting to die.

By the end of the month he was back in bed — and fading fast. A press conference was cancelled, so too a dinner with his old enemies Frankie Fraser and Charlie Richardson. Suddenly it was all very quiet — no press release, no newspaper headlines, nothing at all. The end was indeed nigh.

But legends do not die and news about Ron, Reg and Charlie Kray will continue to make the headlines — long after their deaths. And when the 75-year rule is up, some time around 2040, I am sure they'll make the news all over again. Somewhere, Ron will be smiling, Charlie will be rubbing his hands — and Reg will be once again sticking those two fingers high into the air.

The Kray saga continues.

Watch this space!